T0301574

From Industrial Districts to Local Development

From Industrial Districts to Local Development

An Itinerary of Research

Giacomo Becattini

Professor of Political Economy, University of Florence, Italy

Marco Bellandi

Professor of Political Economy, University of Florence, Italy

Gabi Dei Ottati

Professor of Industrial Economics, University of Florence, Italy

Fabio Sforzi

Professor of Economic Geography, University of Turin, Italy

Edward Elgar
Cheltenham, UK • Northampton, MA, USA

Published by
Edward Elgar Publishing Limited
Glensanda House
Montpellier Parade
Cheltenham
Glos GL50 1UA
UK

Edward Elgar Publishing, Inc.
136 West Street
Suite 202
Northampton
Massachusetts 01060
USA

A catalogue record for this book
is available from the British Library

Library of Congress Cataloguing in Publication Data

From industrial districts to local development: an itinerary of research/
by Giacomo Becattini, Marco Bellandi, Gabi Dei Ottati, Fabio Sforzi.
     p. cm.
     1. Industrial districts—Italy—Tuscany. 2. Industrial policy—Italy.
3. Industrial organisation—Italy. 4. Economic development. I. Becattini,
Giacomo, 1927– .
HC307.T9 F76   2003
338.945'5—dc21   2002034708

ISBN 1 84376 159 9

Printed and bound in Great Britain by Biddles Ltd *www.biddles.co.uk*

Contents

List of figures and tables

FIGURES

TABLES

Foreword

When I was asked by the editors of this volume to contribute a foreword, my very first reaction was hesitant. Would I be able to do justice to the prolific writings of this group over a period of fifteen years or more? I quickly concluded that I could seize this invitation to pay tribute to the formidable intellectual and professional contribution by this group, acknowledge the inspiration I had drawn from them for my own thinking and professional development, and finally, express my gratitude for many years of warm friendship to them as well as to other Italian scholars whose work is dedicated to the subject of industrial districts and local development.

Giacomo Becattini was the first Italian scholar who enlightened me about the Italian districts back in 1986. He convinced me that it was worth looking into local economies as a crucial dimension of economic and social development. The first time I came across the notion of the district was through Mike Piore and Chuck Sabel. For them, the Italian industrial districts served as a chief testimony of the rise of flexible specialisation described in their seminal book *The Second Industrial Divide*, published in 1984. Mike told me about an encounter with Italian producers at an industrial fair that evoked his interest in districts. In contrast to the usual opportunistic behaviour of business persons who secretively guard their knowledge from other producers, the Italians appeared at ease talking freely about their secrets and sharing them with competitors. Later on when I had the opportunity of visiting a number of Italian industrial districts myself I was able to verify Mike's experience. I realised how much the owners of the small firms in the district aligned their own fortune and survival with that of their neighbouring firms, how they compromised their immediate interest for the sake of that of the community. This was in clear contrast to the widespread practice of business seeking to maximise self advantage, even if that meant cheating the community. In my later visits to small firm communities in various countries I frequently tested the willingness of producers to share information and other resources by asking them whether in case of a machine breakdown they would ask for the needed spare part from their neighbouring competitor. The answer was more often 'no' than 'yes'. Rarely have I come across the same blend of competition and cooperation as in the districts of Prato, Sassuolo or Carpi-Modena.

Combining competition and cooperation is one of the distinctive features of the Italian industrial districts, and of dynamic local production systems more generally. There are many other characteristics of industrial districts that have greatly informed modern thinking about industrial organisation and economic and social development. Among them are flexibility arrangements based on the skill and competence of workers and managers and on product and process innovation, rather than just on wage adjustment; the combination of flexibility in labour markets and security of employment and income; collective efficiency through specialisation, agglomeration and coordination; endogenous local and regional development based on adapted technology and self-reliance through the mobilisation and utilisation of local resources, rather than the buying in of know-how or the reliance on subsidies; competent entrepreneurship; the development of trust as a guiding principle of business relations and a source of economic dynamism; the embeddedness of the market in the larger social community; the role and significance for democracy of viable local production systems and local communities; and finally the shift in the role of the State from one of a regulator to one of facilitator and orchestrator of social dialogue.

There was a time of controversy centred on the question whether small firm industrial districts and local development were to be seen as pointing the way to the future, or whether they were to be judged as archaic or unsustainable forms of industrial organisation, representing a temporary aberration from the main path of development. For example, some of the small firms in the district appeared to be absorbed into larger ones and small capitalism to be displaced by big capital. There was also the issue, discussed in trade union and political circles, whether industrial districts that resort to the practice of subcontracting and tend to mix up the status of wage labour, self-employment, home workers and entrepreneurs, should be considered as social progress or not. Today, these issues appear to be settled. While there have been some concentration and re-centralisation in the industrial district, its basic integrity and viability have been preserved. In fact, the small firm districts have performed better than large firms in Italy. Globalisation has not done the harm to local economies that had been predicted. On the contrary, in many instances the local level has been strengthened. It is now understood that it is not the size of firms as such that is decisive for economic performance or social acceptability, but the way firms are organised. Small firms can be efficient and highly performing through collective organisation and linkages. Subcontracting production and services can lead to labour exploitation, but can also comply with labour standards. Trade union density and influence can be just as great in small firm economies as in large firms. Tuscany and Emilia-Romagna, but also Denmark, provide evidence of this.

The industrial districts and the associated local development have aroused great curiosity among scholars in various parts of the world. They have been a spur not only to industrial organisation, but modern development theory, relevant to industrialised and developing countries alike. Since the mid-1980s, Frank Pyke and I have endeavoured to have the International Labour Organisation participate in and benefit from the debate about districts and local development. The 'Florence School' of Giacomo Becattini and his associates has been a central pillar in this debate. They contributed to each one of the following four books published by the ILO's International Institute for Labour Studies: *The Re-Emergence of Small Enterprises: Industrial Restructuring in Industrialised Countries* (1990); *Industrial Districts and Inter-Firm Cooperation in Italy* (1990); *Industrial Districts and Local Economic Regeneration* (1992); *Local and Regional Response to Global Pressure: The Case of Italy and its Industrial Districts* (1996). Starting from the concept of the 'Marshallian district', the Becattini group (Giacomo Becattini, Marco Bellandi, Gabi Dei Ottati and Fabio Sforzi) has contributed to our theoretical understanding, in particular by linking it to classical economic theory. At the same time, the group has contributed to empirical knowledge about the districts, by inter alia analysing and documenting their incidence and location in Italy. It is a worthwhile endeavour to recapitulate and synthesise the principal stages of this work in the present reader. The book deserves to receive wide attention, in both academic circles and among policy makers. Its publication comes at an opportune moment when, economic globalisation notwithstanding, there is a new appreciation of the continued importance of local development for promoting economic dynamism, social cohesion and human dignity.

Werner Sengenberger
International Labour Organisation

Acknowledgements

The publishers wish to thank the following who have kindly given permission for the use of copyright material:

Academic Press Ltd for article 'Trust, interlinking transactions and credit in the industrial district' in *Cambridge Journal of Economics*, 1994, 18(6): 529–46.

Carfax International Periodical Publishers (Journal Oxford Ltd) for article 'On entrepreneurship, region and the constitution of scale and scope economies' in *European Planning Studies*, 1996, 4(4): 421–38.

Carfax Publishing (Taylor & Francis Ltd) for article 'Social concertation and local development: the case of industrial districts' in *European Planning Studies*, 2002, 10(4): 449–66.

Editions techniques et économiques for article 'The incentives to decentralized industrial creativity in local systems of small firms' in *Revue d'économie industrielle*, 1992, 59: 99–110.

Felice Le Monnier for the chapter 'The past in the present: Prato folk' in G. Becattini, *The Caterpillar and the Butterfly: An Exemplary Case of Development in the Italy of Industrial Districts*, Florence: Le Monnier, 2001, pp. 212–21.

M.E. Sharpe Inc. for article 'The economic bases of diffuse industrialization' in *International Studies of Management & Organization*", 1991, 21(1): 53–74.

Pinter Publishers for the chapters 'The development of light industry in Tuscany: an interpretation' and 'The Tuscan model: an interpretation in the light of recent trends' in R. Leonardi and R.Y. Nanetti (eds), *Regional Development in a Modern European Economy: The Case of Tuscany*, London and New York: Pinter, 1994, pp. 77–93 and 86–115.

Rosenberg & Sellier for the chapter 'La molteplicità dei sentieri di sviluppo locale' in G. Becattini, M. Bellandi, G. Dei Ottati and F. Sforzi, *Il caleidoscopio dello sviluppo locale. Trasformazioni economiche nell'Italia contemporanea*, Turin: Rosenberg & Sellier, 2001, pp. 41–63.

Società geografica italiana and CNR-Italian Committee for International Geographical Union for the chapter 'Local development in the experience of Italian industrial districts' in B. Cori, G. Corna Pellegrini, G. Cortesi, G. Dematteis, M.T. Di Maggio Alleruzzo, C. Minca, F. Sforzi and G. Zanetto (eds), *Geographies of Diversity: Italian Perspectives*, Geo-Italy 4, Rome: Società geografica italiana/CNR-Italian Committee for International Geographical Union, 2000, pp. 133–56.

Introduction: an itinerary

This book collects papers written by the four authors over the past twenty years. In this period Becattini and his three disciples have constantly exchanged ideas, sometimes working together, sometimes taking each other's advice on individual works. The common field has been the industrial district, both as a general and open framework for modelling local development, and as an important element in the recent history of Italian industrialisation.

The framework has its roots in the Marshallian concept of territorial external economies. The first paper where such a concept plays a significant role in explaining the industrial development of an Italian region is IRPET (that is, Tuscan Institute for Regional Economic Planning) 1969.[1] The paper resurrected the idea of localised external economies, coming very close to the concept of the industrial district.

In 1975 the IRPET published a report on the light industrialisation of Tuscany[2] edited by Giacomo Becattini, founder and former Director of the IRPET. Central to this book was the concept of 'urbanised countryside' (*campagna urbanizzata*) seen as a sort of incubator of the specialised industrial centres of Tuscany, afterwards called industrial districts.

The first time the term 'industrial district' was actually used was in a paper given by Giacomo Becattini at a meeting of the Italian Economic Association on *Italian Regional Development* (Pisa, 1977).[3] An English version of it was delivered at a Seminar of the European University (Fiesole-Florence) in 1978, and finally published in *Economic Notes*.[4] The first chapter of the present volume reproduces the paper under the new title 'Industrial districts in the development of Tuscany'.

Our second chapter on 'The Tuscan model' was first published in 1993 as a chapter of an Italian book which was the outcome of a joint research study on 'Regional socioeconomic development of Tuscany' by the London School of Economics, the University of Florence and the European University Institute (Florence) with the financial support of the Tuscany Region.[5] Then in 1994 the book was published in English.[6]

The paper focuses on the changes in the Tuscan model of development, placing particular emphasis on the 'different Tuscanies', on the shift to services in the industrial districts and on the de-industrialisation of the manufacturing poles.

The third chapter, on 'Prato's people', translates the last chapter of the concluding essay ('Prato in a changing world, 1954–1993') of Volume IV (*Il distretto industriale*, edited by G. Becattini) of the four volume work: Various authors, *Prato: storia di una città* (Florence: Le Monnier, 1997). It has already appeared in English as the concluding chapter of the English version (*The Caterpillar and the Butterfly: An Exemplary Case of Development in the Italy of Industrial Districts*, Florence: Le Monnier, 2001) of that essay.

It illustrates how all the experiences, both the positive and the negatives, of the Prato community shaped, in a sense, the system of local institutions and the typical character of Prato folk; which are its main resources in a rapidly changing world.

The fourth chapter, on the 'community market', reproduces a paper published in 1991 with the title 'The economic bases of diffuse industrialization' in a special issue of the journal *International Studies of Management & Organization*. That issue was devoted by the guest editor, Giorgio Inzerilli of the Erasmus University of Rotterdam, to 'The Italian alternative: flexible organization and social management, II: Theoretical analysis'.[7] The contents of this paper gather some reflections matured during extensive research on industrial districts, and in particular on the Prato district from the Second World War to the 1990s. An Italian version of the paper was first published in 1986 in the journal *Economia e politica industriale*.[8]

In this chapter some concepts derived from the economics of transaction costs are used to analyse business relations within the district. That enables the individuation of the special governance of normal contractual relations within the industrial district: the 'community market', so called in order to stress the blend of competition and cooperation based on local conventions typical of the district atmosphere. Moreover, in the same chapter the advantages of the 'community market' in facing opportunism, uncertainty and ambiguity are considered.

The fifth chapter, on 'decentralised creativity', corresponds, with minor modifications, to a paper published in 1992,[9] on the explanation of innovation in industrial districts. Italian case studies, for example those conducted by Sebastiano Brusco, started to suggest in the mid-1980s that the roots of competitive performance of industrial districts were to be found not only in small firms' flexibility, but also in strong though peculiar innovative capacities, basically different from the usual coupling 'big science – big R&D'. An Italian version of the paper had started to explore some conceptual foundations, referring both to Alfred Marshall's ideas, and to contemporary research on tacit knowledge, learning by doing, and collective invention.[10] The 1992 version combined a synthesis of those concepts with the results of research on the early diffusion of digital technologies in the industrial district of Prato.[11]

That research suggested a more accurate consideration of one necessary condition for strong innovation in industrial districts, which provides the solution to the incentive problems connected with inter-firm exchange of productive knowledge.[12]

The sixth chapter, on 'Trust', translates with some changes a paper published in 1992.[13] A preliminary version of it was presented in 1991 at the *Incontri pratesi sullo sviluppo locale* (Prato (annual) meetings on local development) held at the Villa Medicea of Artimino (Prato). The origin of this paper relates to the vast body of empirical research and reflection carried out in the framework of the studies on the Prato district.[14]

The aim of the chapter is to investigate how the rise and the development of an industrial district are financed, and what role and form credit assumes in those processes. The chapter establishes that trust relationships are crucial for financing the birth of new firms in industrial districts. In particular, trust based on investments in building up a good reputation is offered as security for informal credit, often interlinked with subcontracting relations. On the other hand, trust relationships of consolidated local firms with (mainly local) banks generate a double financial intermediation which, in normal circumstances, helps to overcome information asymmetries usually associated with credit rationing.

The seventh chapter, on 'entrepreneurship', corresponds, with minor modifications, to a paper published in 1996.[15] A preliminary version of this paper was presented at an international workshop organised by Maria Teresa Costa at the University of Barcelona in 1995.[16]

The paper resulted from the convergence of two streams of reflection: the first, on the mechanisms of change and transition in industrial districts; the other one, on the technical and organisational basis of the constitution of external economies in production systems. From the end of the 1980s to 1992 some important Italian industrial districts went through a prolonged crisis. This prompted debates on the end of Marshallian industrial districts, a new age of big firms, and finally the concentration of the industrial structure of surviving districts in the hands of a few leading firms. The predictions, translating temporary difficulties into sentences of decline and death, were based on the idea that the governance of industrial districts, based as it is only on small firms, markets, and customary cooperative behaviour, cannot cope with economic changes that demand different, more centralised, organisational solutions.

A research group based in Florence (Becattini et al.) and in Modena (Brusco et al.) took the point. The reflection on in-depth case studies suggested that industrial districts might have internal resources for the adjustment to crisis, since they normally develop, in periods of growth and innovation, multiple bases of productive knowledge and business. This same multiplicity helps the transition to new paths of local development.[17] A couple of related points have regard to external economies in production systems.[18] First, the constitution of external economies always demands a framework of specific public goods. Second, this framework is the ordinary object of various collective agencies, embedded within the district. In periods of crisis, collective agencies and, possibly, local private leadership may take a positive, even if transitional role in driving the district towards new paths.

The eighth chapter, on 'Italian industrial districts', was first published in 2000 as one of the Italian contributions to the 29th International Geographical Congress (Seoul, 14–18 August 2000) in the collective book *Geographies of Diversity: Italian Perspectives,* supported by the CNR-Italian Committee for International Geographical Union.[19] Preliminary versions of this paper were presented in Italy, at the ASEM Conference on Industrial Districts in 1999[20] and in Germany, at the ICE Meeting on Industrial Districts in 2000.[21]

This chapter addresses the problem of industrial districts in the Italian economy from the point of view of their economic and socioterritorial significance, as well as their evolution in time. It illustrates: (a) the relationships between the local productive structure and the relative socio-economic environment; (b) the relationships between firms concerning the organisation of the production process; (c) the human and social capital that are at the basis of the constitution of the district as a creative environment; (d) the main processes of a socioeconomic character that led Italy to the district experience. It is argued that the genesis of the districts is not linked to the restructuring processes of major corporations, but is an integral part of the history of Italy in the 20th century. The 'processes of districtualisation' that characterise the Italian economy are underlined; these also extend to the local productive systems dominated by major companies, making it possible to state that there is a convergence between the two pathways towards industrialisation, in the sense that both seek out competitive advantages in the territorial external economies that increasingly entail the intense involvement of local society in the production process, encouraging enterprise processes (in other words, the generation of new firms) and cooperation among firms. The chapter ends with some ideas on the future prospects of the districts, concluding that we can expect consolidation and development of the Italian industrial districts, helped by current processes of re-territorialisation of production and of economic policies.

The ninth chapter, on 'Local governance', translates an article published in 2001 in a volume which collects the contributions to a conference, on the recent evolution of labour and the crisis of trade unions, organised by the journal *Economia e politica industriale* at the Bocconi University in Milan.[22]

A very preliminary reflection on the topic was first presented by the author in a lecture given at a meeting on *Local Concerted Action in Industrial Districts* organised by the Municipality of Pesaro in 1998. In 2001, a first English version of this paper was delivered at a conference on *Kooperation und Interaktives Lernen in der Oekonomie*, organised by the Institut für Institutionelle und Sozial-Oekonomie of the University of Bremen.

This chapter deals with the role played by collective concerted action in local development. Contrary to the common view of industrial districts as examples of spontaneous development, on the basis of in-depth study of some Italian districts the paper argues that the competitive advantage of districts' firms is dependent on a greater social integration. The latter, in turn, is usually the result of concerted collective action among the main district groupings and local government. Moreover, whereas 'normal' acting in concert ensures continual semiautomatic adaptation of district firms and institutions, 'extraordinary' acting in concert is needed to adapt the local system to the major external changes. In conclusion, the generation and the reproduction of the competitiveness of industrial district firms require the process of competition to be directed by concerted collective action at the local level.

The tenth chapter, on 'multiple paths of local development', translates a chapter in a volume of collected papers on the re-reading of the Italian economy from the point of view of local development.[23] The volume puts together the results of a programme of research aimed at building an interpretative framework based on three intuitions: first, that industrial districts are a clear manifestation of a formula of economic and social development alternative to the big firm, (that is, the formula of local development); second, that they are not the only manifestation of such a formula; third, that the Italian economy in the last decades has been profoundly shaped by various paths of local development. The chapter was written in order to give an overview of the present state of research. It takes advantage also of the growing international literature on innovative milieux, learning regions, regional innovation systems, and industrial clusters.

Industrial districts are at the core of the mechanisms of local development that has a different, even if partial, materialisation in dynamic cities, rural developing areas, and company towns. Local development is based on the entrenchment of a population of producers in a local society, combining openness to external exchanges and a rich local reproduction of trust, entrepreneurial attitudes, and complementary specialised competencies.

The eleventh and final chapter, on 'a geographical redefinition of the form of the State', translates a paper given by the author at a meeting of the Fondazione Agnelli (Florence, 14 April 1994) on *Le regioni del centro Italia di fronte alle nuove prospettive istituzionali* (*The Regions of Central Italy*

Facing the New, Prospective Institutional Changes), and published in Italian in the No. 1 issue (September 1994) of the journal *Sviluppo locale.*

This short chapter, which does not claim to be conclusive, explores several aspects of the problems arising from the reorganisation (devolution) of the State suggested by new approaches to the problems of development.

NOTES

1. IRPET (1969), 'Lo sviluppo economico della Toscana: un'ipotesi di lavoro', *Il Ponte*, 25(11–12): 4–32.
2. IRPET (1975), *Lo sviluppo economico della Toscana, con particolare riguardo all'industrializzazione leggera*, Florence: Guaraldi.
3. The Italian version was published only in 1993: 'L'industrializzazione leggera della Toscana: un'interpretazione', in R. Leonardi and R.Y. Nanetti (eds), *Lo sviluppo regionale nell'economia europea integrata: il caso toscano*, Venice: Marsilio.
4. Becattini, G. (1978), 'The economic development of Tuscany: an interpretation', *Economic Notes*, 2–3.
5. Sforzi, F. (1993), 'Il modello toscano: un'interpretazione alla luce delle recenti tendenze', in R. Leonardi and R.Y. Nanetti (eds), *Lo sviluppo regionale nell'economia europea integrata: il caso toscano*, Venice: Marsilio, pp. 115–49.
6. Sforzi, F. (1994), 'The Tuscan model: an interpretation in the light of recent trends', in R. Leonardi and R.Y. Nanetti (eds), *Regional Development in a Modern European Economy: the Case of Tuscany*, London and New York: Pinter, pp. 86–115.
7. Dei Ottati, G. (1991), 'The economic bases of diffuse industrialization', *International Studies of Management & Organization*, Spring, 21(1): 53–74.
8. Dei Ottati, G. (1986), 'Distretto industriale, problemi delle transazioni e mercato comunitario: prime considerazioni', *Economia e politica industriale*, 51: 93–121.
9. Bellandi, M. (1992), 'The incentives to decentralised industrial creativity in local systems of small firms', *Revue d'économie industrielle*, 59: 99–110.
10. Bellandi, M. (1989), 'Capacità innovativa diffusa e sistemi locali di piccole imprese', in G. Becattini (ed.), *Modelli locali di sviluppo*, Bologna: Il Mulino, pp. 149–72. A very preliminary version of this last paper had been presented in 1984 at the 25th scientific meeting of the Società italiana degli economisti.
11. Bellandi, M. and C. Trigilia (1991), 'Come cambia un distretto industriale: strategie di riaggiustamento e tecnologie informatiche nell'industria tessile di Prato', *Economia e politica industriale*, 70: 121–52.
12. Another version of the same ideas was presented as 'Decentralized creativity and innovation within a representative dynamic industrial district', in UNCTAD and Deutches Zentrum für Entwicklungstechnologien (1994), *Technological Dynamism in Industrial Districts: an Alternative Approach to Industrialization in Developing Countries?*, New York and Geneva: United Nations, pp. 73–81.
13. Dei Ottati, G. (1992), 'Fiducia, transazioni intrecciate e credito nel distretto industriale', *Note economiche*, 1–2: 1–30. An English version of that article with some modifications was published in 1994 in *Cambridge Journal of Economics*, 18(6): 529–46. Chapter 6 of this volume corresponds to the latter version.
14. See also Dei Ottati, G. (1995), *Tra mercato e comunità: aspetti concettuali e ricerche empiriche sul distretto industriale*, Milan: Franco Angeli.
15. Bellandi, M. (1996), 'On entrepreneurship, region and the constitution of scale and scope economies', *European Planning Studies*, 4(4): 421–38.
16. 'Impacto de los procesos de globalización económica en los sistemas locales'. The presentation had a direct publication in 1996 as 'Algunas consideraciones acerca de la

creación de economias de escala y la dinámica tecno-organizativa de los sistemas de producción', *Información comercial espanola. Revista de economía*, 754, June: 73–83.
17. Bellandi, M. and M. Russo (eds) (1994), *Distretti industriali e cambiamento economico locale*, Turin: Rosenberg & Sellier. The author presented an English version of these issues at the *Workshop on Regional Innovation Systems, Regional Networks and Regional Policy*, Lysebu, Norway, 1995, invited by Björn Asheim.
18. See Bellandi, M. (1995), *Economie di scala e organizzazione industriale*, Milan: Franco Angeli.
19. Cori, B., G. Corna Pellegrini, G. Cortesi, G. Dematteis, M.T. Di Maggio Alleruzzo, C. Minca, F. Sforzi and G. Zanetto (eds) (2000), *Geographies of Diversity: Italian Perspectives*, Geo-Italy 4, Rome, Società geografica italiana/CNR-Italian Committee for International Geographical Union, pp. 133–56.
20. *Industrial Districts and International Transfer of Technology as Means to Promote Trade in Goods and Services*, ASEM Conference, Bari, 5 October 1999, organised by the Italian Institute for Foreign Trade (ICE).
21. *Distretti industriali: Ein Erfolgsmodell zwischen Tradition und Zukunft*, Berlin, 3 July 2000, organized by Italienisches Institut für Außenhandel (ICE), Berlin.
22. Dei Ottati, G. (2001), 'Concertazione e sviluppo nei distretti industriali', in A. Ninni, F. Silva and S. Vaccà (eds), *Evoluzione del lavoro, crisi del sindacato e sviluppo del paese*, Milan: Franco Angeli, pp. 163–95. For a shorter English version, see 'Social concert and local development: the case of industrial districts', *European Planning Studies*, 2002, 10(4): 449–66.
23. Becattini, G., M. Bellandi, G. Dei Ottati and F. Sforzi (2001), *Il caleidoscopio dello sviluppo locale: trasformazioni economiche nell'Italia contemporanea*, Turin: Rosenberg & Sellier. This volume hosts the results of a set of Italian research groups coordinated by Becattini in the second half of the 1990s.

PART I

The Development of Tuscany:
Industrial Districts

1. Industrial districts in the development of Tuscany

Giacomo Becattini

1. A NOTE ON THE HISTORICAL ORIGINS OF POSTWAR EVENTS IN TUSCANY

The characteristics and potential of a development process can only be understood through an analysis of how it arose, because most of the preconditions for development in terms of its pace and modes were created at an earlier stage. We know that development is the antithesis of socio-economic stagnation, stagnation being a stage in which all the economic, social and cultural variables interact to produce a generalised lack of faith in the prospect of change, an overestimation of the risks of any innovation and a widespread dislike of innovators of all kinds. Any analysis of a development process must therefore take as its starting-point this – fortunately not entirely stable – equilibrium of stagnation and identify within it the embryonic developmental features and potential.

The role of 'social culture' (defined by Bertolino [1961, p. 181] as 'knowledge and faith welded together in a basic doctrine which is present in all the various activities of every individual, whatever his or her place in society') in preserving this 'equilibrium' has been well put by Bertolino (ibid.):

> This culture is inhibitory, and is reflected in the structure of the economy and of society, that is the whole system of institutions in which are embodied, whether in legal or customary form, the principles informing the behaviour of the population, and also in the moral and political philosophy, at various levels of elaboration but always fitting the respective social classes, which is used to justify and defend that structure.

This is, of course, not the appropriate place, nor is the writer the appropriate person, to carry out even a quick historical survey of what occurred in Tuscany between the achievement of Italian national unification

11

and the Second World War. A task of this type must be left to the experts in the field; nevertheless I shall have to devote a few lines, for which I must apologise to my readers, to a brief review of certain limited aspects of the region's history which form an essential background to the situation which we can term the 'starting-point' of development in Tuscany since the last World War.

The question which looms largest in this part of my account, a question which is really rather rhetorical, is whether Tuscany had a 'vocation' for light industrial development. Although these days it is the case that there is so little faith in analyses of so-called 'area vocations' that the question might well be ignored, I think it is both valid and relevant to ask whether Tuscany might have been able to accommodate a classic type of industrialisation in the postwar period, in other words, with more heavy industry and more intensive urbanisation.

In any case, scholars cannot ignore this question, if they wish their research to be of use to people of flesh and blood, since it serves to distinguish, if not to divide, the different analyses of development in the region and to some extent has implications for the choice of practical policies to be applied to it.[1] In fact, because of its considerable mineral resources, its remarkable financial structure and its long history as a centre of trade, Tuscany appeared to be, as early as the first half of the 19th century, a suitable site for a process of industrialisation as intensive, all things considered, as that which occurred subsequently in areas such as Piedmont, Lombardy and Liguria. Yet this potential was not fulfilled. Tuscany – despite certain considerable strides towards the building up of a modern industrial structure – failed to develop, up to the Second World War, the classic sectors of industrialisation (the cotton industry first, and then engineering) and this was due to factors which, in Tuscan terms, can be defined as 'exogenous' as well as to influences stemming from Tuscan society itself, from its structure and cultural outlook.

1.1 'Exogenous' and 'Endogenous' Factors

Among factors which can be regarded as 'exogenous' at a regional level one can certainly include the way in which Italian unification was achieved and the consequences which this had in terms of both power- and role-sharing agreements among the ruling groups of the pre-unification states, and the territorial organisation set up in the country. While I must refer readers to the works of specialists in relation to the first of these factors,[2] since it would require an account outside the scope of this chapter, as regards the organisation of the territory of Italy after unification, I would stress the relative isolation for many decades of the interior of Tuscany in terms of the provision of roads and railways. The mountain barrier of the Apennines and political and military considerations combined to tip the balance in favour of the railway policy which bypassed Tuscany and hinged rather on a central axis running directly from the Po valley down the Adriatic coastline to the heel of Italy (see Mioni 1976, pp. 74–107).

Further exogenous factors, in the sense employed here, appear to have been the change of Italy's capital first to Florence and then to Rome,[3] the tariff policies of the Kingdom of Italy and the differential effect on the different regions of the two World Wars taken together with the periods of preparation, reconversion and reconstruction which preceded and followed them. Each of these events – and doubtless others besides – had important effects in terms of the intranational (interregional) division of labour of which, however, no more than a mention can be made here.

Among the 'endogenous' factors, in my view, first place must go to the 'grand design' which was lucidly formulated and energetically carried out, first in the Tuscany of the grand-dukes and later in the Kingdom of Italy, by that section of the Tuscan ruling group known as the 'Tuscan moderates' (*moderati toscani*).[4] This was actually a very heterogeneous group, in which traditionalists and romantics combined with forward-looking individuals who anticipated subsequent developments but which, taken as a whole, stuck to the maintenance of a status quo assuring ample economic rewards to the small (though not tiny) number of landowners or to the partly overlapping group of coupon-clippers, and even greater social and moral rewards in terms of the enjoyment of a cultural hegemony, in addition to political dominance, over the 'plebeian' mass, as it was then called, in the region.

This policy, which can be summed up as anti-industrial, aimed to spare the streets and squares in Tuscany the social stirrings which were then shaking Europe and its drawing-rooms; the vulgarity of artisans grown rich plays an important role in holding back the formulation in the region of an 'industrial base' while encouraging it, through investment, elsewhere. It should not, of course, be thought that this 'grand design' was so simple and straightforward as may appear from such a brief survey, nor that it prevented all industrial development in Tuscany, where indeed important and significant episodes occurred, especially around the turn of the 19th century, on which ample light has been shed by historians.[5] If this were not so, it would be hard to explain both the political importance and the strong cultural influence of this region in the decades between unification and the First World War, and in some respects also during the Fascist period.

The 'moderate' strategy in fact gives general tone to what happened in Tuscany but leaves untouched many important economic and sociocultural developments,[6] related to the highly differentiated make-up of society in the region, which in turn were the result of a very complex history.

1.2 Controlled Development and the Light-Industrial Specialisation of the Tuscan Economy

It was by the interaction between the exogenous and endogenous factors mentioned above that the relative development of the region was shaped. A few data will suffice to give a fairly clear idea of what happened in relative terms. The strengths of the Tuscan economy at the time of its absorption into the Kingdom of Italy were its financial credit structures and its famous agriculture.

On a much more modest scale, though far from negligible, was the position of manufacturing in the region. Measured in terms of the number of persons employed, the 1881 census shows that in Tuscany about seven per cent of the population was engaged in manufacturing industry, a figure below that of the region's share of the country's total population (7.4 per cent). In terms of its share of the capital of limited companies operating in the industrial sector the figures for Tuscany were (in 1865) still lower (5.2 per cent), illustrating the small number of large and modern units.

This situation of widespread craft-industry and small factories had already been given theoretical expression in the work of Raffaello Busacca, one of the main economists of the 'moderate' group:

> The special characteristic of its manufactures lies in its exquisite taste ... if Tuscany is to become a genuinely manufacturing country it will be when manufactures of this sort grow large enough to satisfy most of the foreign market. (Busacca 1855)

Busacca and his friends believed, indeed, that Tuscany's hopes 'should not rest in manufactures', however artistic, but in the agriculture 'which will always form the main basis of its economy' and above all 'in its rich and diverse mines'. And, in fact, Tuscan mining in the period following Busacca's 'memorandum' (1855) was the object of considerable attention on the part of capitalists from inside and outside of the region.

If we compare these data with those of the years around the First World War we find (a) that Tuscan agriculture in 1908 is still more or less at the level of 1861 (200 kg/ha.), while in regions like Lombardy capitalisation had risen to the order of 366 kg/ha. of livestock; (b) capital in Tuscan limited companies in the credit sector had fallen by 1916 to 25.3 per cent of the national total; (c) large-scale industry had lost ground in relation to the national average as is shown by the unchanged share (5.2 per cent) it had of the capital of industrial limited companies (1916) and by its falling share of employees in the heavy-industrial sectors (engineering, metals and chemicals): from 7.5 per cent in 1881 to 6.7 per cent of the national total in 1921.

The interwar period is complex and contradictory from the viewpoint which concerns us here. Some public support for heavy industry produces a halt in the falling trend of the previous period and even a modest improvement. Tuscany's share of the national total of those employed in these sectors (engineering, metals and chemicals) rises by 1936 to 7.4 per cent. But there is a much greater rise in the numbers employed in the same sectors in the industrial triangle (from 48.8 to 54.4 per cent of the national total) while there is a fall in Tuscany in the number of personnel in industrial enterprises with more than 500 employees (from 7.6 in 1927 to 6.3 per cent in 1937–50). If one adds to this the proliferation of productive units in light-industrial sectors, especially after the Great Depression, it is clear that Fascism does not halt the trend towards regional specialisation which had already started in previous decades.[7]

To conclude this rapid outline of the evolution of industry in Tuscany between unification and the Second World War, I believe one can say that the nature of development there was led rather than leading and that, apart from some important developments in mining, steel and chemicals (due mostly to investment and entrepreneurs from outside Tuscany) it affects sectors which most easily 'fit in with' the social environment of the region. Symbolic of this gradual fading away of the prospect of Tuscany becoming one of the driving forces in Italy's industrial development during this period is what happened to the iron-ore resources on Elba, which for many decades were mined and exported and where it was decided to make use of them only when they were virtually exhausted.[8]

Thus the answer I would give to the question raised earlier – whether development in Tuscany since the Second World War might have taken a different course – is that, as early as the beginning of the war, the process of the interregional division of labour had already gone a very long way towards cutting Tuscany off from the 'heavy' sectors of industry. Clearly, this does not mean that the trend could not have been reversed, but simply that such a shift (had it been clearly conceived and really desired at both regional and national levels – which was not the case, for reasons which do not allow one to pin the blame squarely on any one political party) would inevitably have conflicted with trends already well established both within and outside the region.

2. FORMATION OF THE PREREQUISITES FOR INDUSTRIAL TAKE-OFF

The long series of events between unification and the Second World War had the effect of producing at one and the same time, as we have seen, a relative decline in industrial activity (manufacturing) in Tuscany as compared with the regions of the industrial triangle, and a growing relative specialisation in the 'light' and 'traditional' sectors of industry. This 'controlled development' was, however, accompanied by a gradual modernisation of Tuscan society and a growing diversification of its productive apparatus.

We shall examine, first, the infrastructural aspects, especially those with the greatest influence on the development of industry. From the standpoint of communications the period was marked by steady extension and improvement of both the road system in Tuscany and the region's links with the outside world (the Apennine passes); there was, indeed, little improvement in the railway system between the 1870s and 1934 when the main Florence-Bologna line was opened, overcoming central Tuscany's winter isolation from the Po Valley. The importance of this road and rail network for a region without navigable rivers and canals needs to be stressed.

As regards the distribution network (commerce), Tuscany achieved the same figure per head of population as the 'industrial triangle' did twenty years earlier. In 1936 Tuscany had 366 persons employed in this sector per 10 000 inhabitants, while as early as 1911 the figure was 307 per 10 000 in Piedmont, 443 in Liguria and 352 in Lombardy.

Turning to the educational system and illiteracy levels we find a similar picture of backwardness compared with the regions of the industrial triangle. The number of those employed in teaching (both private and public) in Tuscany was 32 per 10 000 inhabitants in 1911 compared with 37–8 in the triangle as early as 1881. By 1936 the situation was much better (58 per 10 000) but still clearly lagging behind the triangle and, indeed, below the national average. Tuscany was some thirty years behind the triangle with respect to literacy rates. Only in 1931 did the region achieve a literacy rate of 81.8 per cent; the rate in Piedmont was higher as far back as 1901, a level also achieved in Liguria and Lombardy later in the same decade.

A similar backwardness in relation to the triangle is found in Tuscany with respect to the number of those employed in health services: 24 per 10 000 in 1936, which is little better than 21–2 per 10 000 which the triangle regions had achieved in 1881. One hardly needs to point out that Tuscany's backwardness in comparison to the triangle was matched by all the other regions of the centre and south (except for Latium).

All in all, it can be said that Tuscany's infrastructure at the end of the Second World War (ignoring war damage) was on the same scale as the triangle's at the end of the First World War. From the standpoint of infrastructural prerequisites Tuscany was thus ready for a process of rapid industrialisation by about 1949–51. Of course, this means merely that industrial development was a possibility, not that any direct stimulus for it existed.

From the strictly industrial point of view, the situation in Tuscany at the end of the Second World War looks highly differentiated. A vast agricultural area virtually without manufacturing industry, though with some important units in mining, accounted for the south of the region. Along the coast stretched a chain, broken in places, of large and medium-sized industrial establishments operating in engineering (such as the Livorno shipyards), metals (the Ilva and Magona ironworks in Piombino), chemicals (the Solvay sodaworks at Rosignano and so on), and glass (the St Gobain glassworks in Pisa).

In the central valleys, to complete the list, there was a more or less unbroken string of towns and villages with some industry, with considerable industrial concentration and population density especially in the Prato area and in the lower Arno Valley (from Empoli to Cascina). The population of manufacturing firms in this area was made up of a very small number of significant large industrial units, a number of medium-sized firms, and a multitude of small and very small enterprises, these last being connected by a sort of umbilical cord to the independent craftsmen and the world of wage- and agricultural labourers. Thus we have a very broad productive base in which the unchanged craft-character of the organisation of production was mixed up with an attitude to the domestic and foreign market which was no longer just that of the independent craftsman; a market whose demand moreover was met and to some extent stimulated (often through the direct or indirect activity of middlemen) by the production of short-run products, probably differing only in details such as colour, material, trim and so on.

If we deepen the analysis we find that in each of the subsections comprising this system there coexisted different types of productive activities and that almost always the same was true of enterprises differing considerably in size.[9] It is worth pointing out that this gave rise to a social environment in which wage-labourers, particularly skilled ones, lived side by side with independent skilled craftsmen, producing an extremely interesting sociological blend. The world of the non-agricultural labourer (often an ex-agricultural labourer) thus reveals a unique structure which is penetrated by demands for social emancipation stemming from a constructive ideology of the social role of labour. It was from this matrix, which is at once economic and sociocultural, that there flowed the form of development typical to the region, with the results that we shall see.

To employ a concept much used by Alfred Marshall, the course of Tuscan history leads to a form, still incomplete but already clear in outline of 'industrial district' (which I understand as meaning 'an integrated industrial area') which produces economies external to the single firm and even to the industrial sector defined by technology, but internal to the 'sectorial-social-territorial' network.

2.1 Tensions and Tendencies in Tuscan Society

From the standpoint of the search for the forces which may have led Tuscany astray from the path of 'controlled development', the accumulation of civic infrastructures or industrial plants (the physical growth of the basis of production) is less important than the build-up of tensions and the ripening of tendencies favouring a form of development based on economic self-assertion by individuals. The problem is a particularly knotty one and here I can only offer the bare bones of the very tentative results of reflections which really need much more thorough and painstaking comparison and checking.

From what I have been able to grasp of this complex matter, there are three main sociocultural premisses specific to development in Tuscany. First of all, there is a peasant protest, particularly by women and youth, not so much against the country itself as against the rigidity of the pecking-order in the family and against their close economic dependence on its older male members. The share-cropping system (*mezzadria*) in particular, with its considerable economic adaptability and its unchanging social patterns, is crucial to any analysis of Tuscan society: it can be said that, for centuries, the tensions within a social structure so obviously unfair in its distribution of duties and rights had been absorbed or even socially channelled by an appropriate ideology which contrasted, often in a subtle and sophisticated manner, the combined virtues of family hierarchy and solidarity, of the certainty of survival that farming activity provided and the wholesome properties of country air and food, with the unbridled self-seeking, the uncertainty of life, the pollution and stress of factory work and urban system of living.

This ideological superstructure, only a few of whose features we have touched upon (perhaps the most striking ones as opposed to the most important ones) was still in place at the outbreak of the Second World War, as a coherent pattern of political and economic conditions which undermined any strong and determined aspiration for change.

A second premiss for development was, I believe, intimately linked to the first, namely the work ethic which is thrown up by an environment such as the one I have described. As I understand it, this work ethic is made up of three fundamental aspects: first, an arbitrary but categorical dividing-line between those 'willing to work' (as it was crudely expressed, meaning those who are prepared to seek their fortune or at least their survival within the existing framework of institutions) and the 'workshy'.

This distinction is made, in my view, right across the social and political spectrum: even the gospel of socialism is taken to mean that labour is then a source of legitimation for all wealth and material prosperity as opposed to the non-labour of both the bosses and of parasites and idlers. The notions of 'alienated' labour and of 'the right to leisure' of a part of the Marxist and semi-Marxist tradition would have seemed to the great mass of Tuscan workers as no more than the twittering of intellectuals.

Second, a high esteem for work well performed, a 'mastery of the craft', provided social discriminators of great importance. Third, we find an acceptance of the risk of industrial accidents as a normal physical feature of work activity.

This work ethic is the result of a social formula and historical process in which low average wage rates are associated – for a number of reasons both historical and natural (the mild climate and the ideological conditioning of most Tuscans), but also because of restraint in pursuing tendencies to harsher exploitation implicit in the original 'grand design'– with living conditions which as a whole were not abysmal, so that work as such was not felt to be purely negative in its characteristics.

It is hard even to guess at the role played in the creation of this work ethic by the Catholicism with which the Tuscan people's worldview was so deeply imbued. I shall merely point out that Catholicism is more in line with the principle of work well done than with that of unremitting toil.

It may be of interest to quote the words of an official of the British Embassy in Florence in November 1870:

> As former physician to a hospital in London, relieving from 30 000 to 40 000 yearly, I often met with diseases resulting from overwork, either too prolonged or too severe. For many years I attended the Florence Hospital, but I do not think I ever met with a case of illness from a similar cause.[10]

A third premiss of development was what may be called the cultural-touristic open-mindedness of the region – an open-mindedness obviously assisted by the wealth of its traditional artistic resources and by the fact that the national language came to correspond with the speech of Tuscany, but which might not have exerted much influence had it not been nourished and supported by a well established tradition of foreign links and of warm and efficient 'hospitality'.[11]

Trading in relation to a continuing, though declining, rich export trade, should be added to the still important regional traffic in imports and exports, and to the commerce of ideas in relation to the whole great coming and going of foreigners, tourists and merchants, artists and scientists who flocked to Tuscany. The long tradition of business, cultural and tourist contacts with foreigners, often merging together, embodied in highly specialised interme-diary structures (such as international banks, travel agencies, buyers, hotels, and so on), constituted privileged channels, indeed almost pipelines, for economic relations with the outside world. On the other hand they were

instrumental in training Tuscan town-dwellers for the trauma-free absorption
of the 'modern' way of life.

2.2 The 'Priming-Mechanism' of Development

I should now like to refer to certain aspects of the situation during and
immediately after the Second World War which acted in a way as a 'priming
mechanism' for the developmental process in Tuscany. The first of these is
the war damage and the subsequent intensive rebuilding which occurred in
the region. Tuscany and Emilia-Romagna are recognised as being the two
regions which suffered most from the campaign in Italy: bridges, tunnels,
road and railway junctions, factories and houses were all largely destroyed as
the battle raged. By a paradox now generally accepted by researchers and
embodied in the literature, this higher rate of destruction caused a higher rate
of public expenditure, an exceptional renewal of industrial and civic structures and a greater effort at reconstruction. In a climate of common
determination, looms come out of their hiding-places, warehouses are re-
paired, houses, roads, bridges and railways rebuilt. Real incomes rise rapidly
if inflation spreads unequally, expenditure is accelerated and both official
and 'black' markets pass on the stimulus to industry itself.

A second element is represented by the different impact of the process of
reorganisation of national and international markets following the disruption
of the Second World War. The economic rebirth of Tuscany did not get
much help from the Allied Military Government at first, or from the central
Government later. Large-scale light industry got started on its own: Prato
with the odds and ends of clothes, the furniture industry with local timber,
the footwear factories with any raw and semi-finished materials to hand.
Against this prompt recovery of light industry we find in the central and
southern regions of Italy an enormous delayed demand for consumer goods
of all kinds, mainly durables and semi-durables. Even abroad the situation is
favourable for anyone capable of producing anything.

The reconstruction period is thus marked by an outstanding boom in
textiles from Prato, reinforced and spurred on by the currency exchange
measures adopted by the Government to encourage exports. But the boom is
not confined to Prato: several light sectors and several geographical areas
quickly get off the mark.

A third element, whose relevance may be open to argument, but which I
do not believe can be ignored without losing sight of an essential and
singular aspect of this development process, is the effects of the difference
between the balance of social and political forces in Tuscany and that
prevailing elsewhere in Italy. Numerous symptoms can be found of an
overall plan of disengagement on the part of the major industrial groups in

respect of regions such as Tuscany, where the parties of the left and the CGIL (General Confederation of Labour) are much stronger than elsewhere. The effects of this plan merit a more thorough investigation than I have been able to carry out; I will do no more than refer to an aspect which cannot fail to be intriguing because it represents a unique feature in Tuscan regional development, a feature with very serious consequences. Much of the political and trade-union leadership after 1948 found it difficult or impossible to remain inside the large factories in the region and so set up their own small firms, often with an alacrity on a par with their feelings of anger and political frustration, and thus contributed to the economic development of the region.

More generally, the dissipation in 1947–48 of the cultural atmosphere of the postwar period – an atmosphere full of uncertainties but also rich with hope – channelled energies into economic self-assertion which might have been directed, and would have preferred to be directed, to political activity in the broad sense (trade unions, running public concerns, and so on).

3.   THE 'MECHANISM' OF DEVELOPMENT

3.1   The Flight from the Land

The logical and historical starting-point for the mechanism of development in Tuscany must be sought, in my view, in what is termed the labour market. A labour market which, in this case, at the start of the period we are concerned with, possessed a singular feature which has already partly been touched upon: behind what is usually defined as the primary labour supply, and behind a secondary supply which, as is usual, comprised the very young, the elderly, women and those workers willing to take on two jobs, there was in Tuscany a potential supply of farmworkers, both male and female, mainly young people, anxious to escape the living and working conditions associated with the 'family farm' and hopeful of finding elsewhere an environment less redolent of poverty and stagnation and above all less inimical to individual initiative and personality. This group comprised a huge pool of underemployed who had been affected by the breakdown of age-old psychological barriers as a result of war, resistance, foreign invasion and the recovery of civil liberties.

It was a mass of farm labourers who rejected the paternalism and subordination of yesterday's world but not its faith in the providential connection between effort and reward, between commitment to a job and social success. Just how this came about, by virtue of precisely what sociological and economic processes, in response to what political promptings, is still semi-virgin soil which needs to be approached with both rigour and open-mindedness: it points, in my view, to a good many of the reasons for that sociocultural process whereby the Tuscany of yesterday, to all appearances still imprisoned within a hegemony of 'moderatism', has been transformed into the Tuscany of today, in which, despite factors of continuity (whose significance and role are currently the subject of lively debate in the region), the characteristics of the region's culture seem to foreshadow new social relationships.

The INAIL (National Institute of Insurance for Accidents at Work) data on workers' earnings and accidents at work, for all their well-known limitations, do seem to fit this hypothesis of exogenous pressure by the peasant masses in Tuscany on the region's labour market: they show indeed, for the 1950s, a slower rate of growth in wages in Tuscany than in the country as a whole and a rise in the number of accidents at work greater than the national average. These figures, and the others used to test the hypothesis of the existence of a surplus of pressure on the labour market stemming from a local potential labour supply, are not of course unambiguous: nevertheless they seem on the whole to allow us to regard it not merely as plausible, but as highly likely (see Becattini 1975, pp. 95–6).

3.2 The Expansion of World Trade

Of course this pressure by the peasants on the local labour market, despite its new intensity and new characteristics in the postwar period, had also existed beforehand and might have been relieved in the form of emigration as it was elsewhere (for instance, in share-cropper regions such as Marche and Umbria). That this did not occur is apparently due to the influence of special features, one peculiar to the postwar period and the other to Tuscany as it then was. The first is the exceptional expansion in world trade; and from the standpoint of the Tuscan region in trade with other regions of Italy, Tuscany found itself operating for some twenty years in a very rapidly expanding 'external' market, both national and international. This expansion, I must stress, was due to factors outside the control of Tuscan manufacturers.

Without this exogenous extension of the external market, the development of the region, given the social and economic structures which had been consolidated there in earlier decades, would simply not have taken place. This obviously does not mean that the tension would have found no outlet, merely that the outlet would have been different, probably in the form of emigration to other parts of Italy or abroad. I consider that this would have occurred even had there been a radical reform of agriculture, since the latter would in any case have had to reduce the size of the rural population which even in 1951 was still over 40 per cent of the total.

3.3 The Interaction of Economic and Sociocultural Factors

Even the condition just mentioned would not, however, have sufficed to ensure expansion as can be seen from the fact that the external market was enlarged for all the regions of Italy: for Lombardy which did develop as for Lucania which did not; the factor which differentiates some of them and brings others into line is, in my view, the existence in Tuscany of that 'sectorial-territorial-social' network of industrial activity and infrastructures already described. Although not yet, at the start of the period, a genuine 'integrated industrial area', it was certainly rather more than just the embryonic form of one: it represented a set of activities which still had large gaps, both sectorial and territorial, but was already arranged in a non-random way across the region and was easily capable of filling the gaps once the process of expansion was underway. It was from this continually growing network of industrial activities and concentrations of manpower that there arose a simultaneous and linked occurrence (by a process of proliferation whose analogies may be sought more in the realm of biology than in that of mechanics). On the one hand we have the catalysing factor of entrepreneurship, and on the other the ceaseless flow of external and internal economies which gave Tuscan goods a decisive competitive edge compared with those of firms which, despite having manpower available willing to accept even lower wage rates, were not working within such a rich and diversified socioeconomic network.

It should be noted that the bulk of Tuscan industrialists in the postwar period was not coterminous with the prewar industrial bourgeoisie but was made up of a mixture of entrepreneurial types with a preponderance of very small-scale industrialists, most of whom began as craftsmen, workers and peasants and grew in step with the environment, both entering and leaving the field of industry, but which even when throwing its hand in left behind its deposit of know-how, wealth produced and aspirations baulked but not abandoned.

All the same, it would be very odd and almost incomprehensible for a capitalistic industrial development to be brought about by 'new men' alone, without the involvement of the social classes which previously controlled the process of capital accumulation.

And in fact when we move from the numerical and quantitative plane to the 'qualitative' one, we have to recognise that the role of certain sections of the industrial bourgeoisie and especially of the mercantile and financial bourgeoisie of the region was far from being a minor one. One example will suffice: the brokers (buyers acting for foreign firms who were already installed in Florence before the Second World War, international banks, and so on) played a considerable part both in channelling international demand towards Tuscany and in inducing Tuscan manufacturers to adopt the price-quality combinations enabling them to compete in the mass markets of the industrialised countries.

Another important aspect was represented, right from the start, by the 'unified budgeting' of the Tuscan family, in both financial terms and allocation of time, which acted as an invisible transmission belt between the sectors of production in which different members of the family were working. A fall in the income of one member tended to produce a fall in the supply-price of the services of the other members; a change in the hours one member had available for leisure produced a corresponding overall redistribution of the tasks assigned within the family. The consequence of this is a linking-up, outside the workplace, of the production costs in the different sectors of industry, and this made it increasingly unsatisfactory to deal with the problem of industrial competition in terms of industrial sectors defined by their technology alone. The production cost of any given product in Tuscany thus became an extremely complex function of all the technical, economic, social and cultural factors which interacted within the 'sectorial-social-territorial' network.

3.4 Industrial Development without Vertical Integration

A necessary step in this formula for development, as in all others, is its comparative capacity for absorbing technological progress: this is even more important and urgent after a period of partial isolation such as occurs in wartime. In a period of intensive innovation, such as that which in fact took place after the Second World War, the sectors of production typical of Tuscany also had to face the challenge of the technological progress which had gone on elsewhere. To cope with this necessity there exist two general strategies: the first aims for a gradual development of the firm as a whole so as to maximise within it the advantages of line organisation of production and of the advanced specialisation of labour which the former permits and promotes. This naturally requires an enlargement of both technical and economic units in accordance with fairly precise economic and technical laws. Any innovation which increases the economic minimum unit size (flow per unit of time) requires a complex reorganisation of the whole process which in turn leads to enlargement or rearrangements of the organisational and managerial structure and, after a certain point, a move towards a legal status which will ensure an ample supply of capital.

This is the classical strategy of capitalistic industrial development, but it is not the only strategy, and not even necessarily the most rational from the microeconomic viewpoint in cases where the following two conditions apply at the same time: where the process of production is comprised of stages which can be technically separated from each other; and where demand is diversified and varies over time. In such cases a second strategy is possible which brings about the same advantages of line organisation (overcoming the problems of the elimination of idle time, of what Georgescu-Roegen (1971) calls the 'fund-factors') without the need for any substantial enlargement of premises and management.

The strategy concerned is not one of integration, but is just as intensively specialised, and the shrewdest economists from Adam Smith onwards have always been aware that it represents a viable alternative to the obvious model of capitalistic centralisation and vertical integration. All the same it would be quite misleading, in my view, to say purely and simply that this strategy was chosen by industry in Tuscany: there certainly was an element of choice but it was by no means a free one: it was clearly conditioned by external circumstances and choices made elsewhere, and invisibly but no less effectively by sociocultural traditions prevailing in the region. The work ethic and the rejection of share-cropping were not the reasons for choosing a particular type of firm: they did no more than enable the choice to be made, but the strong identification with the firm of a first-generation population of entrepreneurs was what prevented any shift towards types of firms based on the association of anonymous sources of capital. This cultural bottleneck, which might have had a negative effect on a form of development moving towards mass-production on a large scale, proved to be harmless as part of a model of development whose main direction, in line with that followed in previous decades, was towards typical products.

There thus occurred a development by proliferation of industrial units which were predominantly diversified and specialised within those sectors allowing such a strategy of growth: textiles, clothing manufacture, furs, leather, furniture and others. Among these 'others', it should be noted, there were significant subsectors belonging to quite untypical statistical categories such as papermaking and packaging, plastics, secondary processing of non-metal minerals and even engineering. This was the process of 'non-integration' (rather than 'disintegration') which characterised the 'classical' stage of development in Tuscany.

This diversification and specialisation did not stop at industries producing finished goods such as those just mentioned, but reached into the huge and decisive area of industrial services. The extension of the overall size of the process actually allowed an increasingly detailed specialisation in the sectors of road transport, technical servicing, administrative and fiscal wholesale trades advisory services, brokerage services for trade, and banking and insurance services. An increasingly detailed and ramified specialisation thus developed which was translated into a growing capacity to meet the specific needs of the sector directly concerned with production of goods in terms of both the quality and the speed with which services became available on (and were required by) the market.

3.5 The Characteristics of the Labour Supply

Faced with this rapid multiplication of productive enterprises, but also largely as a result of it, there arose an extremely complex diversification of the labour supply: the most obvious aspects of this are those relating to primary supply, both original and induced, local or otherwise. This part of the development of the labour supply in Tuscany is the most visible one, although it is far from having been adequately explained, and indeed cannot be explained in isolation. But it is the other part of the labour supply, the so-called secondary supply, which is most interesting. It was a supply dependent on both objective and subjective conditions, a supply that could not or would not be fully integrated into the production process of the firm, which provided industry with a few hours per day or a few years in a life, which may have been of great value to industry (such was the case of the physically active and experienced retired worker) but those who supplied this labour had not made a firm and irrevocable decision to work for others and in particular to do a specific job which would be a continuing and not merely temporary feature of their existence. This supply of 'uncommitted' labour, which was often involved, because of the haphazardness of the labour legislation, in unregulated or illegal forms of work, naturally encountered and easily fitted in with a demand for labour which, by the very nature of the goods produced, fluctuated greatly over a period of time: production grew, incomes grew (though unevenly) and ever higher levels of expectation among the working population were produced and reproduced. To a certain extent the mechanism was self-sustaining: bits of an archetypal ideology of consumption, which was the expression of the way in which a population only just emerging from poverty sought to benefit by the expansion of capitalism, merged with bits of the work ethic previously mentioned to produce peaks of hectic and single-minded dedication to money-making (as, for example, at Prato in certain aspects) reminiscent of the heyday of early capitalism.

But the picture is even more complex than that investigated in the classics of the sociology of capitalism: the shortening of the working day, improved transportation, the introduction of machines for doing housework, the changed standards socially acceptable in relation to the latter, all this leaves time and energy free, to capture which, in a somewhat bewildering and muddled way, employers and sociocultural structures frantically compete with each other and with the time objectively needed to use and maintain the ever-growing mass of privately owned consumer durables which clutter people's lives. The picture of the contradictions within the 'affluent society', even in an often cheap and wasteful version of such a society, is just as instructive as that of the contradictions within poverty.

Yet the Tuscan industrial formula serves remarkably well, at least to a certain extent, to turn this supply of surplus hours in people's lives to productive purposes, as demonstrated also by the good response of the Tuscan economy to cyclical fluctuations (see Bianchi 1976).

This process of development, in which I have tried to connect the strictly economic aspects with the sociocultural ones, has given rise to the formation of a new socioeconomic entity: the industrial district of central Tuscany. The future prospects of Tuscany depend largely on the capacity of the decision-makers to understand the peculiarities and the contradictions of this industrial district and to develop its potential.

NOTES

1. Against the approach originally formulated in the two overall interpretations put forward by IRPET (1969) and Becattini (1975), one can contrast the essay by Cantelli and Paggi (1973), which has also inspired a number of papers on the Tuscan economy.
2. Besides the classic monograph by Salvestrini (1965), I would draw attention to the shrewd lecture by G. Mori in Mori (1977, pp. 65–82).
3. For a good account of the social and political background to the drama of the transfer of the capital from Florence to Rome, see Ciuffoletti (1977).
4. The essential lines of this 'design' have been clarified by the specialised historical literature. Among the more important manifestations before Italian unification, see Carpi (1974). For the subsequent period see Mori (1977). On the 'reactionary' epilogue of this moderate plan, see Pinzani (1963).
5. On this point see G. Mori's ample treatment in Mori (1977).
6. Many examples of 'anomalous' developments have been revealed by historians of this period, to whom I refer the reader. I will merely mention, since its importance has only recently been given due weight and is therefore not widely known, the foundation even before the end of the Grand-Ducal period (1857) of a Tuscan Technical Institute which became the main prop of the attempts made by Tuscan craftsmen to industrialise themselves and market their goods. It is certainly an accident, but a highly significant one, that the first nucleus of the Galileo engineering works in Florence was born from the closure of the technological laboratory at the Technical Institute. For this episode and others relating to this rather anomalous initiative in the Tuscan context see the brief but informative introduction by Galluzzi (1977).
7. On this topic see G. Mori, 'Materiali, temi ed ipotesi per una storia dell'industria nella regione toscana durante il fascismo (1923–1939)', in Mori (1977).
8. On this point see Lungonelli (1978).
9. For a survey of what has been written on these subsectors I refer the reader to the 'comprehensive bibliography' by V. Spini, in Becattini (1975, pp. 185–241).
10. *Further Reports from Her Majesty's Diplomatic and Consular Officers Abroad Respecting the Condition of the Industrial Classes and the Purchase Power of Money in Foreign Countries*, London: Harrison and Sons, 1871, p. 245.
11. 'On our arrival at Schneider's, a most excellent hotel (I know no better anywhere), we found a good dinner quite ready for us and every accommodation we could desire', wrote a truly exceptional traveller, David Ricardo, from Florence on 13 October 1822 (Ricardo 1951).

REFERENCES

Becattini, G. (ed.) (1975), *Lo sviluppo economico della Toscana*, Florence: IRPET (large part of which is now available in G. Becattini (1999), *L'industrializzazione leggera della Toscana: ricerca sul campo e confronto delle idee*, Milan: Franco Angeli).

Bertolino, A. (1961), *Cooperazione internazionale e sviluppo economico*, Florence: La Nuova Italia.

Bianchi, G. (1976), 'Congiuntura e prospettive dell'economia toscana 1976: primi appunti', *Il Ponte*, 2–3: 189–97.

Busacca, R. (1855), 'Memorie economiche sulla Toscana', extract from *Atti dei Georgofili*, n.s., Vol. II, Florence: Tipografia Galileana.

Cantelli, P. and L. Paggi (1973), 'Strutture sociali e politica delle riforme in Toscana', *Critica marxista*, 5.

Carpi, V. (1974), *Letteratura e società toscana del Risorgimento: gli intellettuali dell'Antologia*, Bari: De Donato.

Ciuffoletti, Z. (1977), 'I moderati toscani, la caduta della destra e la questione di Firenze (1870–1879)', *Rassegna storica toscana*, 23–56: 229–71.

Galluzzi, P. (1977), 'L'Istituto Tecnico Galilei nella cultura e nelle società toscane del secolo Ottocento', introduction in *Catalogo dell'esposizione di un saggio delle collezioni scientifiche dell'Istituto tecnico Gaetano Salvemini (già Galileo)*, Florence.

Georgescu-Roegen, N. (1971), *The Entropy Law and the Economic Process*, Cambridge, MA: Harvard University Press.

IRPET (1969), 'Lo sviluppo economico della Toscana: un'ipotesi di lavoro', *Il Ponte*, November.

Lungonelli, M. (1978), 'Le miniere di ferro dell'Isola d'Elba dall'Unità al 1987', *Rassegna storica toscana*, January–April: 47–56.

Mioni, A. (1976), *Le trasformazioni territoriali in Italia nella prima età industriale*, Venice: Marsilio.

Mori, G. (1977), *Il capitalismo industriale in Italia*, Rome: Editori Riuniti.

Pinzani, C. (1963), *La crisi politica di fine secolo in Toscana*, Florence: Barbera.

Ricardo, D. (1951), *The Works and Correspondence of D. Ricardo*, edited by P. Sraffa, Vol. 10, Cambridge: Cambridge University Press.

Salvestrini, A. (1965), *I moderati toscani e la classe dirigente italiana (1859–1876)*, Florence: L.S. Olschki.

2. The 'Tuscan model' and recent trends

Fabio Sforzi

INTRODUCTION

This chapter analyses the most recent changes in the Tuscan development, placing particular emphasis on its territorial organisation. Subsequent to the interpretation of the Tuscan development covering the period from the end of the Second World War to the end of the 1960s (IRPET 1969; Becattini 1975), there have been a number of attempts to analyse the tendencies and structural changes that have impacted on the territorial and socioeconomic configuration of the region (Mori 1986; Falorni and Sforzi 1989). Nevertheless, it is necessary to take up this issue once again and begin from the conclusions initially formulated by Becattini (1975). It is necessary to validate the capacity of the 'Tuscan model' of development which Becattini put forward to interpret and explain the tendencies and changes that have intervened in the region during the last two decades. New elements have been introduced into the analysis of the region's development – such as, for example, the genesis of the metropolitan system in Central Tuscany, which has not been used to modify or update the interpretation of the Tuscan development (Regione Toscana 1984). It has been argued that the explanatory capacity of the 'Tuscan model' has disappeared given the decline in the competitiveness of the Tuscan productive formula of flexible specialisation. On this basis, the need to develop a 'new' interpretative model involves also the analysis of the ability of the Tuscan form of production to enable its local productive systems localised in urbanised countryside – and in particular its industrial districts – to continue to maintain their specific competitive advantages in a national and international socioeconomic context that has changed profoundly.

   The chapter will discuss the role played in the region by the urbanised countryside, which since the beginning of the 1970s presents itself as the peculiarity of Tuscany's development in relation to the other regions of the country. During a twenty year period (1971–91) regions in Italy had also developed along the same urbanised countryside model as Tuscany by specialising in similar sectors of light industry and becoming competitors in allied product lines. A similar process had also surfaced among competitors in newly industrialised countries in the Far East while traditionally industrialised countries, which had in the past abandoned light industrial manufacturing and sectors judged too hastily to be on the decline, had resumed production in response to new forms of international competition.

The 'Tuscan model' is capable of explaining even the more recent transformations in the socioeconomic and territorial structure of Tuscany within the confines of the mechanisms that are described within it – in other words, the industrial districts of urbanised countryside. However, the deindustrialisation that has manifested itself in the region's tourist-industrial areas – that is, the manufacturing poles concentrated around heavy industry – cannot be explained by the 'Tuscan model'. This consideration also holds true for a part of Tuscany's urban areas because many of the mechanisms operating in them are of the same nature as those present in the urbanised countryside; the difference is that since current service activities are concentrated more on the information-handling services than goods-handling services this consideration has a greater influence on the process of change and the prospects for development.

1. THE TUSCAN DEVELOPMENT MODEL

1.1 Industrialisation through Light Industry

The development model that surfaced in Tuscany during the course of the two decades following that of the Second World War (1951–71) brought to completion a process of industrialisation whose characteristics were already evident in the form assumed by the territorial localisation of industry during the late 1920s. The territorial pattern saw the steel and chemical industry localised along the coastline, and industries producing consumer goods (above all textiles but also clothing, leather goods and furniture) geographically concentrated in the Arno Valley, thereby significantly favouring the latter.

The reasons why Tuscany proceeded along the path of expansion of light industry have already been explained by Becattini (Chapter 1). Here, we need to examine the 'Tuscan model' based on the conviction that it represents the foundation for understanding the reasons for the proliferation of light industry in the region.

Once the first clusters of light industry have been localised they operate as an impulse for growth. In this manner, the initial infrastructure of industries functions as a vital growth mechanism in favouring the territorial concentration of industry through the creation of external economies, by virtue of the fact that the firms all belong to the same industry and are localised in the same place.

The reasons why an industry, once established in a place, decides to remain and consolidates itself are to be sought in the advantages it derives from the skills which are developed locally and shared due to geographical proximity. The increase in technical skills, tied to a progressive increase in the know-how of the population, stimulates innovation which is reflected in both the quality and variety of goods produced and in the improvement of the machines used in the production process. It is also the basis for the creation of new firms, both in the principal industry dominating the local economy and in the auxiliary industries that provide supporting instruments and raw materials as well as commercialising the products. The sum total of these activities provides an advantage in costs derived locally for the local enterprise system.

The social division of labour found in local systems provides the basis for the formation of efficient firms of relatively modest size specialising in phases, products and parts of products according to the specific industrial organisation they belong to. Connected to this mechanism of firm proliferation is the increasing differentiation of functions that involves the production, planning and commercialisation of the goods produced. The very nature of industrialisation through the growth of light industry activates the development of support service activities.

These services – in addition to those tied directly to the production process – involve important activities that meet the exigency of connecting single local producers to the final markets, maintaining stable direct relations with clients, and undertaking the search for new buyers and even new producers.

A locally concentrated industry offering a constant market for specialised labour generates new entrepreneurial initiatives internally and is able to attract them from the outside. As a consequence, it stimulates the influx of workers and their respective families, and it creates the basis for further penetration into the community and the expansion of the productive base. In fact, to the complementarities in economic activities created by a locally concentrated industry (that is, increase in the variety of production) must be added the complementarity that gradually penetrates into the immediately contiguous areas through the growth of the labour market (that is, increase in the variety of employment) as well as in the creation of employment opportunities for the female population.

Complementary to the variety of production is the variety of employment which results from the increased density of connecting networks between economic activities and different localities where people live and work, thereby increasing the earning power of families and attributing a specific local identity to productive systems.

1.2 The 'Four Tuscanies'

In Tuscany the process of light industrialisation created an articulated territorial configuration in which four distinct socioeconomic contexts, corresponding to individual mechanisms of local development, can be identified: the urbanised countryside; the touristic-industrial areas; the urban areas; and the countryside, as illustrated in Figure 2.1.

The urbanised countryside represents a composite of the local systems of light industry. Its dominant characteristic is constituted by the phenomena directly connected with the development of clusters of specialised small firms in typical Tuscan light industry (textiles, clothing, footwear, leather goods and furniture) in addition to other significant concentrations of firms operating in the production of utensils, machines and other equipment for light industry. In the urbanised countryside we find complementary and auxiliary firms whose birth is directly correlated with the growth of light industry; the simultaneous presence of primary product and auxiliary firms in the same territory creates an intense and complex network of inter-industry relations and local commercial exchanges. The fact that the development of the industrial sector took place primarily through the proliferation of small manufacturing firms has favoured the expansion of autonomous productive units in the service sector to carry out accounting, consulting and inter-mediation functions. In general, the productive units in light industry are particularly endowed with flexibility in the combination of the factors and organisation of production, permitting them a rapid level of response to market requests and an equally rapid adjustment in employment patterns. The extended family guarantees a supply of labour that is compensated by the offer of social services on the part of local government – at times integrating with the supply from the private market and at other times substituting for it – and favours extended participation in the production workforce through a variety of different forms of employment. A typical example is piecework subcontracted to females staying at home to take care of their children. But the extended family ties also function to create a sense of familial identity with the firm owner, and the transmission of skills and vocational training from one generation to another or between different components of the family.

The touristic-industrial areas prevalently coincide with the coastline and islands and cover only a few other limited areas in the interior of the region. These areas are characterised by the presence of important manufacturing poles specialised in heavy industry, which were localised here during the first phases of industrialisation initiated at the turn of the 20th century. These coastal cities, along with their local productive systems, offer a demand for labour proportional to the considerable dimensions of the productive structures. The large vertically integrated firms in the manufacturing poles are flanked by the presence of a tourist industry whose characteristics are those of a typical form of mass tourism (artistic sites and 'sun-sea-sand' beach attractions). The progressive growth of national as well as international tourism has come about through a combination of service production, oriented toward individual wants by highlighting the use of human capital, in addition to the wide diffusion of both house and apartment lettings, and forms of family and seasonal management of many hotels and commercial enterprises. The parallel presence on the territory of large plants is reflected in the aggravated competition between different land uses, especially for residential-touristic and industrial requirements. A similar competition arose in the property market between accommodation for tourists vis-à-vis that for the resident population.

The urban areas are identified as the principal cities of the regions in which are found the important decision making centres in the public and private sectors, and the headquarters and affiliates of the major industrial and commercial firms. Here are principally concentrated the supply of administrative, financial and commercial services; and in these localities we find the universities, important social and health service structures, and cultural and recreation services whose localisation is also stimulated by the presence of substantial tourism flows. In Northern Tuscany (for instance, Florence) the urban areas are the localisation of important centres of mechanical industry, endowed with a substantial level of technology, along with light industry and traditional artisan pursuits. Small artisan shops can be found in the historical centres, while the larger concerns are localised in the suburban boroughs and in specifically designated industrial zones in the immediate vicinity. The potential separation of economic activities and social classes concentrated in urban areas is attenuated by the relative dependence of some of these activities – such as the export firms and, in general, the firms concerned with commercial and financial services – on manufacturing, which is usually more prevalent in the urbanised countryside.

The countryside includes the areas in Tuscany which have been negatively impacted by the effects of the industrialisation process. It has provided to light industry a high number of its residents in the form of salaried workers and piecework at home, in addition to a significant amount of human capital in the form of non-salaried workers and small entrepreneurs. The cultivation of agricultural products has been limited to typical regional produce – such as grapes and olives. The raising of livestock, a typical Tuscan agricultural occupation in the past, has declined considerably, though it still plays an important role espe-

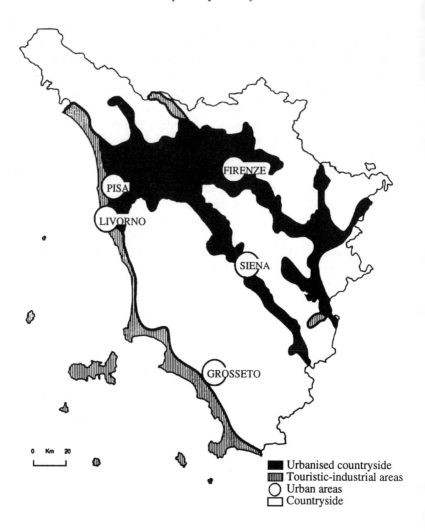

Figure 2.1 'The four Tuscanies', 1971

Source: Becattini (1975)

cially in the food-processing industry. Even if in the production of wages the countryside remains of primary importance for the resident population, being heavily dependent on 'other Tuscanies' in satisfying its demand for consumer goods. As a consequence, the recurrent changes in population flows toward the 'other Tuscanies' – motivated mostly by educational and employment reasons – continue along with the occasional, temporary shift of people spurred by the use of social and health services, more specialised distribution services, or recreation and cultural activities offered elsewhere.

Organisational dependence on the 'other Tuscanies' does not only involve the countryside. It is also manifested in the exchanges that take place between the urbanised countryside and a few of the urban areas, especially that of Florence, due to the presence of numerous administrative and commercial activities indispensable for the functioning of the light industry operating in the urbanised countryside. The relationship between the urbanised countryside and major urban areas reflects elements of complementarity and conflict that are capable, over time, of modifying the territorial configuration of the region's development pattern, to the extent that service activities are concentrated in the urban areas and labour flows to them from the urbanised countryside.

In summary, if the urbanised countryside is the part of Tuscany where we find the highest concentrations of employment in manufacturing, the urban areas represent the Tuscany of services; the tourist-industrial areas manifest their duality in the territorial concentration of industrial and commercial employment, even if the latter often reaches levels above the regional average; finally, the countryside is defined in the last analysis by the commercial activities localised there, as illustrated by the data in Tables 2.1 and 2.2.

Table 2.1   Location and share of employment in the 'four Tuscanies', 1971

Four Tuscanies	Location quotient			Percentage share		
	Industries	Commerce	Services	Industries	Commerce	Services
Urbanised countryside	1.16	0.81	0.66	49.11	34.45	27.96
Touristic-industrial areas	0.96	1.15	0.89	14.42	17.27	13.37
Urban areas	0.84	1.13	1.45	31.00	41.69	53.74
Countryside	0.96	1.16	0.87	5.47	6.59	4.93

Note:
The location quotient (LQ) is LQ = $(e/E)/(n/N)$, where e and n are local and regional employment levels in individual economic activities; E and N are local and regional total employment levels in all economic activities. The percentage share is related to Tuscany.

Source: Calculated by the author from ISTAT data

*Table 2.2   Location and share of manufacturing and other industrial
            employment in the 'four Tuscanies', 1971*

Four Tuscanies	Manufacturing		Other industries	
	Location quotient	Percentage share	Location quotient	Percentage share
Urbanised countryside	1.26	53.31	0.77	32.67
Touristic-industrial areas	0.85	12.77	1.39	20.84
Urban areas	0.83	30.76	0.86	31.95
Countryside	0.55	3.16	2.56	14.54

Note:
As Table 2.1

Source: As Table 2.1

1.3   Contradictions and Limitations of the 'Tuscan Model'

The advantages in terms of social and economic development produced in Tuscany by the formula of flexible specialisation have been amply documented, but it is necessary to recall that the quality of this development is inexorably linked with the urban polycentrism of the urbanised countryside. The geographical distribution of industry and population according to a tight network of small and medium-sized semi-urbanised centres, connected by differentiated relationships of employment and residence, is confronted by the challenge posed by the formation of large urban agglomerations and by the relative peripheralisation of industrial areas that is typical of the process of industrialisation based on large, vertically integrated industrial establishments. The latter is visible in the manufacturing poles even if the presence of a single or a few large enterprises limits the demographic dimensions of the residential centres, but it certainly does not eliminate the polarisation of residential or social patterns.

The model of socioeconomic territorial development that has established itself in Tuscany is not without its contradictions and limitations. These depend, above all, on the way in which the localised industry reproduces itself and the professional profiles which find employment within the territory in response to the mechanism of industrial expansion and the levels of socioeconomic well-being that the model generates.

With regard to the economic activities, it should be remembered that the services to industry required by the formula of flexible specialisation are not entirely produced locally. In fact, there are some that are excluded or seriously ignored by this 'automatic' mechanism of generation, and they are the ones – as, for example, scientific research and initial technical training – that the enterprise system does not succeed in giving expression to or which one single firm is not able to realise on its own, because the major part of the utility produced remains only for a short time as its exclusive property. With the local system there is a great propensity for know-how to escape and be distributed – quite quickly, even – among other firms.

These advanced services, given that they are necessary for the functioning of the localised industries and the maintenance of the level of competitiveness, develop outside of the urbanised countryside, and there is a tendency on the part of these advanced services to concentrate their production in the urban areas. To the extent that they manifest themselves locally, one observes the paradox that a decentralised and rural industrial model leads to a centralised and urban services model. One needs to add that the spontaneous nature of the tendency is also supported and accelerated by the action of public authorities, because various regional and local administrations have identified in these service functions the main constitutive element of the development of the regional capital city or of the corresponding metropolitan area, and have elaborated programmes to make them the centres of 'higher service' activities (Fuà and Zacchia 1983).

Such an approach represents a typical example of the underutilisation of the overall benefits produced by the model of light industrialisation discussed above. Focusing on the role of urban areas as the centres of service activities runs the risk of seriously compromising the continued viability of the 'Tuscan model' of development which has seen the affirmation of the importance of light industry.

What has just been said for services can also be said for the 'new' occupations created in the countryside – even if they remain at low levels – following the high levels of well-being created by the development of localised industry. Given that the wants to which they respond tend to expand in correspondence with the increase in the level of well-being, one would expect that they would absorb an increasing percentage of the active local labour force. It is towards these jobs that the children of the workers and small entrepreneurs who pursue higher-level education (upper secondary diplomas or university degrees) point instead of taking the place of their parents in productive endeavours. Accordingly, we witness the second paradox involving the valorisation of human capital within the productive formula of flexible specialisation, that operates against the interests of reproducing through generation change the prevalent industrial structure.

Social mobility assumes two basic forms. The first is characterised by various paths of mobility that permit, with a certain ease, the passage of workers across different forms of employment: from salaried work to self-employment and all the way to entrepreneurial activity, based on a continual change in status that makes new jobs available and accessible. The second is tied to the provision of higher levels of education on the part of the new generations as a mark of the higher social status achieved by the family. This change in educational base can determine the creation of a workforce whose specialised skills do not find an adequate demand in the local enterprise system; in addition, they are not adequate for the skills and qualities necessary to become the head of a family enterprise. In this manner the increase in the level of education might block, rather than ease, children taking the place of parents in productive roles and provide the stimulus to search for alternative forms of employment different from those focused on industry, that are normally found outside of the urbanised countryside and in particular in the urban areas.

Nevertheless, the process of generational change in the entrepreneurial class seems to be strongly limited if it depends exclusively on changes within the family group. In reality, things are different, at least in part, because continuity in entrepreneurial roles in localised industries is assured by the salaried workers who become self-employed given that they have the necessary technical skills, managerial capacity and access to sufficient capital to initiate production, assisted by commercialisation firms which find them their customers.

What we have discussed here calls attention to the exigencies that the industrialisation model based on flexible specialisation and localised small enterprise systems requires in terms of local public policies, that is, locally differentiated industrial and social policies formulated and managed on a territorial basis and oriented toward the support of diverse types of external economies. If the access to external economies was decisive in the initial phase of development of light industry, and found support in the long-term plans of the local authorities who often directly contributed to their development or favoured the private initiative that stimulated their growth, these types of public inputs are even more important during the phase of consolidation. It becomes vitally important if among the objectives of the local authorities there is the goal of blocking the phenomenon of polarisation towards urban areas and peripheralisation of industry in the urbanised countryside.

In the final analysis, what is necessary is the recognition of the principal lesson to be drawn from the model of light industrialisation: the genesis of production does not reside within the enterprises, considered in their individual form or separately within the context of their localisation, but rather in the local territorial system that the firms constitute together with the working population. A consolidation of the development model that wants to block the dismantling and removal of the obstacles to social reproduction requires the formulation of policies that have, as their objective, intervention into the local system in its entirety, and are oriented not towards the single firm but towards the entire productive system as well as towards the local community.

2. THE MAJOR CHANGES DURING THE 1970s

2.1 The Consolidation of Light Industry

The dynamism of light industry, which in the 'Tuscan model' sustains the process of industrialisation and represents the motor of regional development, moves during the 1970s along the lines already explored and discussed above. If we consider the region according to the division into the 'four Tuscanies', we find that between 1971 and 1981 it is the urbanised countryside which registers the largest amount of growth in jobs in manufacturing followed by the touristic-industrial and urban areas. The effect of this growth is that the urbanised countryside again increases its regional share of manufacturing jobs and contributes to a further territorial concentration. In contrast, the other areas register a decrease in industrial employment (Table 2.3).

Table 2.3   Location and growth of manufacturing employment in the 'four Tuscanies', 1971–81

Four Tuscanies	Location quotient	Employment (percentage share)		Share of job growth
	1981	1981	1971	1971–81
Urbanised countryside	1.31	56.65	53.31	32.77
Touristic-industrial areas	0.82	11.78	12.77	9.49
Urban areas	0.77	28.66	30.76	8.87
Countryside	0.56	2.91	3.16	7.53

Notes:
The location quotient is described at Table 2.1.
The share of job growth (SG) is $SG = [(e/81) - (e(71)]/[(E/81) - (E/71)] \times 100$, where e is local employment level in individual economic activity and E is local total employment level in all economic activities; 81 and 71 are the initial and terminal observations, respectively.
The percentage share is related to Tuscany.

Source: As Table 2.1

In the touristic-industrial areas we find the largest employment growth in commerce, a sign of the expansion of tourist activity that becomes predominant over industrial employment. More generally, the decade consolidates the respective occupational profiles of the 'four Tuscanies' in such a manner that the urbanised countryside becomes more than before the Tuscany of industry; the urban areas represent the Tuscany of services, and the touristic-industrial areas constitute the Tuscany of commerce; the countryside remains characterised by levels of sectoral employment located around the regional means (Table 2.4).

Table 2.4   Location and growth of employment in the 'four Tuscanies', 1971–81

Sectors/Four Tuscanies	Location quotient	Employment (percentage share)		Share of job growth
	1981	1981	1971	1971–81
Industry				
Urbanised countryside	1.23	53.10	49.11	38.94
Touristic-industrial areas	0.90	12.94	14.42	7.19
Urban areas	0.78	29.19	31.00	11.08
Countryside	0.91	4.77	5.47	3.10
Commerce				
Urbanised countryside	0.82	35.52	34.45	8.92
Touristic-industrial areas	1.30	18.69	17.27	19.87
Urban areas	1.07	39.81	41.69	7.09
Countryside	1.15	5.98	6.59	5.01
Services				
Urbanised countryside	0.75	32.42	27.96	52.13
Touristic-industrial areas	0.96	13.89	13.37	72.93
Urban areas	1.30	48.28	53.74	81.84
Countryside	1.04	5.41	4.93	91.89

Note:
As Table 2.3

Source: As Table 2.1

2.2 The Industrial Districts

The consolidation of industrial manufacturing in the urbanised countryside was made possible through the growth of inter-industry relations between firms specialised by phases, products and parts of products in the typical production process of light industry, firms engaged in the production of capital goods (such as the machine industry) and auxiliary industries supplying materials and components in the production process, including specialised services. This phenomenon multiplied the territorial interactions between productive and residential areas rather than sifting it out. The process was also sustained by a local redistribution of population that took place according to the mechanism of gradual adjustment, which tended to bring together within a daily temporal-spatial dimension places of residence and of production. The outcome of the transformation was the formation of localised networks of socioeconomic interaction which took place in relatively self-contained territorial contexts where residence and place of work operated to create a sense of self-identity. This explains also the persistence of the industrial geography of the region and the fact that outside of the urbanised countryside new local systems of light industry were not created. There was, instead, the formation of an increasingly precise productive identity on the part of those that already existed, a few among which we can now recognise as having the outlines of industrial districts.

The industrial districts are local systems characterised by the active co-participation between a community of persons and small firms specialised in different parts of the production process. Co-participation consists of the process in which the community of persons exercises an autonomous function in relation to the organisation of production based on the contents of a common social culture. The system of values and normative orientations is dominated by the spirit of initiative widely shared by the general public, as is the case in relation to attitudes toward the principal aspects of life such as employment, consumption, savings and economic uncertainty. Such a widely shared base of common values serves to create a cultural context favourable to economic enterprise; it influences industrial relations and the activities of local government and administration. The high capacity and availability of individuals and their families to engage in non-salaried activity in its various forms (such as piecework at home, artisanry, small business, self-employment) favours the formation and diffusion of managerial capacity, creativity, pragmatism and ability to act individually and collectively.

On the other hand, the organisation of production that is realised through independent small enterprises – more or less coinciding with the single phased production units – and connected by networks of specialised transactions and coordinated by forms of more or less explicit cooperation, is made possible by the technical ability to subdivide the productive process and take advantage of the external localisation economies. Such a division of labour between firms is the product of an expansion in demand for non-standardised products, characterised by a high level of fragmentation in quality and temporal differences.

Tuscany's industrial districts are found in urbanised countryside along the lower Arno Valley and its tributaries in that part of the region comprising the urban areas of Florence, Pisa and Siena, while only one district is found in the south-east of Tuscany (Figure 2.2).

Figure 2.2 The industrial districts, 1981

Source: Compiled by the author

These districts register a percentage of regional employment (20.2 per cent) higher than their share of population (17.2 per cent), and an even greater share of manufacturing employment (29.5 per cent), which is the equivalent of a coefficient of territorial concentration that is greater than the percentage of manufacturing employment in the region (Table 2.5).

Table 2.5   Location and growth of employment in the industrial districts, 1981

Sectors/Population			Retrospect analysis		
	Location quotient	Percentage share	Location quotient	Percentage share	Share of job growth
	1981	1981	1971	1971	1971–81
Industry	1.33	27.00	1.22	24.76	45.44
Commerce	0.77	15.60	0.72	14.66	10.08
Services	0.63	12.69	0.57	11.54	44.49
Manufacturing	1.46	29.52	1.37	27.72	38.32
Employment	–	20.25	–	20.29	–
Population	–	17.20	–	16.32	–

Note:
As Table 2.3

Source: As Table 2.1

The principal industries in Tuscany's industrial districts are those in fashion (textiles, clothing, tanning, leather goods, footwear) and in furniture (wood furniture) accompanied by secondary industries specialised in the transformation of non-metal minerals, in particular glassware. Other manufacturing, such as mechanical industries, machines and related items, even though present, does not possess a sufficient territorial concentration (Table 2.6) to constitute an industrial district. Nevertheless, its localisation is reflected in the form of different levels of specialisation in a manner similar to that reflected in the industrial district (Table 2.7).

Table 2.6 *Location and level of employment in the industrial districts, 1981*

Industrial districts	Non-metallic mineral products	Chemicals, rubber and plastics	Food products, beverages and tobacco	Textiles	Tanning, leather goods and footwear	Wearing apparel	Furniture and wood products	Paper, printing and publishing	Other manufacturing industries
Location quotient [a]									
Lamporecchio	c	1.06	c	1.04	9.01	c	2.46	1.06	c
Montecatini-Terme	c	c	1.03	c	10.73	1.21	c	1.29	c
Castelfiorentino	1.46	c	c	c	6.36	2.42	1.91	c	c
Empoli	3.55	c	c	c	2.55	4.78	c	c	c
Prato	c	c	c	10.01	c	c	c	c	c
Santa Croce sull'Arno	c	c	c	c	16.83	c	c	c	c
Poggibonsi	3.17	c	c	c	c	c	3.84	c	c
Sinalunga	2.93	c	c	1.43	1.15	1.41	3.83	c	1.45
Employment level [b]									
Lamporecchio	d	8.94	d	8.91	43.82	d	19.29	5.19	d
Montecatini-Terme	d	d	7.45	d	52.18	9.54	d	6.32	d
Castelfiorentino	8.54	d	d	d	30.96	19.07	14.96	d	d
Empoli	20.81	d	d	d	12.41	37.64	d	d	d
Prato	d	d	d	85.72	d	d	d	d	d
Santa Croce sull'Arno	d	d	d	d	81.86	d	d	d	d
Poggibonsi	18.57	d	d	d	d	d	30.16	d	d
Sinalunga	17.15	d	d	12.27	5.61	11.14	30.10	d	2.47

Notes:
(a) The location quotient (LQ) is $LQ = (e/E)/(n/N)$, where e and n are local and national employment levels in individual economic activities; E and N are local and national total employment levels in all economic activities.
(b) Percentage share of industrial employment.
(c) Location quotient less than 1.
(d) Employment level is ignored because location quotient is less than 1.

Source: As Table 2.1

Table 2.7   *Location and specialisation of manufacturing employment in the industrial districts, 1981*

Industrial districts	Location quotient	Specialisation index	District-dominant manufacturing industry
Lamporecchio	1.85	50.27	Tanning, leather goods and footwear
Montecatini-Terme	1.23	55.24	Tanning, leather goods and footwear
Castelfiorentino	1.66	43.48	Tanning, leather goods and footwear
Empoli	1.62	46.43	Wearing apparel
Prato	1.75	85.97	Textiles
Santa Croce sull'Arno	1.78	82.20	Tanning, leather goods and footwear
Poggibonsi	1.56	45.53	Furniture and wood products
Sinalunga	1.46	40.88	Furniture and wood products

Notes:
As Table 2.6.

The specialisation index of manufacturing (Sp) is $Sp = \sqrt{\left[P_1^2 + P_2^2 + P_3^2 + \ldots P_n^2 \right]}$, where P is

the percentage of local total manufacturing employment of each local industry in turn.

Source: As Table 2.1

2.3 The Metropolitan System of Central Tuscany

The process of residential and occupational sub-urbanisation manifested in the Florence area has reversed the tendencies of urbanisation which were manifest until the end of the 1960s. Movement of manufacturing firms and population into the surrounding urbanised countryside has contributed, together with the change in the flows of daily travel for work reasons, to the completion of an interactive network of relations and dualistic flow of traffic between the city and its surrounding territory.

What is involved here is a dynamic common to a large number of urban areas in Italy. In Florence this dynamic is less developed than it is in other urban areas of Northern Italy, in particular in the urban areas in the industrial triangle (Milan, Turin and Genoa). The phenomenon is also characteristic of Bologna's urban area which in the decade 1971–81 passed through a phase of dis-urbanisation. Both population and employment declined in the Bolognese urban area as a whole (Table 2.8).

Table 2.8 Stages of development in urban areas of selected metropolitan systems, 1971–81

Metropolitan systems	Employment[a]			Population[a]			P PStage of development	
	Inner	Outer	Total	Inner	Outer	Total	Employment	Population
Florence	1.04	42.06	13.76	-2.07	16.70	4.54	II3 [b]	II4 [c]
Turin	-8.62	7.41	-4.30	-4.35	2.38	-2.55	III5 [d]	III5 [d]
Milan	-11.34	20.10	-4.57	-7.35	13.16	-1.53	III5 [d]	III5 [d]
Venice	1.49	38.19	9.15	-4.66	15.57	2.64	II3 [b]	II4 [c]
Bologna	0.59	48.89	16.25	-6.41	11.99	-0.35	II3 [b]	III5 [d]

Notes:
(a) Percentage share of change 1971–81.
(b) II3 = Suburbanisation with relative decentralisation.
(c) II4 = Suburbanisation with absolute decentralisation.
(d) III5 = Deurbanisation with absolute decentralisation.

Source: As Table 2.1

What has just been highlighted suggests that the Florence area may be transforming itself into a metropolitan system covering Florence and the other local systems in Central Tuscany. Such a metropolitan system would go from the local system of the upper Valdarno, concentrated on Montevarchi, all the way over to the local system centred on Pistoia (Figure 2.3).

This hypothesis is based on the observation that in localities of light industrialisation the metropolitan system tends to transform itself into a 'network of local systems' connected by complex mechanisms of interdependence rather than according to relationships of hierarchical dependence on the part of the various local systems to the principal one. This phenomenon derives from the fact that each single local system remains strongly marked by its own economic-territorial identity in addition to a sociocultural one, and it is this identity that confers on the metropolitan system a multi-centre nature (IRPET 1986).

The nature of the metropolitan system of Central Tuscany superimposes itself upon, but has not succeeded in substituting itself for, the structure of local systems which continue to possess a primary identity and role in the explanation of socioeconomic change in the region. In order to understand the relevance of the above, it is necessary to recall the fact that in the metropolitan system of Central Tuscany we also find the industrial district of Prato, which certainly does not represent an industrialised periphery; nor is its industry dependent on the services localised in the urban area of Florence. On the other hand, it is not surprising that this so-called 'system of local systems' existing around Florence represents a remarkable percentage of the region's entire employment and population (respectively, 38.6 and 35.5 per cent).

If we can no longer reasonably argue that the metropolitan economy dominates each individual local system incorporated into the metropolitan system of Central Tuscany and that it has succeeded in suppressing their individual identities, it is possible to draw the implication that such a transformation is not desirable, and its realisation should not become part of public policies.

The 'metropolitan scheme' of analysis can usefully be used to understand developments relative to the specific relations between economic and social spheres in this part of the region. In a similar manner, it is useful for the formulation of public policies oriented towards the localisation of infrastructure and activities for the development of the service sector in the prospect of promoting further consolidation of the productive structure of each constituent local system, producing synergies among development activities, and having a generally positive impact on the development of the rest of the region.

The development of Tuscany

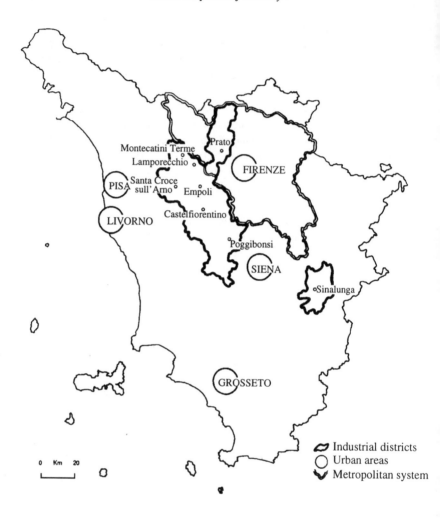

Figure 2.3 The metropolitan system of central Tuscany, 1981

Source: Compiled by the author

3. THE RECENT TRENDS

3.1 An Overall View

At the beginning of the 1990s, Tuscany visibly demonstrated in an accentuated manner the different processes of industrialisation that had characterised its territorial mode of development. We do not have sufficient information to provide a comprehensive overview of the structural changes which had taken place between 1981 and 1991, but what emerges clearly from the available data shows the break with the past. The long and practically uninterrupted trend of growing industrial employment had come to an end.

This is a phenomenon present in the entire country. On the basis of data from the 1991 census, the clearest change in the Italian workforce is the one registered in the general decline in industrial jobs and the parallel increase of jobs in commerce and services. The fall in industrial employment did not hit Italy in an equal manner; it was clearly evident in the oldest industrialised areas and regions. It was most evident in the regions of the industrial triangle while the regions with light industry – that is, the Third Italy – registered a lower level of decline. Despite the drop in total number of industrial jobs, the regions in the Third Italy increased their overall percentage of national industrial employment, even surpassing that of the industrial triangle (Table 2.9).

Tuscany's performance was in a position between those of the regions in the industrial triangle and the regions of the Third Italy given its dual industrial structure. The region was caught between the manufacturing poles of heavy industry in the touristic-industrial areas and the industrial districts of the urbanised countryside. This combination was unique among the regions with light industry (Table 2.10).

The fall in industrial jobs in the decade between 1981 and 1991 took place in each of the 'four Tuscanies', even if with different tendencies and, above all, with different results in each of the single economic structures (Table 2.11). The urbanised countryside experienced a fall in industrial employment much higher than that in the urban areas but small vis-à-vis the countryside. The areas worst hit by the fall in industrial jobs were the touristic-industrial areas along the coast. The consequences of this pattern were that the share of the industrial workforce present in the urbanised countryside and, to a lesser extent, present in the urban areas increased; it declined very little in the rural areas while it dropped considerably in the touristic-industrial areas. The latter continued to register a relative decline that had already manifested itself in the previous decade (1971–81) in the number and percentage of industrial jobs vis-à-vis the regional mean. Its coefficient of industrial workforce was now equivalent to that of the countryside.

Table 2.9   Location and growth of employment in the 'three Italies', 1981–91

Sectors/Three Italies	Location quotient	Employment (percentage share)		Share of job growth	Location quotient
	1991	1991	1981	1981–91	1981
Industries					
Industrial triangle	1.19	38.65	39.96	−171.19	1.16
Third Italy	1.12	39.00	37.85	−33.00	1.09
South	0.68	22.35	22.19	−16.95	0.72
Commerce					
Industrial triangle	0.93	30.22	30.84	52.98	0.89
Third Italy	1.00	34.69	34.82	25.45	1.00
South	1.07	35.09	34.34	21.19	1.12
Services					
Industrial triangle	0.87	28.24	29.79	218.21	0.86
Third Italy	0.90	31.19	30.55	107.55	0.88
South	1.24	40.57	39.66	95.76	1.29

Notes:
LQ and SG are calculated as noted in Tables 2.3 and 2.6.
The percentage share is related to Italy.

Source: As Table 2.1

Table 2.10 Location and growth of employment in Tuscany, 1981–91

Sectors	Location quotient	Employment (percentage share)		Share of job growth	Location quotient
	1991	1991	1981	1981–91	1981
Industry	1.04	37.20	47.70	−101.33	1.08
Commerce	1.04	24.10	22.01	51.66	0.97
Services	0.94	38.70	30.29	149.67	0.92

Note:
As Table 2.9.
The percentage share is related to Tuscany.

Source: As Table 2.1

*Table 2.11   Location and growth of employment in the 'four Tuscanies',
1981–91*

Sectors/Four Tuscanies	Location quotient	Employment (percentage share)		Share of job growth
	1991	1991	1981	1981–91
Industry				
Urbanised countryside	1.29	54.87	53.71	−150.00
Touristic-industrial areas	0.86	11.76	13.21	−532.51
Urban areas	0.75	28.88	28.29	−43.13
Countryside	0.86	4.49	4.79	−142.62
Commerce				
Urbanised countryside	0.87	37.18	35.72	72.81
Touristic-industrial areas	1.30	17.73	18.25	193.79
Urban areas	1.02	39.14	39.84	30.61
Countryside	1.14	5.95	6.19	53.30
Services				
Urbanised countryside	0.80	34.20	32.74	177.19
Touristic-industrial areas	0.95	12.93	13.43	438.72
Urban areas	1.23	47.46	48.51	112.51
Countryside	1.04	5.41	5.32	189.32

Note:
As Table 2.3

Source: As Table 2.1

On the other hand, the touristic-industrial areas registered the highest
increase in employment in commerce and transformed themselves into the
areas with the highest percentage of commercial employment in the region.
Even in services, these areas registered the highest concentration in the
region, though the comparisons with other areas in Tuscany did not reflect
large differences. Service employment also increased in a sustained manner
in all of the other areas in Tuscany. The short-term impact on the trend in
industrial employment was the drastic reduction in the industrial component
in employment in favour of the tertiary sector, and the traditional duality of
coastal Tuscany – large industrial plants on one side and tourism on the other
– had seen the rising supremacy of the latter. Large manufacturing poles in
Tuscany and elsewhere in the country had undergone a strong process of
deindustrialisation.

The urbanised countryside had increased its overall concentration of industrial jobs in such a manner that, despite the shift to services, an important

industrial occupational component had been maintained. Thus, in 1991 the urbanised countryside contained a concentration of both industrial and commerce/service jobs above the regional means.

The industrial districts demonstrated an accentuation of the phenomena already observed in the urbanised countryside as a whole. Both the negative growth in industry and positive growth in commerce and services demonstrated a greater dynamism, and what seems to have most characterised the decade was the process of shift to services. The percentage of industrial employment remained unchanged between 1981 and 1991, but it increased in relation to the regional mean while employment in commerce and services increased from every point of view (Table 2.12).

Table 2.12 Location and growth of employment in the industrial districts, 1981–91

Sectors/Population	Location quotient	Employment (percentage share)		Share of job growth
	1991	1991	1981	1981–91
Industry	1.39	27.03	27.30	−436.71
Commerce	0.85	16.46	15.77	157.68
Services	0.72	14.06	13.00	379.03
Manufacturing	–	–	–	–
Employment	–	19.46	20.43	–
Population	–	17.90	17.20	–

Note:
As Table 2.3

Source: As Table 2.1

The phenomenon of diffused tertiarisation, subject to different types of interpretations depending on where it takes place, explains the lack of evolution in the metropolitan system of Central Tuscany. The urban areas reduced their own percentage of occupation in commerce and services while industrial employment remained unchanged, but the percentage decreased in relation to the regional mean in a manner that reduced its specific characteristic as the focus of service employment. This phenomenon was very evident among the local systems in the metropolitan system of Central Tuscany if we compare what had taken place in the principal local system – that is, the urban area of Florence – and the others. The increase in commercial and service sector jobs had proceeded in a sustained manner, but even more so in the local systems that constituted the other parts of the metropolitan system (Table 2.13).

Table 2.13 Location and growth of employment in the metropolitan system of central Tuscany, 1981–91

Metropolitan system of central Tuscany	Location quotient	Employment (percentage share)		Share of job growth	Location quotient
	1991	1991	1981	1981–91	1981
Metropolitan system					
Industry	1.03	40.77	39.33	−61.31	1.02
Commerce	0.93	36.89	36.01	41.07	0.93
Services	1.02	40.40	39.70	120.24	1.03
Urban area (Florence)					
Industry	0.84	20.24	18.97	−28.45	0.84
Commerce	1.00	24.05	23.63	31.04	1.05
Services	1.15	27.57	27.19	97.40	1.21
Other local systems					
Industry	1.31	20.53	20.36	−227.34	1.25
Commerce	0.82	12.84	12.38	91.72	0.76
Services	0.82	12.83	12.52	235.61	0.77

Note:
As Table 2.3

Source: As Table 2.1

The changes in employment during the 1980s offer a number of points for discussion in the interpretation of Tuscan development. One of these is the evaluation of the capacity of the 'Tuscan model' to explain what had taken place in the industrial districts in the urbanised countryside – that is, in the shift to services that appears to have been the fundamental element in their evolution.

The shift to services which took place in Tuscany touches a fundamental aspect of development that is linked to the other changes: the so-called deindustrialisation, the change in industrial employment in the urbanised countryside and touristic-industrial areas rather than in urban areas, the transformation of the industrial districts and urban areas. If we separate the processes from the territorial context where they occur, it is more difficult to understand both aspects – that is, the nature of the processes as well as that of the transformation of the territorial contexts where change takes place.

3.2 The Shift to Services in the Industrial Districts

The principal explanation of the shift to services in the industrial districts has to be sought in the mechanism of firm proliferation which is at the base of the productive formula of flexible specialisation that distinguishes localised industry.

In the 'Tuscan model' the interpretation of light industrialisation is based on the idea that the increased demand for goods produced by typical Tuscan industry and the expansion of production do not take place through an increase in the size of firms – that is, by taking advantage of internal economies of scale; it takes place, instead, through a proliferation of small firms by way of a specialisation in production by phases, products and parts of products – in other words, by taking advantage of external organisational economies.

The proliferation of firms is made possible by the characteristic of the 'fragmentary and variable' nature of demand for goods produced by localised industry found in the industrial districts, and by the characteristics of the local labour market that permit the clusters of specialised manufacturing firms a considerable level of non-integration of productive processes. Small firms are fundamental to the process in that productive phases and operations can be technically separated from the process of transformation and delegated to independent producers (small firms and non-salaried workers) external to the enterprise.

The evolution of productive phases – that is, the localisation of firms specialised in productive phases – takes place under conditions of geographical proximity within a contiguous and relatively restricted territory. The geographical proximity of specialised phase firms is necessary for the recomposition of the productive process given that the determination of whether the phases can take place nearby or far away depends on the exigencies of production – in other words, if the nature of the product needs a constant supervision of the details – required by a product (for example, if it requires a frequent variation of its characteristics) and by the rapidity with which the order has to be delivered to the client. The efficiency of the productive formula is the combined result of the methods of production, design, collection of orders and distribution of the final products. The commercialisation network uses the input of commercial agents and independent intermediaries, in addition to shippers who provide a specialised understanding of the market as well as additional capital.

In any case, both in the initial stage of the firm proliferation process as well as in that of consolidation, forces for territorial agglomeration predominate. This depends on the fact that the productive system has to develop through the formation of a common base of skilled workers, the growth of auxiliary industries capable of responding to the specific requirements of the dominant product line, and development of habits that favour the exchange of ideas between producers, which combine to form a common local consciousness. Only when the process has proceeded sufficiently far is it reasonable for an inverse tendency to emerge, moving functions outside of the district. De-agglomeration can assume the connotations of a relative dispersion in the territory of a few functions which are often the least important ones for the production process, are the most easily standardised, or require a particular ability not commonly present within the district. Internal restructuring through the expulsion of functions can take place in such a manner that the district expands by increasing its territorial allocation of productive units and employment to other local systems in the region, the country or the rest of the world. De-agglomeration also takes place when the district is still growing. In this version de-agglomeration represents a reaction to negative factors localised within it.

The basic causes of externalisation are to be found in the emergence over time of external diseconomies. Increased labour costs, high value of land, urban saturation and high levels of pollution represent some of these external diseconomies. As a consequence, phases of the productive process concerned with the transformation of the product more easily adapted to standardisation or conducted elsewhere can be effectively transferred outside of the district. It is possible to affirm that these can be transferred elsewhere because they lose their local specificity, and there is no longer an advantage in their being localised in the district. As a consequence, the producing firm can seek cost advantages in the production of standardised products or process – that is, where the crucial input is not the quality of the human skill – through the use of machines. The cost of transportation in bringing the manufactured goods to market is more than compensated by the cost of labour inside and outside of the district.

On the other hand, other phases are given increased importance – such as the design of the pattern and commercialisation of the product – which might not find an adequate response within the district. Obstacles to their expansion can be traced to the sociocultural attitudes of the population as well as to the role of these phases in the production process. If this were the case, they would tend to emigrate from the district and relocate themselves in urban areas or be carried out by firms and individuals operating within them. These urban service firms are in a better position to produce services – such as the commercialisation of products among retail and wholesale and specialised and generic firms – tied to the promotion of publicity, than are their counterparts in the districts, because the city is a larger place for the exchange of ideas and information. It is also more easily accessed from the outside by buyers as well as by visitors.

If among the phases that tend to relocate the outside of the industrial district there is a prevalence of design and commercialisation rather than production, in the long run we would expect to see a progressive peripheralisation of the district and, following certain lines of urban growth, even its metropolitanisation. A large part of the shift to services in the industrial district, therefore, is generated by the same mechanism that is at the base of its growth and is explained by the model of light industrialisation.

The 1991 results related to the Prato textile district indicated that there had been a doubling of services to firms in terms of the percentage of workforce employed (from 3.2 to 7.3 per cent), while commercial intermediation had also doubled (from 1.7 to 3.4 per cent). In the services-to-firms category, the major increases were registered in management consultancies (from 0.7 to 11.2 per thousand) and data processing services (from 2.8 to 10.7 per thousand). It is useful to remember that in 1981 commercial intermediaries operating in the sector of typical Tuscan products (textiles, including raw materials and semi-processed goods; clothing; footwear; and leather goods) represented a ratio of 9.5 workers per thousand employed in the Prato textile district, which was more than half (4.4 per thousand) of those employed in the urban area of Florence. Similar situations were found in services provided to industry; the quantitative difference between industrial districts and urban areas was not sufficient to support the thesis of the supremacy of the city over the district. One can reasonably conclude that the increase in service functions had also been motivated by the relocation of some manufacturing phases outside the district.

The increase in employment in the service sector represents, therefore, a manifestation of the indirect and increasingly complex means by which production was being undertaken. Manufacturing and the distribution of finished products took place between firms that employed productive relations extending outside of the district. This translated itself in a greater opening of the district to the outside world and the bringing into the productive process of other districts, regions, countries and continents and different economic sectors. The coordination of such a complex set of activities created new demands for increasingly diversified and specialised services. A few of these services may even seem trivial, but their localisation inside the districts increased the potential to create external organisational economies.

However, there is another explanation of what underlay the shift to services of industrial districts in the urbanised countryside. It was tied to the increase in well-being of the population. The general increase in well-being of the local community gives support to economic activities that respond to new wants, and the tendency is to increase the amount and variety of services in proportion to the wealth of the population. Given that these new service activities do not derive their immediate impulse from technological or organisational innovation and in many cases they represent labour-intensive processes, their increased presence on the local market is realised above all through increases in employment.

The shift to services of the industrial districts was in contrast to the hypothesis of metropolitan development formulated in Tuscany during the 1980s; in general, the idea was that the productive relations between the major urban areas and industrial districts in the urbanised countryside should have evolved in the direction of a territorial division of functions, thereby reserving service activities to the city and manufacturing ones to the district. A closer look at this argument reflects a basic rejection of the Tuscan formula of flexible specialisation, because it establishes a 'limit of development' on districts due to the proposed inability of the districts to generate additional service functions capable of meeting the requirements of the manufacturing firms, other than that of the commercialisation of their products.

3.3 The Deindustrialisation of the Manufacturing Poles

In light of what has been stated above, the trend of deindustrialisation does not function well in explaining the decline of manufacturing jobs in the urbanised countryside nor in the industrial districts which represent its productive focus and more dynamic element. We are not trying to affirm that all of the industrial districts found themselves in the same situation in terms of development. Many differences existed between the various districts given that they were characterised by different industries and lines of production, and the existence of different levels of industrial specialisation reinforced the differentiation in response to external economic shocks such as a decline in consumer demand. The result is that the process of shift to services did not present itself within all industrial districts at the same level and intensity, even if it was implicit in their mechanism of internal regeneration.

Deindustrialisation, interpreted as a progressive reduction in the guiding role of the principal industry in the development of the local economy through an extensive and systematic disinvestment in its productive capacity, is in a much better position to explain the fall in employment in the manufacturing poles in the touristic-industrial areas than it is elsewhere. Here, the collapse of primary industry – the vertically integrated large plants – had the effect of a progressive destruction of the local productive and social fabric. In these areas there was a lack of alternative forms of employment for a population of salaried workers with few technical skills – given the Fordist-Taylorist organisation of the plant – and accustomed to moving between different jobs inside the factory and 'temporary unemployment' rather than finding jobs in different firms. Thus, even if disinvestment in the 'old' industry were motivated by a reallocation of capital toward 'new' industries localised in the same local system, the workers who lost their jobs would rarely have the opportunity to find a new job in an alternative industry. What is more likely is that the manufacturing pole would be abandoned and the capital reallocated elsewhere, usually in localities that permitted a new process of industrialisation on the basis of lower salaries and a lower propensity toward unionisation.

The social costs of deindustrialisation through the closing of industrial factors and the transfer of capital elsewhere have had a permanent impact on the workers and their families. Individual families as well as the local community underwent a significant loss of purchasing power. But there were also costs for the national economy. In addition to wasting human capital, the State was forced to collect less in taxes while at the same time being obliged to transfer more scarce resources to the local community in terms of unemployment compensation and other types of social support for the unemployed.

The shift to services undergone by Tuscany in its manufacturing poles cannot be interpreted as a sign of post-industrial vitality. If that were the case, we would be able to identify the new professional and technical skills and occupations, using theoretical understanding and scientific know-how as the basis for innovation, or the way in which the provision of services has become dominant over manufacturing. Such an alternative is only possible if, after all, a post-industrial society really exists and is not merely a more complex form of a developed industrialised society.

Even when the phenomenon of deindustrialisation relates to local systems that are poles of manufacturing development, it is legitimate to express doubt as to whether the decline in industrial employment needs, by necessity, to imply a reduction in the size, productivity and competitiveness of local industry. In some manufacturing poles in Tuscany, like those focused on the steel industry, the loss of jobs reflects the impact of innovation aimed at the acquisition of efficiency through the reduction of employment. Such processes are part of industrial policies aimed at the modernisation of production facilities, reorganisation of the productive cycle, and the introduction of technological innovation, to which are attributed the growing difference between increase of productivity and decrease in employment.

The actions that can be carried out by local government to block the process of deindustrialisation of a manufacturing pole are minimal, in that it has a low level of input and, therefore, little sway over the local economic system. This is true even if the process of deindustrialisation is relatively long and the signs of crisis clear enough to enable government to develop alternative economic policies and productive investments capable of creating new economic capacity and employment, before the local community finds itself in an irreversible and catastrophic situation. But when the process of deindustrialisation reaches an advanced stage, generic appeals for a process of reindustrialisation are not sufficient to face the problem of a loss of jobs in industry and high levels of unemployment without investments in education through local programmes of vocational and higher education.

CONCLUSIONS

According to the interpretation that has been proposed here, the changes that took place between 1981 and 1991 accentuated the differences in development between the 'four Tuscanies'. While the touristic-industrial areas went adrift, there was a growing affirmation of the industrial districts of the urbanised countryside in relation to the other Tuscanies, including the urban areas, and a marginalisation of the countryside.

In a national overview, the general fall in industrial employment in Italy created a more territorially concentrated industrialisation than was the case ten years previously. In the local systems of light industry existing in Tuscany and the Third Italy, industry was more territorially concentrated in the urbanised countryside, in particular in the industrial districts. This involved a relative phenomenon that at the time had still to attract the attention of analysts and public and private decision makers. In a similar vein, the fall in industrial employment was not necessarily directly connected with the rise of service employment.

If it is true that these changes correspond to a development process contained in the interpretative model of light industrialisation, it should also be said that the conditions of national and international development in 1991 are different from those of twenty years before. Italy had a much higher level of public debt, and the economy had undergone a rapid opening and internationalisation. The consequences were that the shift to services of the districts required at that time an active contribution from local industrial and social policies and not a renunciation from intervening. The districts had demonstrated their ability to fend for themselves in an era of global changes by creatively interpreting the tendencies of development, but nevertheless local changes had not been without negative ramifications. If the relocation of manufacturing activities outside the district were to be misinterpreted as a sign of 'modernisation' and public policies insisted on favouring the trend, public policies ran the risk of destroying the skills and activities that characterised the district. All that would be achieved would be a Pyrrhic victory.

What was necessary at this point was a thoughtful policy reflecting a combined goal of reinforcing productive capacity and the maintenance of local consumption levels through an efficient use of the human capital available locally. Local entrepreneurship had to be favoured rather than discouraged, and it needed to be able to make use of the local service networks, services to industry, vocational education, and laboratories of scientific and technological research with the aim of increasing the knowledge base of individuals and the community.

In Tuscany the urban areas remained 'the dark object of desire' of regional development. The hope was that they could become the motor of development, but on the whole the motor was 'utterly exhausted'. As we have seen, this role was still being carried out by the urbanised countryside and the industrial districts. Excluding Florence, the service sector was a local one, and in general it had very little global or metropolitan in its content. It should be recognised that the role of urban areas in relation to Tuscan development does not pass exclusively through local metropolitan relations based on a growing interdependence between industrial districts and urban areas; instead, it depends on the capacity of single urban areas to develop global, service metropolitan functions. These are such when they belong to a national and international network capable of directly accessing global exchange networks. In this light, in Tuscany only the urban area of Florence presents itself in a similar manner, on the basis of its cultural function. On this basis, it is possible to move on to the search for competitive advantages. The artistic and cultural patrimony and the scientific research and university centres – along with other activities such as publishing houses – which are present in the major urban areas in Tuscany (Florence, Siena and Pisa) needed to be considered assets to be used as an economic resource in competition with other urban areas in Italy and the world, through the stimulation of local entrepreneurial initiatives or attracting them from abroad. In fact, it was not a matter of taking advantage, through the development of local services, of the past and the tradition of diffused light industry, but of becoming competitive at the international level. Individual urban areas endowed with their own peculiarities and development capacity could face the competition from other urban areas whose activity was characterised by the processing of information and promoting the exchange and diffusion of know-how.

The objectives of regional and local planning needed to change from being those of merging into one large socioeconomic territorial area the 'four Tuscanies' to being those of contributing to a better development of the characteristic features that each enjoyed in the cases of both local growing systems as well as those of local systems in decline. This could only be done through the formulation and implementation of public policies designed to safeguard the interests of the individual local communities and by taking forward the valorisation of the local human capital.

REFERENCES

Becattini, G. (ed.) (1975), *Lo sviluppo economico della Toscana con particolare riguardo all'industrializzazione leggera*, Florence: IRPET.

Falorni, A. and F. Sforzi (eds) (1989), *Materiali per un'interpretazione dello sviluppo economico della Toscana*, Florence: IRPET.

Fuà, G. and C. Zacchia (eds) (1983), *Industrializzazione senza fratture*, Bologna: Il Mulino.

IRES Toscana (1988), *Toscana che cambia: economia e società nella Toscana degli anni '80*, Milan: Franco Angeli.

IRPET (1969), *Lo sviluppo economico della Toscana: un'ipotesi di lavoro*, Florence: Il Ponte.

IRPET (1986), *Mutamento economico e trasformazioni urbane nei sistemi metropolitani medi in Europa*, International seminar, Florence, 18–19 December.

ISTAT (1971a), *11° Censimento generale della popolazione*, Rome, 24 October.

ISTAT (1971b), *5° Censimento generale dell'industria e del commercio*, Rome, 25 October.

ISTAT (1981a), *12° Censimento generale della popolazione*, Rome, 25 October.

ISTAT (1981b), *6° Censimento generale dell'industria, del commercio, dei servizi e dell'artigianato*, Rome, 26 October.

ISTAT (1981c), *6° Censimento generale dell'industria, del commercio, dei servizi e dell'artigianato*, Rome, 26 October.

ISTAT (1991a), *13° Censimento generale della popolazione e delle abitazioni*, Rome, 20 October.

ISTAT (1991b), *7° Censimento generale dell'industria e dei servizi*, Rome, 21 October.

Mori, G. (ed.) (1986), *La Toscana. Storia d'Italia: le regioni dall'Unità a oggi*, Turin: Einaudi.

Regione Toscana (1984), *Processo di urbanizzazione nell'area Firenze-Prato-Pistoia*, Florence: La Casa Usher.

3.   The past in the present: Prato's people

Giacomo Becattini

Prato today is certainly not the culturally integrated community of fifty years ago; things have been so stirred up in the last half-century that in current behaviours the sharp outlines of 'Pratosity' have surely been blunted; nevertheless life in Prato has preserved, as everything changed around it, a set of values, rules and institutions – that have also changed of course but perhaps less than elsewhere and in any case following the same direction – around which its economic, political and cultural life revolves. Such at least is my impression, which is confirmed moreover by many inquiries.

As I cannot attack, for reasons already cited as well as my own want of the necessary skills, the problem of the effects of technological, organisational and merchandising changes of the last forty years on Prato's 'typical character' (or on the typical make-up of its typifying features) the only thing I can do is to touch upon that large topic by mentioning some aspects of the observable behaviours of Prato folk that appear to be most clearly connected to the process of change in the district. This is a brief addition to my arguments, therefore, that I am proposing as my last word of helpful advice to the city, I believe, if only to indicate where further inquiry and consideration are needed.

The three features of the typical behaviour of Prato folk that I am about to weave into my argument are the following: their acute sense of belonging to the community; their 'fierce' dedication to work; and the rich breadth of their imagination.

In order to deal with these features I shall start from the questions posed by Giovanni Cherubini, at the end of the first volume of *Prato, the History of a City*:

> Is it really so fanciful a notion to suppose that something ... of the merchants, of the woollen-drapers of Francesco Datini's time is still present in the Prato folk of today? And could that same blunt realism, which does not necessarily mean lack

of aspirations and dreams, that devotion to work which distinguishes the Prato folk of today and which appears so obvious to any outside observer, not be to some extent the legacy of the realism, the sense of proportion, and the dedication to their work of the Prato folk of the Middle Ages ... obliged to steer a prudent course between cities more ancient and more powerful? (Cherubini 1991, p. 1006)

The devotion to work Cherubini speaks of was certainly obligatory for a small, though lively, community such as Prato, that emerged around the end of the first millennium without an adequate 'lebensraum' in a world already divided up politically and economically. To assert itself in such a world it needed, though it might not have sufficed, an intense commitment (in terms of the pace of work in that period, of course) to the production of some goods that could be sold widely; also needed were a certain unity and mutual cooperation between the local producers, as well as the ability to build up, boldly and ruthlessly when needed, their outlets in markets beyond the city. It was in the combined grip of the need to overcome through 'exports' the shortage of food supplies essential for survival and growth and of the need to keep up with the level of technology set by its joining first the 'regional' market, where the jealous competition of the surrounding populations was at work, and then the national and international markets, that were forged, I believe, the two attitudes, but certainly not the only ones, that typify Prato folk: a certain tendency to stand together to defend their common interests (such as the Prato 'colony' in the city of Ragusa in Dalmatia) and the capacity for calculated gambles that goes with being a long-range merchant.

These processes unfold, from the very origins of Prato, around the production and sale of woollen cloths, but not without significant variants over the centuries – though so far transient – in its specialities (from copper to paper and straw goods) and the organisation of manufacturing (from the scattered workshops of Datini to the vertically-integrated Fabbricone – the big factory – down to the team of firms of today). It was around woollen textile manufacturing essentially that the 'culture of unsparing hard work', in Giorgio Mori's words (Mori 1988, p. 1479) was forged. By building up experience in the heads of the local operators this generated the wealth of textile know-how that Prato folk are famed for. It was on trade, especially long-distance trade (as per Datini, Marcovaldo or Mazzoni and Pacciani), however, and on activities connected to trade (money-changing) that the speculative and entrepreneurial spirit of Prato folk was forged and grew strong in the rapidly changing fortunes of different kinds of goods. And this was to be fully reflected in the rag and shoddy trades, where Prato in the 19th century became the capital and main receptacle for the whole world.

The history of Italy [exclaimed Malaparte in a bitter but also prideful invective] ends up in Prato, and in rags ... And not just Italy's ... but flags of all nations, uniforms of generals and privates of every army, and priests' cassocks, prelates' breeches, cardinals' purple robes, judges' gowns, policemen's and gaolers' tunics, bridal veils, yellowing lace and babies' nappies. Even the civilian clothes worn by King Umberto at Monza when Gaetano Bresci, who came from Prato, emptied his revolver into him, ended up in Prato in a bale of rags ... It's Prato where everything ends up: the world's glory, honour, piety, pride, and vanity. (Malaparte 1994, p. 66)

I cannot help conjecturing whether just that daily comparison of the sacrifices required by manual labour with the experience of the rapid enrichment of a few merchant woollen-drapers was the thing that fostered the famous 'propensity to set up on one's own' of Prato folk. To quote Simonetta Soldani, there was in Prato in the early part of the 19th century, along with a full recognition of the 'nobility of manual labour', a widespread longing to 'escape being a slave to it' (Soldani 1988, p. 679). A French historian, Corine Maitte, has written that Prato was: 'a city where self-help, as elsewhere in Italy and perhaps more than in other countries, was the driving force of a common identity that encouraged people to look for independent jobs, to be their own masters' (Maitte 2001, p. 446).

A useful contribution to understanding this aspect of the identity of Prato folk comes to us, I believe, from the pen of the already quoted Curzio Suckert Malaparte:

The history of the people of Prato is the history of little people, without tragedies or dramas, nor epic disasters: it is the story of people that has never bred nobles in its bosom, and so has never had to bow the knee to local gentry nor be roused by trumpet blasts nor tumble out of bed to take part in great campaigns nor run behind be-plumed horses clad in armour. (Malaparte 1994, pp. 56–7)

Setting aside his historiographical simplifications and his colourful language, this passage conveys a good picture of a community that grew up naturally, without great cleavages within it, as if in a play constantly re-enacted; a community where the ambition to demonstrate, before an audience of one's peers, just what one is made of, constitutes a social force of the first order. Standing united against outsiders, and especially the Florentines and the men of Pistoia, but equally so on occasion against the Catalans or Dalmatians, yet intensely argumentative amongst themselves, almost as quarrelsome as the Florentines, this has been the character of the Prato folk since anyone can remember: 'there does not exist in this disrespectful Tuscan commune any immunity from criticism and argument' in the words of Raveggi, referring to the first half of the 14th century (Raveggi 1991, p. 668).

This urge to demonstrate – in the field of economic activities where the results are easier to compare rather than in warfare or politics – what stuff one is made of tends to produce, whenever the right conditions are there, a social structure in the city in which one stratum of the population, perhaps not very large in absolute terms, but also not negligible in number, and in any case socially and economically 'central', constantly revolves between, in employment terms, independence, semi-dependence and dependence, with relatively few going from rags to riches and few falling into poverty and social exclusion. A fairly intense circulation of wealth, to which corresponds an uncommon social and political mobility, thus appears to have characterised Prato over a long period of time. We can find confirmation of this, albeit with obvious variations, in every historical period. Take, for instance, the period around 1500:

> the dominant class certainly enjoys a very diverse degree of mobility from period to period, but is always present ... Many clans and families disappear, many new names are found, perhaps revealing the turnover of wealth ... Thus the renewal of the ruling class never stops and its speed significantly keeps pace with changes in economic and social mobility. (Fasano Guarini 1986, pp. 844 and 846)

Renewal in continuity therefore: 'on the one hand changes in leadership, albeit at different speeds from one time to another, prevail over continuity, on the other hand social barriers remain fluid and economically diversified forces co-exist' (ibid.).

It does not appear absurd to suggest that the solidarity between the citizens of Prato that seems likely to have arisen in the 13th and 14th centuries, if not earlier, from the need to unite in defence against 'outsiders', especially in foreign markets, becomes stronger in the intervening centuries from the 15th to the 18th because of a remarkable blossoming of religious and charitable institutions that lock Prato into a web of personal and family alliances. In fact, assuming that the fabric of Prato's spirit of community was made up of an alliance of economic interests to repel outsiders, in the period of the take-off of the free commune, it may have been knitted together more tightly by the closer ties between the families and classes in the city that becomes fully apparent with the weakening of industrial activities from the 1400s to the 1700s (Stumpo 1986, Chapter IV).

The second half of the 19th century marks an 'ideological' break in the culture of Prato whose effects are hard to assess; it was certainly the case that part of the local textile industry, partly because of the influx of foreign capital, tended to model itself on the organisational formulae of the capitalist large factory (Lungonelli 1988; Pescarolo 1988). This brought about, albeit still partially and in a rather odd way, separation and confrontation between the ownership of the material means of production (the factory and its machinery) and the ownership of labour, certain sections of which remained, it must be remembered, saturated with a contextual knowledge of production that was hard to replace. A gulf then opened up between the two alternative concepts of the changes taking place (Becattini 2001): on one side the concept that prevailed among the industrial classes and the trade union members in the factories, which, in tune with the dominant ideologies of the day (liberalism and socialism) stressed the break with the past and tended to view the city's textile industry as one episode in the more general process of capitalistic industrialisation; and on the other the concept, still anchored to the popular perception of the profound continuity of the structures of everyday life, which tended to see special value in the aspects of the Prato manufacturing formula that had not changed and remained their own peculiar selves. The distance between the two pictures reached its peak, as already mentioned, in the post-1945 period, during the metamorphosis of the caterpillar into a butterfly, and then the gap was finally closed in more recent decades in the image of the industrial district.

Turning to the second point made by Cherubini, Prato starts out as a small town lacking room to develop between Florence and Pistoia, so is unable to oppose them successfully. The precocious industrial take-off (late 13th–early 14th centuries) of the commune of Prato is not supported by valid political plans, so that Prato wavers between distant protectors (the Angevins of Naples) and small local tyrants (the Alberti family) until, in 1651, its fate is sealed by subjection to Florence (Fantappié 1991). This leads to an unbroken series of protests, demands, attempts (though really not very serious) at rebellion against the Mistress City. Elena Fasano Guarini speaks of 'need running through the whole history of Prato from the 1500s to the 1700s to defend its own lebensraum and its own identity within the rigid context of the dominant state in the region' (Fasano Guarini 1986, p. 847). Nor does the problem disappear in the 19th century, when, in the words of Soldani, Prato is 'ever anxious to be different from Florence and to maintain a strong and distinct self-image, able to contain and repel the centripetal energy of its big neighbour' (Soldani 1986, p. 750). As for more recent times, for instance the first half of the 20th century, the 'widespread and deeply-felt sense of belonging to the community' with which Giorgio Mori concludes the third volume of the story of Prato (Mori 1988, p. 1479) is enough to confirm that the problem had not disappeared nor the attitude changed even on the eve of the Second World War. Finally, even during the time-span I have dealt with in this essay, there were many times when evident signs of resentment and rivalry were to be found. It seems plausible, indeed, to link the strong sense of belonging shared by the Prato folk also to this persistent, perhaps deliberately cultivated, self-image as being a group that was undervalued and discriminated against[1] (Absalom 1997).

Yet one gets the impression that this posing by the Prato folk as the victims of Florentine prevarication does not cover the whole history of the

Prato-Florence relationship. I think there is certainly a complex relationship stemming from economic complementarity and cultural reflection, of competition and emulation, that does not fit at all well into the stereotype of the oppressor and the oppressed.

The fact that the Prato folk have had to struggle, firstly in order to get into the remaining bits of the woollen cloths market left to them by the dominant state of the region, and later into those left by the big players in the world market might thus explain the way the Prato folk persisted in their defence of the common interests that had, as often happens, become part and parcel of their own, partly real and partly of course imaginary identity as a city. In this supposed process nothing automatically derives from real developments, as is shown by the examples of many other industrial communities where similar experiences have not led to the same outcomes.

And so I come, finally, to the thing that comprises the strategic strength – the rich imagination – of a people condemned by their specialisation in particular products to steer a course through a market reality that changes with the play of uncontrollable outside forces.

My hypothesis is that the multiplicity and the variety of the expedients, constantly being thought up by the Prato folk in order to defend their markets in outside contexts they cannot control, have created over the centuries a cast of mind that could be defined as that of a handyman.

A proof of this that can certainly not be suspected of coming from any preconceived sympathy for the 'Prato businessman' can be found in the words of 'Anonymous 54'. From the quotations cited earlier it seems fairly clear that the Prato entrepreneur of the early 1950s, at least in the opinion of this observer, was an extrovert personality who hated defeat, to which anyway he never yielded, and relished just as much his successes, blatantly boasting about them within his social circle. In a word, he lived life to the full – jumping nimbly from one fabric or one yarn to another – in a situation of constant market turbulence. And he lived it in a frame of mind that from infatuation with being a 'shoddyman' who feels he is an industrialist (a Mario Sala, but less gloomy) (Mastronardi 1962) quickly merged into being a citizen protesting against everything and everyone. What is certain is that, amidst the oscillations and uncertainties of the textile situation, the Prato putter-out (*impannatore*) of the immediate postwar period was in his element. It is hard to imagine a human type more suited to the market situations that were in the making.

People who are 'too earnest', who 'takes things literally', who avoid unjustified risks, who worship the 'cautious' and the 'reasonable', do not prosper when change is constant. The constant shattering of the optimum mixture of forms of knowledge that goes with globalisation certainly requires a growing level of cultural information and training, but also and especially a great degree of intellectual versatility, a great capacity for 'lateral thinking' (de Bono 1971). Its is a capacity that today's education system does not provide and which, in the case of Prato, has been formed in the field by working over a long period, I believe, at the edges of a market that is as hard to grasp as Proteus.

The famous, and often denigrated, 'art of getting by' of Prato folk, of adapting a thing to a use it was not intended for, is merely in my view the normal manifestation of this 'rich, unbridled imagination' of theirs.

There is a passage in a book by Roberto Benigni that seems to symbolise very well this capacity to 'think laterally', creatively combining images that belong to different spheres of daily life:

> we got there at dawn and found ourselves looking at an astonishing picture: the fields were all coloured in red, and green ... and from the trees dangled threads of cloth: they were the waste bits from the spinning mills. Instead of throwing them away they were being used as manure. But I believed that in Prato cloth grew from the soil, that you could plant a shirt or sow a jacket, that there were trouser trees and suit-plants. (Melani 1993)

The kaleidoscope of images flitting from farm labour (Benigni was from the countryside near Arezzo) to the typical operations in textile production or clothing manufacture, carried along by the myriad facets of using nature (sowing, planting, manuring, spinning, weaving, cutting, sewing ...) that reminds us irresistibly of the roofless workshops of the frantic postwar reconstruction of Prato's industry or the bold decision of the Prato folk, when faced with the collapse of carded woollens in 1982, to apply the techniques of carding to new and different materials. So it is this remarkable aptitude and willingness to reshuffle the pack, in this 'unbridled imagination' that the true, lasting heritage of Prato really lies, far more than in its famous textile know-how, which is its historical content but which can lose much of its value as outside circumstances change. If the Prato folk do not surrender to the besieging economic gospel nor become smugly self-satisfied, but stay faithful to the old saying of theirs 'when you think you've finally made it, it's all up with you', the 'Prato system' can face the period of globalisation that is before us with quite a few arrows in its quiver.

In conclusion to this attempt to grasp, against the double background of change in Italy and the world, the overall meaning of what has been happening in Prato over the last forty years, may I express the hope that the globalisation of markets and whatever may follow on from it may preserve the Prato folk, with all their vices and virtues, just as they are! After all, the world would be a duller place without them.

NOTE

1. The following passage from Alfred Marshall seems to have been written just to describe the relationship between Florence and Prato: 'When a group of people in daily intercourse with one another had to earn their living under difficulties, and to rely on one another in contending with those difficulties, a feeling of brotherhood almost invariably grew up. If the difficulties were partly of man's creation, and had in them any savour of injustice or oppression; then to contend with them was more then mere enterprise. It became a religion, and a source of inspiration; and by its aid the community was knit together in living bonds, which grew with its growth' (see Marshall 1919, p. 685).

REFERENCES

Absalom, R. (1997), 'Liberazione e ricostruzione a Prato: il ruolo degli alleati', in Various authors, *Prato: storia di una città*, Vol. IV, pp. 85–146.

Becattini, G. (2001), *The Caterpillar and the Butterfly: an Exemplary Case of Development in the Italy of Industrial Districts*, Florence: Le Monnier.

Cherubini, G. (1991), 'Ascesa e declino del centro medievale (dal Mille al 1494)', in Various authors, *Prato: storia di una città*, Vol. I, pp. 965–1012.

de Bono, E. (1971), *The Use of Lateral Thinking*, Harmondsworth: Penguin Books.

Fantappié, R. (1991), 'Nascita e sviluppo di Prato', in Various authors, *Prato: storia di una città*, Vol. I, pp. 613–762.

Fasano Guarini, E. (1986), 'Sintesi conclusiva: un microcosmo in movimento (1494–1815)', in Various authors, *Prato: storia di una città*, Vol. II, pp. 827–80.

Lungonelli, M. (1988), 'Dalla manifattura alla fabbrica: l'avvio dello sviluppo industriale (1815–95)', in Various authors, *Prato: storia di una città*, Vol. III, pp. 3–49.

Maitte, C. (2001), *La trame incertaine: le monde textile de Prato: XVIIIe–XIXe siècles*, Villeneuve d'Ascq: Septentrion.

Malaparte, C. (1994), *Maledetti toscani*, Milan: Leonardo editore.

Marshall, A. (1919), *Industry and Trade: a Study of Industrial Techniques and Business Organization, and of their Influences on the Conditions of Various Classes and Nations*, London: Macmillan.

Mastronardi, L. (1962), *Il calzolaio di Vigevano*, Turin: Einaudi.

Melani, M. (1993), *Polvere di stelle in Prato*, Prato: Coop. editoriale.

Mori, G. (1988), 'Il tempo dell'industria: sintesi conclusiva', in Various authors, *Prato: storia di una città*, Vol. III, pp. 1419–98.

Pescarolo, S. (1988), 'Modelli d'industrializzazione, ruoli sociali, immagini del lavoro (1895–1943)', in Various authors, *Prato: storia di una città*, Vol. III, pp. 51–134.

Raveggi, S. (1991), 'Protagonisti e antagonisti nel libero comune', in Various authors, *Prato: storia di una città*, Vol. I, pp. 479–612.

Soldani, S. (1988), 'Vita quotidiana e vita di società in un centro industrioso', in Various authors, *Prato: storia di una città*, Vol. III, pp. 663–806.

Stumpo, E. (1986), 'Le forme del governo cittadino', in Various authors, *Prato: storia di una città*, Vol. II, pp. 281–347.

Various authors (1986–1997), *Prato: storia di una città*, 4 vols., Florence: Le Monnier.

PART II

Inside the District:
Clues for Theoreticians

4. The governance of transactions in the industrial district: the 'community market'

Gabi Dei Ottati

INTRODUCTION

In recent years in Italy (and also in other countries), an ever increasing group of scholars, including numerous economists, sociologists, and other experts in the social sciences, have examined the question of the economic development attained by territorial systems of small and medium-sized firms.[1]

At first, the idea that this development was intrinsically precarious, based on organisational forms that seemed to have survived from the past, was the most widespread.[2] Later, the diffusion and persistence over time of small-firm systems forced scholars to examine their specific advantages. This line of inquiry has now developed to such an extent that some feel the territorial systems of small firms can be one of the models for industrial organisation in the future.[3]

However, since small firms have often been known to achieve competitiveness either by keeping wages low or by tax evasion, it is easy to understand why scholars are sceptical that 'real' economic growth can be attained via small firms.

This scepticism is fostered not only by the empirical data on how some small firms operate, but also, in part, by the relative lack of theoretical frameworks capable of throwing light on relations among these firms (or between the firm system and the community), which are essential to an understanding of how small-firm systems function.[4]

Hence, however important the small-firm system may be, both today and in the future, the effectiveness of which depends mainly on elements of economic rationality, it might seem useful to trace an ideal typical model of production organised in a territorial system of specialised small private firms.

73

To this end, I have made use of existing research on the subject,[5] as well as of writings on transaction costs.[6] In fact, by focusing on single transactions rather than on single firms, the latter writings seem to indicate that the coordination of economic activity can be effectively achieved via governance mechanisms *different* from the one typical of vertically integrated corporations.

Furthermore, these writings have underscored the fact that one must take transaction costs into account in order to evaluate the effectiveness of a specific form of economic organisation, and that transaction costs are positively correlated to problems of opportunism, uncertainty, and ambiguity.[7] Therefore, I shall first sketch the 'industrial district' model, as the conceptualisation of a territorial system of small private firms (section 1), and then consider its performance with regard to these problems (sections 2, 3, and 4).

1. THE INDUSTRIAL DISTRICT AS AN INTERPRETIVE MODEL OF ECONOMIC ORGANISATION

1.1 The Single Firms and their System

Over a hundred years ago, Alfred Marshall (thanks to his knowledge of contemporary industrial development in Sheffield and Lancashire) had discovered that the 'industrial district', an agglomeration of specialised small and medium-sized firms in the same area, could be an alternative mode of organising production in certain manufacturing industries to that of the large firm, without relinquishing the advantages generally attributed to the division of labour.[8] In *The Pure Theory of Domestic Values*, Marshall explained that 'the advantages of production on a large scale can in general be as well attained by the aggregation of a large number of small masters into the district as by the erection of a few large works' (Whitaker 1975, Vol. 2, p. 196).

This brief quotation immediately reveals the very special nature of Marshall's industrial district, namely, (1) the moderate size of the single firms of which it is made up; (2) their large number; and (3) their clustering in one geographical area or district.

In order to sketch the industrial district as a theoretical model of economic organisation, it may be useful to start by examining these three aspects, leaving any remarks on the complex network of relations, whether market relations and other forms that unite and separate firms and individuals within the industrial district, to the next section.

The first aspect, the small size of the single firms in the district, can be regarded from at least two perspectives.[9] It means that the number of employees, the value of capital goods, and the output of each firm will not, in general, be very high. However, the size of a firm also depends on the number of stages of production it performs. Thus, its small size implies a tendency to specialise in one or a few stages – in other words, a tendency to vertical disintegration, rather than vertical integration.[10]

Insofar as the smallness of the single firms in the industrial district depends on specialised production and therefore on an essentially horizontal rather than vertical division of labour, machinery will tend to be the most productive possible, given the existing techniques,[11] and workers will generally possess a broad range of skills.[12]

The typical size of a single firm in the district also produces effects on its internal organisation. Indeed, because of its reduced size, the firm may well be run by one family or by one person, and the entrepreneur may be directly involved in production, performing both technical and managerial tasks in person.

The quotation from Marshall reveals two other aspects of the industrial district: the large number of firms involved and their clustering in one area. Taken together, these three aspects indicate that, if the single firms making up the district are small, their aggregation will form a large system. It is precisely because the overall size of the industrial district is large that the single units composing it can, under certain circumstances, benefit from the advantages of specialisation and of large-scale production, mostly under the guise of external economies.

To understand how economic activity can be effectively organised within the industrial district (as an interpretive model), we should then focus on the relations among its firms rather than on individual firms.

1.2 Competition and Cooperation in the Industrial District

The fact that the industrial district is made up of a large number of small specialised firms, clustered in one area, has effects on the economic relations among individuals living and working in that area.

If the firms within that area are numerous, quite small, and specialised, then for each production stage in the economic process a local market will be generated in which the firms that demand and those that supply a given (generally intermediate) product or service will compete with one another.[13]

On the other hand, the relatively stable aggregation of business agents in the same area usually implies they are from roughly the same social environment. They will probably possess a common culture (language, meanings, values, and so forth) and, above all, a common body of implicit rules of behaviour (customs).

The fact that agents belong to the same cultural environment is, therefore, one important aspect of the industrial district. However, if such a model of economic organisation is to work, the social context in which the specialised firms are embedded should be one in which cooperation has long been customary and where this custom has been extended to economic relations. Thus, only where such a custom exists (even if it crystallised before the area's industrialisation), or where conditions favour the development of a spirit of cooperation, can the economic process be organised as an industrial district. The industrial district, as a model of economic organisation, is distinguishable by the special relations that link the firms. This is because competition in the district markets is combined with a local custom of mutual cooperation.

This is a distinctive feature of the industrial district. Not only does it make the working of a governance mechanism of transactions particularly cheap (see subsection 1.3), but the reciprocal integration of competition and cooperation also encourages people to try to find less expensive ways of producing their goods or services, and hence stimulates continuous change.

In markets for specialised intermediate products and services that intervene between one stage and another of the economic process of an industrial district, competition is a dynamic factor that motivates agents to offer better and better results. In these markets, competing agents strive to save on resources and invent new devices that will increase productivity.[14]

The function of competition in promoting efficiency and change in the industrial district is reinforced by the custom of mutual cooperation. This can help the economic process from various perspectives. First, it helps to keep it dynamic because it reduces the risks for those who start their own firms, or who decide to invest in new machinery and new products. This is because these decisions are taken, within a framework of mutual cooperation, in the hope that should things not work out, all would not be lost. A person can always go back to being an employee (possibly in the same firm as before he struck out on his own), or continue to produce for other firms, or for subcontractors, rather than work on his own. Thus, cooperation favours a process of continuous change, which is essential for the success of the industrial district.[15]

Insofar as the custom of cooperation is a guarantee against the major risks of the economic game, it helps to increase the number of those prepared to play. But, for the same reason, it helps to economise on initiative and on the propensity to take risks that are essential resources for development. Thanks to cooperation, the failure of a firm or of an innovation is not considered a definitive failure, but can be tried again, later on, when either circumstances have changed, or the agent has gained greater experience. Furthermore, cooperation helps to foster change, because it allows the process of innovation to be split among the firms in the district.[16]

Second, cooperation helps promote the coordination of closely complementary activities, in other words, those that need to be matched quantitatively and *qualitatively*.[17] This double requirement usually accompanies all transactions among firms specialised in different phases of a production process. If one considers how the economic process is divided up among the various firms, it is easy to see the importance of coordinating complementary activities. Since the latter require the volume *and characteristics* of the product to be matched, they need some kind of agreed-upon coordination; in the industrial district this coordination is achieved by cooperation.

Third, cooperation helps to lower production costs, enabling firms in the district to take advantage of external economies deriving from the overall size of the industrial district. Indeed, interdependence in the latter does not concern only those firms with complementary activities; it is a general phenomenon, because the productivity of single firms depends also on their enjoying the benefits of external economies (of scale, of coordination, of skill, and so forth) produced by all the agents of the district taken together. These economies can be reaped by firms thanks to their links of cooperation.[18]

1.3 The Mechanism of Transaction Governance: the 'Community Market'

In the previous section, I described how economic relations, among both individuals and firms in a district, are peculiar because they are compounded of an original mixture of competition and cooperation. Indeed, thanks to that mixture, transactions in the district can be governed by a mechanism that is particularly effective in cases of widespread uncertainty and ambiguity.

As scholars writing on transaction costs have pointed out, economic exchanges could not take place without some mechanism, whether formal or informal, that would provide the parties with the necessary information on the degree of reciprocity, or equity, between both sides.[19] These writers have identified three main ideal types of mechanism governing transactions, according to the information used: (1) markets, which allow agents to evaluate transactions by referring to prices; (2) hierarchies, or bureaucracies, in which people refer to explicit rules enforced by authorities with discretionary powers; (3) communities where people follow an implicit code of behaviour acquired by socialisation.[20]

Now, if one bears in mind the peculiar interlacing of relations typical of the industrial district, one can understand that in this case the mechanism governing transactions is a form that lies halfway between two of the ideal types mentioned above: the market and the community. And, since this mechanism uses elements taken from both the market and the community, it can be called the 'community market'.

Indeed, if on the one hand, competition in the district's markets helps to locate rewards capable of stimulating the initiative of its agents, then on the other hand, the custom of cooperating allows them to believe that the reciprocity between performance and reward will be respected, at least over a certain period.

Naturally, this is a way of integrating the market that cannot be planned ex ante. The custom of cooperating may possibly evolve among people who live and work in the same area, but it is a slow process whose study is not even within the normal scope of economic inquiry.

However, once the custom of cooperation exists, the ways of organising the economic activity typical of the industrial district help to perpetuate it, because its advantages (in terms of reduced costs and of support to development) are there for all to see. Besides, personal contacts, which occur frequently because each unit is small and *non-routine* transactions are relatively numerous, can (and often do) stimulate loyalty, esteem, and even friendship among the agents. Insofar as this actually takes place, interdependence is increased and cooperation is developed.

Before I examine the advantages of the 'community market' as a mechanism for governing transactions, I should like to mention one aspect that is important for an industrial district if it is to maintain its capacity for development over a certain period of time. This aspect is related to the fact that a district could close in on itself, or obstruct the entry of 'new shrewd energy to supplement that of native origin' (Marshall 1923, p. 287), because some of its economic advantages derive from local custom and, since the latter is a body of implicit rules, it can only be learned by socialisation. On the whole, however, it seems that such a danger can be avoided.

The necessary amount of socialisation for the working of the industrial district does not include the entire cultural system of its members, but only the habit of correct behaviour and, when circumstances require it, a spirit of cooperation in work and trade relations. Such a code of behaviour is easily learned by simply living and working for a while in the district. During this period of 'apprenticeship', people (even those from other areas) can learn the skills required by their job, as well as the habit of cooperating in economic relations, and in exchange receive monetary and social rewards in the form of earnings and esteem.

The advantages of using a governance mechanism of transactions based in part on community factors, is that it considerably reduces transaction costs. Since these costs derive mostly from the need to maintain a certain reciprocity in performance on either side, whenever this reciprocity is to a large extent guaranteed by a social mechanism (rather than by contract or bureaucratic structure), transactions will cost less. Usually, it will not be necessary to stipulate complicated contracts, nor to apply to bureaucratic authorities to settle possible disputes. Should these occur, they will be settled directly by the parties concerned.

However, the greatest advantage of the 'community market' is that it allows members of an industrial district to make transactions that otherwise would not be possible, or would cost far more. Such is the case, for instance, with transactions whose value is uncertain or ambiguous, whether because the parties are interdependent, or because of innovation.

Having outlined the industrial district as an interpretive model of economic organisation, the next three sections will examine its performance with regard to the problems of opportunism, uncertainty, and ambiguity. In fact, most scholars writing about transaction costs feel that it is precisely these problems that usually raise transaction costs, and hence require the creation of special structures of governance.

2. THE INDUSTRIAL DISTRICT AND OPPORTUNISM

2.1 Opportunism and the Custom of Cooperation

From the point of view of the behaviour of the parties, opportunism has been defined as 'an effort to realise individual gains through a lack of candour or honesty in transactions' (Williamson, Wachter and Harris 1975, p. 258). Therefore, it implies some kind of information manipulation, both by giving distorted or incomplete information and by making false promises, before concluding or during the execution of a transaction.

Consequently, if numerous people are prepared to behave opportunistically, transaction costs will increase, because it will be necessary, for instance, to inquire into the reputations of one's counterparts, or to make sure the various points of a contract are respected.

Thus, since the subjective tendency toward opportunism can hobble economic activity by increasing transaction costs and reducing its effectiveness, it may be useful to see whether a subjective propensity to behave opportunistically is widespread or not in the industrial district.

Obviously, if there is a custom of cooperation that extends to economic relations, this should prevent people from following their instinct to behave opportunistically, or at least to curb it considerably. This is so because those who live and work in the industrial district ought to have absorbed a rule of social behaviour contrary to the craftiness of self-interest.[21]

Insofar as the custom of cooperation is characteristic of the industrial district as an economic organisation, one can assume that opportunistic behaviour will not be very common. However, since the propensity to behave opportunistically in general can create economic problems when circumstances make such behaviour highly profitable, I shall now consider some of these circumstances.

2.2 Opportunism and Asymmetry between Parties to a Contract

As writers on this subject have emphasised,[22] on the whole opportunism is a serious obstacle to economic efficiency whenever there is a significant asymmetry between the parties in a transaction, as regards information, substitutability, and/or specificity of (that is, non-marketable) investment.

Since information is relatively transparent in an industrial district, thanks to the joint effect of competition and cooperation, I shall examine the other two forms of asymmetry, which enable opportunism to be transformed from a subjective propensity into a serious transaction problem.

As I have said, we are dealing with asymmetry between the parties vis-à-vis substitutability (in other words, the fact that it is hard and/or expensive to find a valid substitute for a specific transaction) and vis-à-vis specific investments (the costs of acquiring knowledge, equipment, or whatever else is necessary for a given transaction). Now, to understand how these asymmetries can give rise to economic problems, one has merely to bear in mind that the more lopsided the relations between parties, in terms of substitutability or specific investments, the greater the benefit (and cost for the other party) that the less substitutable party, and/or the one who has contributed less to the specific investment, will enjoy by behaving opportunistically.

For this reason, it seems possible to say that there is a positive association between economic problems deriving from the propensity to behave opportunistically and the frequency with which transactions are asymmetrical in matters of substitutability and specific investments. If this is so, then it will be possible to evaluate whether objective circumstances that make opportunism highly profitable are widespread in an industrial district or not.

First, let us examine substitutability between contracting parties in a productive structure of the type I have just described. As already mentioned, the industrial district is made up of a considerable number of relatively small firms clustered in the area. Taken together, these characteristics should lead to contractual relations that are roughly balanced in matters of substitutability. This should be so because the aggregation in one district of several firms, specialised in the same phase of a production process, should considerably reduce the cost of any possible substitution, both in relations between subcontracting firms and subcontractors, and in relations between entrepreneurs and workers. Besides, since the units are more or less small, they will tend to develop relations of interdependence rather than of dominance-dependence.

Since it appears that, as far as substitutability is concerned, there is not much room for opportunism, let me now take a look at the other form of asymmetry considered here: transaction-specific investments. When substitutability is lopsided, to attribute the cost of transaction-specific investments to the less substitutable party can be a good way to discourage opportunism (one side may find it hard to obtain a substitute, but the other will find substitution more expensive). When substitutability is fairly symmetrical, transaction-specific expenses can be distributed among the contracting parties. Precisely because the production process is split up in the industrial district, investments are spread among the agents, even though subcontracting firms (which are relatively less substitutable) may contribute, in more or less direct form, to their financing.[23]

Furthermore, if firms are numerous in the industrial district, single investments (whether in physical or in human capital) can be recycled fairly easily in similar transactions with other contracting parties, or else they can be sold to other local agents without great loss. The relative ease with which investments can be recycled allows economic specificity to be reduced, without reducing its technical or professional specialisation. Thus, the hazards to individual capital goods are limited and their overall volume is increased by circulation.

This leads one to conclude that, even without considering the custom of cooperation, circumstances that make opportunism highly profitable in the industrial district are not frequent.

2.3 Opportunism and Mobility within a Stable Framework

In any case, in a system as diversified and mobile as the industrial district, situations may occasionally arise that leave room for opportunistic behaviour. This is always possible, for instance, in transactions that are new in some respect, because there is a certain amount of uncertainty and ambiguity in evaluating them.

It has been remarked that the foreseeable length of economic relations is an important ingredient for opportunism.[24] If they are expected to last fairly long, opportunistic behaviour is discouraged, because it is more likely to be discovered and consequently to provoke retaliatory behaviour.

In an industrial district, with its relatively small firms and the trend toward continuous change, single transactions will be treated as transitory and (for that very reason) given scant formal expression. This could encourage opportunistic behaviour; yet if one takes a closer look at normal economic relations in the industrial district, one can see that, however short-lived, they occur frequently and each of the parties will have recurrent business relations with other members of the same district. This is both because firms are mutually interdependent (due to vertical disintegration), and because markets and techniques are continuously evolving. Furthermore, despite the great mobility of labour (both horizontally and vertically), people tend to be stable, in other words, they go on living and working in the same district, however often they may change jobs and positions.

If one takes all these points into account, it is easy to understand why opportunism is discouraged: the need for and frequency of economic relations among members of a district, the fact that people continue to live and work there, the fact that positions of advantage are more or less transitory, and also the transparency of information and the personal nature of contracts typical of the industrial district, make it fairly easy to discover opportunistic behaviour, and to render the corresponding economic and moral sanctions onerous.

3. THE INDUSTRIAL DISTRICT AND UNCERTAINTY

3.1 Vertical Disintegration and Flexibility

Having examined how opportunism is kept in check in an industrial district, in this section I will consider the performance of this economic organisation with regard to the problem of uncertainty, which, as we all know, is a basic issue for modern industrialised economies.

I have already suggested that the industrial district is particularly effective in cases of uncertainty; let us now see why this is so. First, let me take the distribution of investments. As I said earlier (subsection 2.2), in the industrial district the splitting up of the economic process into a large number of small firms helps to spread the distribution of investments. Thus, the risk involved in owning capital goods is distributed. Second, consider the capacity of the industrial district as a whole and of its firms to adapt to the evolution of markets and techniques. Since single units are technically efficient and small, they can easily multiply[25] and be reconverted, because (1) only a few elementary phases of the productive process need to be changed; (2) only a small proportion of capital goods needs to be renewed, and chances for using them elsewhere are numerous; and (3) as we shall see shortly (subsection 3.2), workers will usually adapt to innovation in both process and product. All this makes the reconversion of single units easier whenever return prospects change.

Besides, the synergistic effect of the peculiar mixture of competition and cooperation in the industrial district encourages behaviour suited to external circumstances and therefore leads to a fairly rapid and consistent overall adaptation of the district. Thus, the industrial district is particularly suited to facing situations of continuous change, since its organisational flexibility allows it to circumvent many of its hazards.

3.2 The Custom of Cooperation, Social Institutions, and Mobility of Labour

Although a model of productive organisation such as the industrial district has the right sort of structure to adapt to the constant redefinition of processes and products, this would never come about if people were not themselves ready to accept change. In particular, labour must be such as to allow for systematic horizontal and vertical mobility. In other words, firms in the district should be able to count on workers who (1) have a wide range of skills and therefore are fairly versatile; and (2) are capable of initiative, that is, able to respond autonomously to new situations.

Given the characteristics of firms in an industrial district, one can surmise that people who have worked there for some time do possess these qualifications. But, taken on their own, these qualifications are not sufficient to guarantee flexible production. The other element is that people who live and work in the district feel confident, even in adverse circumstances, that they will be able to find a job in their area.

Such confidence may derive from the custom of cooperation, which limits competition whenever the latter could destroy the degree of cohesion necessary for the functioning of an industrial district by unloading the costs of uncertainty on its weakest members. One might even suggest that its members are fairly aware of this, since the spirit of cooperation prescribed by custom also corresponds to individual self-interest, at least over a medium- or long-term period. Generally, observance of the custom of cooperation not only corresponds to individual self-interest over a medium-term period, but will be guaranteed, directly or indirectly, by the institutions that exist in the district.

Local trade associations (of workers, artisans, and employers), for instance, will be expected, among other things, to set the normal prices for single products of the various phases of the economic process in the district. In this way, individual agreements will be made easier and, above all, the contracting parties will be guaranteed against the risk of excessive exploitation of temporary asymmetries of market power. Consequently, although in an industrial district prices are influenced by the state of the market, to a certain extent they are under the control of local institutions, including the above-mentioned associations which represent the employers and workers of the district and respect the local customs of cooperation.[26] These institutions play a double role: they moderate the fluctuations of prices dependent on temporary changes in demand and supply conditions, and they help to set rewards that the parties will consider fair, thereby helping to encourage and maintain the habit of cooperation.[27]

Another particularly important institution for the proper functioning of the industrial district is the family.[28] This is because the socialisation process carried on within a family is so important to the economy of the district. Indeed, family firms (which in the production structure typical of an industrial district still have an economic role) do a great deal to socialise individuals into the world of work; but, above all, the family makes sure that the custom of cooperation is transmitted and observed.

Thus, it is precisely this custom that allows production in the industrial district to be so flexible, since it is a source of confidence for its members that some degree of stability exists within the mobility of the system. Just as the splitting up of the economic process allows the costs of capital goods and their corresponding risk to be shared, so the habit of cooperation can to a certain extent spread the risks deriving from the loss in value of work. Therefore, within an industrial district, even if no one (or almost no one) is completely free of uncertainty, yet everyone can feel fairly certain of not being overwhelmed by it.[29]

3.3 Innovation and Uncertainty

If the custom of cooperation extending to economic relations allows people to set mutually agreed-upon wages and returns and, when in trouble, to expect on-the-spot help from someone else whose business is doing better than expected,[30] then competitive pressure will tend to encourage continuous change.

A considerable number of people will be willing to set up on their own, to renew machinery or convert production, whenever this proves necessary or convenient. Those who have specialised in the various stages will strive to adapt their machinery, to make it as highly productive as possible according to the requirements of the moment; whereas those who have specialised in marketing and design will be spurred to seek new markets and to think up new products. Since the ability of the firms in an industrial district to innovate is a crucial feature, it is worth pausing to examine how that ability can be exerted in such a model of economic organisation.

As in the case of production and marketing, in an industrial district innovation is also split up.[31] Here the process of innovation is usually sparked off by the intuition of an agent who, normally, will possess neither all the necessary skills nor the necessary machinery to put this idea into practice on his own. Hence, he will turn to other agents in the district who do possess these skills and machinery. Thus, by combining different specialised contributions, the original idea often produces a profitable new line of business.

The process of innovation is to be carried out in this way, both because each firm is highly specialised and because of relationships among firms and agents. Owing to its specialisation, each unit needs the help of nearby firms doing complementary work whenever it has to solve a complex problem. Nevertheless, it is the cooperative element typical of interpersonal relationships in the district that makes it possible to distribute innovation among a number of firms and individuals, each with an original contribution to make in terms of knowledge, experience, and initiative, so that one can almost speak of collective innovation.[32]

Now, it is possible to assert that in the industrial district everyone, or almost everyone, plays some part in the general process of production and change. However, taken on its own, cooperation seems insufficient to guarantee that all the single efforts are efficiently coordinated. For this purpose, cooperation is assisted by the activities of firms that specialise in maintaining contacts with the external markets, since they serve as a link with the outside world and can offer information on the various business opportunities.

The way in which the process of innovation comes about in an industrial district seems doubly suited to encouraging innovation. First, since such a process is split up, even new ideas, which taken separately might have been overlooked, can produce results that are far from negligible when combined with others. Besides, the fact that the processes of production and innovation are distributed among a large number of independent units is a stimulus to initiative and sharpens the wits of individuals at all levels.[33]

However, if the ability of firms in an industrial district to innovate is, on the whole, substantial in both quality and quantity, then it would appear these firms are capable of influencing the evolution of demand and technology to a certain extent. Yet there is a considerable difference between such a case and that of a large corporation. In an industrial district, market power is not concentrated, but roughly distributed among units. Furthermore, production and innovation are to a great extent collective. Thus, for the single firms in the district, market power tends to be transformed into positive externalities.

In conclusion, considering how flexible and innovative the industrial district can be, one can indeed see the advantages of such a model of economic organisation in cases of highly differentiated and variable demand. Its flexibility and capacity to innovate can indeed reduce the costs of uncertainty, not only because the industrial structure adapts rapidly to external changes, but also (at least in part) because it stimulates such changes by continuous efforts to improve techniques, and also to diversify and specify demand.[34]

4.   THE INDUSTRIAL DISTRICT AND AMBIGUITY

4.1   Ambiguity and the 'Community Market'

It seems probable that ambiguity exists whenever one has trouble in evaluating or interpreting correctly the contents of a given transaction. Ambiguity is an economic problem because it makes it expensive both to determine rewards that are commensurate with a given performance,[35] and to solve disputes between the parties over the interpretation of a contract.[36]

Various circumstances lead to ambiguity. Leaving aside problems of language and related difficulties of interpretation, ambiguity often arises out of economic interdependence in complex organisational situations, or from technological inseparability. It may also depend on the fact that in innovative transactions there are no proper terms of comparison, so that their value cannot be determined at once (Barney and Ouchi 1984).

If one bears in mind the industrial districts' characteristics of economic interdependence, widespread innovation, and continuous change, one might expect many of the transactions among members of the district to be fairly ambiguous. However, as we have already seen (subsection 1.3), in this case the market is supported by significant community elements that enable agents to accept transactions even if they are unprofitable to them in the short run, because they feel confident of righting the balance later on.

Thanks to the peculiar governance of transactions in the district, ambiguity does not seem to prevent efficiency. However, since ambiguity is probably a widespread element in the industrial district, it may be useful to examine in greater detail how the issue is solved, both with regard to production and with regard to marketing.

4.2 Ambiguity and Production

Alchian and Demsetz (1972) have shown that the firm is an economic organisation suited to facing problems of ambiguity in the work performance in cases of team production. The reason for this is that entrepreneurial monitoring allows rewards to be paid to workers according to their productivity, whereas the fact that the entrepreneur is the residual (profit) claimant would guarantee that his monitoring is efficient. However, if the firm is a large one, the entrepreneur cannot monitor directly all the various activities carried out in it. He will have to employ assistants and will have to lay down explicit rules on how the various activities should be executed, in order to monitor individual performance.

If one remembers how the productive and innovative processes are carried out in an industrial district, as well as the characteristic way in which work is organised within each unit (workers doing several jobs, deciding for themselves what to do whenever minor unforeseen circumstances occur, and responding to the demands of new requirements), it would be not only difficult but very expensive to lay down a set of rules that could be applied with fairness in the majority of cases. If there is a rule, it is that each case differs from the next, which jeopardises any resort to bureaucratic control.

Thus, since most forms of work performance are highly ambiguous (and often highly uncertain, due to continuous change), the most efficient form of control seems to be direct control. Indeed, so idiosyncratic is work performance that control might best be done by a workmate, not by a hierarchical supervisor. In point of fact, this is what happens in most firms in the district run by one person or by one family (subsection 1.1).

Hence, the small size of a firm helps to determine agreed-upon fair rewards, and thus encourages efficient performance. Besides, if performance is not standardised, rewards for apparently similar jobs can be differentiated, for instance, by payments made outside the wage packet or for piecework, or even by some kind of profit sharing.

By being small, firms can also overcome ambiguity for another reason. The internal organisation of a small firm is informal; thus, those working in it can acquire norms, values, and suitable skills for the functioning of an industrial district. Within each firm, direct and continuous contact among a small number of workers with different skills, and between them and their employer (often a former worker or technician), helps each one to develop the wide range of skills necessary for flexible production in the district. Yet, as already said (subsection 1.3), by working in this kind of firm (which is often owned by relatives or friends), members learn to cooperate and to coordinate their activities by reciprocal adaptation.[37]

Hence, in the district, rewards roughly in accord with individual productivity (evaluated by one who knows the work inside out), together with personal relations of mutual trust, make it easy to keep ambiguity within each firm in check.

4.3 Marketing and Ambiguity

Besides checking work performance, an entrepreneur must usually decide what and how many goods to produce, given the expected trends in the market. This is extremely important, especially in industries with a fragmented, variable demand, in which, as we have seen (section 3), the industrial district seems to enjoy a comparative advantage.

This task normally requires rather different knowledge and ability than does the control of work performance. The latter mainly requires technical skills and the ability to organise production. On the other hand, deciding what and how much to produce requires the 'power of forecasting the subtler movements of trade' (Marshall 1920, p. 247). This, in turn, is possible only with intimate knowledge of the finished product and supply markets for the industry in which the firm operates – not to mention information on the state of demand in general, on economic policy, and on exchange rates in the case of foreign trade. If one remembers how production is organised in an

industrial district, it is impossible to believe that all entrepreneurs are capable
of doing this second task well. Whereas a small manufacturing firm is able to
keep ambiguities of work performance in check, it seems rather inadequate
as far as marketing the final goods is concerned. Marketing requires a broad
knowledge of the production process, as well as the ability to weigh up a
large quantity of heterogeneous information. These qualities are not easily
fostered in entrepreneurs who have specialised in a particular phase of production.

Consistent with the organisational logic of the industrial district, contacts
with the external markets are maintained by specialised firms, splitting up
even the role of the entrepreneur. Whereas production is in the hands of
small and medium-sized phase firms, marketing is handled by specialised
market firms. In general, these latter deal mostly (or exclusively) with buying
raw materials and other inputs from outside the district, as well as the sale
and even the design of products made therein. This activity is based on the
collection, sifting, and interpretation of the manifold signals which come
from both the outlet markets and the supply markets, so as to forecast new
business opportunities.

Although it is comprehensible that the expectation of profit is a sufficient
incentive for agents specialised in marketing, at first it may seem surprising
that, even though these agents have no hierarchical power over phase firms,
yet they manage to steer production. However, this is made possible by the
district's mechanisms of transaction governance (subsection 1.3).

Competition among the firms in the various stages of production ensures
that there will always be some people willing to try to manufacture a new
product or to use a new technique. Likewise, in case of success, there will
always be others ready to imitate them. On the other hand, the custom of
cooperation (with the support, if necessary, of the activities of such
institutions as local government and the local trade associations mentioned
earlier, in subsection 3.2) will diminish the risk deriving from the excessive
reduction of rewards to workers and phase firms.

Furthermore, because of their specialisation and the fact that the overall
situation is in continual flux, any possible position of advantage for those
dealing with marketing will be neither stable nor absolute. Consequently, at
least over the medium-term period, it is also in their interest to keep agreed-
upon fair rewards, since their profits depend in part on the skill, the capacity
to innovate, and the willingness to cooperate of workers and phase firms.[38]

The way in which the problem of ambiguity is overcome in the district
(both in production and in marketing) has brought us back to the 'community
market'. Indeed, in the industrial district as a model for economic organisation, coordination of its many and diverse units (whether they are phase firms
or marketing firms) is achieved mainly by the two 'invisible hands' – the

market and the community – by a combination of the price system and the practice of mutual adaptation.

FINAL REMARKS

Taken together, the observations advanced in this chapter show that those systems of small firms most resembling the industrial district, from an economic point of view, *can be as effective* as large firms. As a matter of fact, in certain circumstances, they can be even more effective.

In any case, the industrial district is substantially *different* from the economic organisation of a large, vertically integrated firm. This is even more obvious if one considers how transaction problems are faced in the two models. In an industrial district, opportunism is discouraged without recourse to expensive hierarchical control, as in large firms. Uncertainty is faced with flexibility and innovation that tend to differentiate the final demand, rather than standardise it as in large corporations (Berger and Piore 1980, pp. 23–54). Ambiguity is overcome by dividing and distributing the economic process and by splitting entrepreneurial functions as well, through the units specialised in buying and selling, rather than by introducing bureaucratic rules and by entrusting command to salaried managers.

In more general terms, the quality of intersubjective relations is different in the two forms of organisation. In the industrial district, most relations tend to be symmetrical, whereas in large firms relations are hierarchical, that is, asymmetrical by definition.

Finally, the territorial systems of firms that possess the characteristics of the industrial district model seem to be less short-lived than would appear at first sight. This is because the effectiveness of the industrial district is based on the professional capacity, in the strict sense (specialised skills), and, above all, in the broad sense (a capacity for initiative and cooperation), of people who live in a given geographical area that, within certain limits, tends to be transmitted by the process of socialisation. This process, in turn, is encouraged by the economic result it helps to achieve.

If all this is true, in some circumstances *real* economic development can be achieved by systems of only small and medium-sized firms.

It is almost superfluous to underscore the fact that not all clusters of small and medium-sized firms can be regarded as industrial districts. For instance, small satellite firms dependent on a large private or public corporation do not possess the prerequisites, such as the relative symmetry of relations between subcontractors and subcontracting firms, or the importance of community elements in the coordination of the economic process.[39] But, whenever most firms are of a moderate size, are financially independent, are clustered in the same area so as to form a fairly stable, though diversified, network of social and economic relations, then this may come close to the interpretative model of economic organisation I have described.

I feel I can say that postwar development in Italy has led to the formation of various territorial systems grouping small and medium-sized firms (especially in the regions of the 'Third Italy') that do to some extent belong to the industrial district model. If this is so, then the arguments put forward in this chapter may help to throw light on some of the most controversial aspects of these systems.

NOTES

1. Of the numerous writings on the territorial systems of small firms, I mention only the most recent, such as the articles in the volumes edited respectively by Varaldo (1979), Goglio (1982), Fuà and Zacchia (1983), and Piore and Sabel (1984).
2. However, some scholars, for instance Frey (1974), had already seen in the proliferation of small and medium-sized firms 'an enduring aspect of the organisation of manufacturing' (7 and 11).
3. On this point, see Sabel (1982) and Piore and Sabel (1984).
4. On relations among firms, see Mariti (1980).
5. Some of the scholars who have written about the functioning of the Italian territorial systems of small and medium-sized firms are: Tani (1976); Becattini (1979a and Chapter 1 in this volume); Brusco and Sabel (1981); Brusco (1982 and 1986); Bagnasco (1985); Fuà (1985).
6. Analysis on these lines has been fairly recent and is based on the idea of transaction costs, introduced by Coase (1937) to compare different ways of organising economic activity. A more recent contribution on the possibilities of transaction-cost economics is to be found in Williamson (1985).
7. To simplify, I treat opportunism, uncertainty, and ambiguity as similar problems that require a suitable governance mechanism of transactions. These are, however, complex and interconnected issues. Take, for instance, *opportunism* – the term usually refers to self-interests that override, totally or in part, the rules of correct behaviour and loyalty. Opportunism depends both on the capacity of the parties to behave disloyally, and on an asymmetry of 'market power' between the parties that makes opportunism advantageous to one side. On the other hand, *uncertainty*, typical of complex transactions or of those with long-term effects, is tied up both with subjective elements such as bounded rationality (see Simon 1957), and/or the tendency to behave opportunistically (see Williamson 1986), as well as objective ones, such as circumstances changing over a period of time. *Ambiguity*, the difficulty of evaluating and interpreting the contents of transactions, usually depends either on the technical and organisational inseparability of the economic process, or on different interpretations due to semantic shortcomings, or even on new events.
8. On this point, see Becattini (1979a) and Bellandi (1989).
9. Since I use Marshall's definition of the industrial district, I apply the idea of the firm's size throughout this chapter, even though in the transaction-costs approach the question of firm size is not central, because the focal point of the analysis is no longer that of the firm but that of the single transaction.
10. See Tani (1976) for a rigorous definition of the equivalence, from the technological point of view, of a vertically integrated production and specialisation by phase, or by component, of a production process that can be split up. See also Brusco (1975).

11. Marshall himself had already pointed out that small firms, operating within the same area, could use costly and efficient machinery. See, for example, Marshall (1920, p. 225), as well as Bellandi's analysis of Marshall's ideas on the industrial district (1989).

12. On the difference between the horizontal and vertical division of labour, as on the whole range of skills workers require when the division is horizontal, see Leijonhufvud (1986), especially pp. 211–13. For data on the high technological and professional levels achieved by small firms specialised in engineering in Emilia-Romagna, see Capecchi et al. (1981, pp. 125–225).

13. The importance of markets for intermediate products and component parts in industrial districts has been pointed out by Brusco (1982 and 1986).

14. On the role of competition as a 'contest', in a dynamic version that is quite different from that of perfect competition, see Nalebuff and Stiglitz (1983).

15. On cooperation between firms as a trigger for economic development, see Becattini (1979b).

16. On this point see subsection 3.3.

17. On the definition of closely complementary activities, and on cooperation as an effective way of coordinating these activities when they require different specialised capabilities, see Richardson (1972). See also Loasby (1986).

18. On the capacity of mutual cooperation, or 'limited altruism', to increase efficiency so long as the parties involved carry on complementary activities, see Matthews (1981), especially 303–6. An interesting study, based on the 'prisoner's dilemma' game, in which it is shown how cooperation may evolve among self-interested individuals so long as they have some common interest in doing so, and if continuous or frequent interaction is likely, has been written by Axelrod (1984).

19. See, for example, Barney and Ouchi (1984).

20. In using the term *community*, on the whole I mean the kind of governance mechanism of transactions that has been called 'collective' by Butler (1982) and 'clan' by Ouchi (1980). I prefer the term *community* because I feel it expresses better the fact that the various parties coordinate their actions after a reciprocal adjustment rather than at the command of a superior, as in a hierarchy; besides, relations among the parties are based mainly on cooperation rather than on competition as in a market in its pure form.

21. I should point out that socialisation leading to a tendentially cooperative and anti-opportunistic behaviour, which I have said is typical of the industrial district, is usually true of relations among people who live and work in the district.

22. On opportunism, see, for example, Williamson (1975) and Klein, Crawford and Alchian (1978).

23. For example, during the second half of the 19th century in the district of Birmingham, the *factor*, who was the middleman between local producers and national and foreign buyers, usually lent money to small producers to buy their machinery; see Allen (1966, pp. 151–72). However, this practice still exists in industrial systems made up of small and medium-sized firms. On this point, see Lorenzoni (1979, p. 54), who also describes some indirect forms of financing, nowadays used in Prato, such as agreements fixing a minimum quantity of work to be ordered from the firm specialised in marketing by those specialised in production.

24. On this point, see Barney and Ouchi (1984).

25. The typical size of single enterprises in the industrial district, which allows individuals endowed with normal ability and modest capital to set up on their own, helps to spread the investment capacity à la Hirschman. On the concept of investment capacity see Hirschman (1963).

26. It is worth noting that trade associations and even trade unions in the industrial district are partially different from their counterparts elsewhere because, like other locally based institutions, they contain community elements that are typical of the industrial district.

27. For empirical evidence of the role played by local trade associations in the district of Prato, as guarantors of a certain reciprocity between performance and reward and of the partial stabilisation of prices, see Lorenzoni (1979, pp. 66–70).

28. On the importance of the family in the economic process, typical of territorial systems of small firms see, for example, Bagnasco and Trigilia (1984) and Bagnasco (1985).

29. Since the productive structure of the industrial district is made up of a large number of firms, all fairly small in size, rather than of a few large firms surrounded by satellite units, the labour market is characterised by *continuity* rather than by dichotomy (dualism) as to possibilities of acquiring skills, opportunities for earning, and even the certainty of getting a job one way or another. The theory that the dualism of the labour market is connected with the problem of uncertainty in modern industrial economies is put forward by Piore in Berger and Piore (1980). Furthermore, the flexibility of the industrial district should also be connected with the employment, made so much easier by the high number of family firms, of all those persons who, for various reasons, would not be available for regular or full-time work.

30. In other words, in the industrial district, relations among the various economic agents are governed by something similar to the principle of communicating vessels. This means that, when a given product is no longer in demand or is not successful, those who manufacture it could work for the firms that operate in segments of the market where demand is higher than their internal capacity for production.

31. The splitting up of innovation, like that of production, means that the process must be capable of being disassembled. On the spreading of the capacity for innovation throughout the industrial district, see Bellandi (1987).

32. The idea that innovation in the industrial district is a collective process is to be found in Brusco and Sabel (1981, p. 109).

33. On the capacity of industrial districts to stimulate initiative at all levels, see Brusco (1983, pp. 118–19).

34. On the capacity of certain famous 19th century industrial districts (textiles in Lyons and Roubaix, or metallurgy in Solingen, Remscheid, and Sheffield) to promote the evolution of demand and diversification, see Sabel and Zeitlin (1985, p. 144).

35. On the particular ambiguity of identifying and metering individual contributions in team production, and on the firm as an economic organisation capable of dealing with such a problem, see Alchian and Demsetz (1972). For a careful critical assessment of the modern theories of the firm and of Alchian's contribution to the subject, see Silva (1985).

36. On possible 'contractual ambiguity' due to semantic shortcomings, or to incomplete and/or divergent information, see Williamson (1975).

37. On the probable development of implicit rules of behaviour that help to save on the cost of monitoring performance, should this be ambiguous and work groups fairly restricted, see Jones (1983).

38. Take, for example, how important it is to respect delivery times when demand is high, or to accept innovative orders. On the partial dependence of subcontracting firms on their subcontractors within the system of small local tanneries in the Lower Valdarno (Tuscany), see Bellandi (1979).

39. One should bear in mind that the spread and importance of community elements in the coordination of economic activities are typical of the industrial district, as compared to the productive structure of a large firm surrounded by satellite units, and also to a disintegrated productive structure in which pure market relations prevail.

REFERENCES

Alchian, A.A. and H. Demsetz (1972), 'Production, information costs and economic organization', *American Economic Review*, December: 777–95.

Allen, G.C. (1966), *The Industrial Development of Birmingham and the Black Country, 1860–1927*, London: Frank Cass Ltd.

Axelrod, R. (1984), *The Evolution of Cooperation*, New York: Basic Books.

Bagnasco, A. (1985), 'La costruzione sociale del mercato: strategie di impresa e esperimenti di scala in Italia', *Stato e mercato*, 13: 9–45.

Bagnasco, A. and C. Trigilia (1984), *Società e politica nelle aree di piccola impresa. Il caso di Bassano*, Venice: Arsenale.

Barney, J.B. and W.G. Ouchi (1984), 'Information cost and organizational governance', *Management Science*, 10: 125–47.

Becattini, G. (1979a), 'Dal settore industriale al distretto industriale: alcune considerazioni sull'unità di indagine della economia industriale', *Rivista di economia e politica industriale*, 1: 7–21.

Becattini, G. (1979b), 'La cooperazione tra imprese come strumento di sviluppo economico', *Cooperazione di credito*, 68: 130–42.

Bellandi, G. (1979), 'Lavorazioni per conto terzi e strategie di sviluppo delle imprese minori nel settore conciario', in Varaldo (1979), pp. 241–73.

Bellandi, M. (1987), 'Capacità innovativa diffusa e sistemi locali di impresa', *Studi e discussioni*, 44, University of Florence, Department of Economic Science.

Bellandi, M. (1989), 'The industrial district in Marshall', in E. Goodman and J. Bamford (eds), *Small Firms and Industrial Districts in Italy*, London: Routledge, pp. 136–52.

Berger, S. and M.J. Piore (1980), *Dualism and Discontinuity in Industrial Societies*, Cambridge: Cambridge University Press.

Brusco, S. (1982), 'The Emilian model: productive decentralization and social integration', *Cambridge Journal of Economics*, 6: 167–84.

Brusco, S. (1983), 'Flessibilità e solidità del sistema: l'esperienza emiliana', in Fuà and Zacchia (1983), pp. 103–24.

Brusco, S. (1986), 'Small firms and industrial districts: the experience of Italy', in D. Keeble and E. Wever (eds), *New Firms and Regional Development in Europe*, London: Croom Helm.

Brusco, S. and C. Sabel (1981), 'Artisan production and economic growth', in F. Wilkinson (ed.), *The Dynamics of Labour Market Segmentation*, London: Academic Press.

Butler, R. (1982), 'A transactional approach to organize efficiency: perspectives from markets, hierarchies and collectives', *Administration and Society*, 10: 323–51.

Capecchi, V., L. Lugli, V. Rambaldi and S. Ruggeri (1981), 'L'industria delle macchine utensili in Emilia Romagna', in V. Capecchi, A. Enrietti and A. Rollier (eds), *Innovazione e ristrutturazione nel settore delle macchine utensili*, Milan: Franco Angeli.

Coase, R.H. (1937), 'The nature of the firm', *Economica*, November: 386–405.

Frey, L. (1974), 'La problematica del decentramento produttivo', *Economia e politica industriale*, 6: 5–27.

Fuà, G. (1985), 'Les voies diverses du développement en Europe', *Annales économies sociétés civilisations*, 3: 579–603.

Fuà, G. and C. Zacchia (eds) (1983), *Industrializzazione senza fratture*, Bologna: Il Mulino.

Goglio, S. (ed.) (1982), *Italia centri e periferie*, Milan: Franco Angeli.

Hirshman, A.O. (1963), *The Strategy of Economic Development*, New Haven, CT: Yale University Press.

Jones, G. (1983), 'Transaction costs, property rights and organizational culture: an exchange perspective', *Administrative Science Quarterly*, September: 454–67.

Klein, B., R.G. Crawford and A.A. Alchian (1978), 'Vertical integration, appropriable rents, and the competitive contracting process', *The Journal of Law and Economics*, October: 297–326.

Langlois, R.N. (ed.) (1986), *Economics as a Process*, Cambridge: Cambridge University Press.

94   *Inside the district*

Leijonhufvud, A. (1986), 'Capitalism and the factory system', in Langlois (1986), pp. 202–23.
Loasby, B.J. (1986), 'Competition and imperfect knowledge: the contribution of G.B. Richardson', *Scottish Journal of Political Economy*, May: 145–58.
Lorenzoni, G. (1979), *Una politica innovativa nelle piccole medie imprese: l'analisi del cambiamento nel sistema industriale pratese*, Milan: Etas Libri.
Mariti, P. (1980), *Sui rapporti tra imprese in una economia industriale moderna*, Milan: Franco Angeli.
Marshall, A. (1920, reprinted 1959), *Principles of Economics*, London: Macmillan.
Marshall, A. (1923), *Industry and Trade*, London: Macmillan.
Matthews, R.C.O. (1981), 'Morality, competition and efficiency', *The Manchester School*, December: 289–309.
Nalebuff, B.J. and J.E. Stiglitz, (1983), 'Information, competition and market', *American Economic Review*, May: 278–83.
Ouchi, W.G. (1980), 'Markets, bureaucracies and clans', *Administrative Science Quarterly*, March: 129–41.
Piore, M.J., and C. Sabel (1984), *The Second Industrial Divide. Possibilities for Prosperity*, New York: Basic Books.
Richardson, G.B. (1972), 'The organisation of industry', *The Economic Journal*, September: 883–96.
Sabel, C. (1982), *Work and Politics: The Division of Labor in Industry*, Cambridge: Cambridge University Press.
Sabel, C. and J. Zeitlin (1985), 'Historical alternatives to mass production: politics, markets and technology in nineteenth-century industrialization', *Past and Present*, August: 133–76.
Silva, F. (1985), 'Qualcosa di nuovo nella teoria della impresa?', *Economia politica*, 1: 95–134.
Simon, H.A. (1957), *Administrative Behavior*, New York: Macmillan.
Tani, P. (1976), 'La rappresentazione analitica del processo di produzione: alcune premesse teoriche al problema del decentramento', *Note economiche*, 4–5: 124–41.
Varaldo, R. (ed.) (1979), *Ristrutturazioni industriali e rapporti fra imprese*, Milan: Franco Angeli.
Whitaker, J.K. (ed.) (1975), *The Early Economic Writings of Alfred Marshall, 1867–1890*, London: Macmillan.
Williamson, O.E. (1975), *Markets and Hierarchies: Analysis and Antitrust Implications*, New York: The Free Press.
Williamson, O.E. (1985), *The Economic Institutions of Capitalism*, New York: The Free Press.
Williamson, O.E. (1986), 'The economics of governance: framework and implications', in Langlois (1986), pp. 171–202.
Williamson, O.E., M.L. Wachter and J.E. Harris (1975), 'Understanding the employment relation: the analysis of idiosyncratic exchange', *Bell Journal of Economics*, 6: 250–78.

5. The incentives to decentralised industrial creativity in local systems of small firms

Marco Bellandi

'No one is so wise as all the world.'

(Marshall [1919] 1927, p. 174)

INTRODUCTION

Big research and development (R&D) divisions need the funding of big firms and/or central governments. And big firms and governments proudly advertise their commitment to R&D and the ensuing flows of innovations. But the potentiality for innovation depends also on the mobilisation of the energies of ingenuity and creativity of large groups of people involved in product processing and using. Local production systems based on specialised small and medium-sized firms are relatively strong in this respect. Their potentiality for innovation is not always inferior to that of big firms, supposedly strong in R&D, but often weaker in regard to what I am going to call decentralised industrial creativity (DIC).

In this chapter I will try to define the concept of DIC, and then I will study the relations between DIC and an idealised form of local system of small firms, the so called Marshallian industrial district (MID). In particular I will concentrate on some seemingly important incentive problems for DIC within the MID.

1. THE CONTEXT OF DECENTRALISED INDUSTRIAL CREATIVITY

Nathan Rosenberg (1982, p. 122) defines three types of learning which may be useful for the growth of productivity: the first one is R&D, that is the specialised arrangement of specific facilities and scientific skills for the production of new economically useful knowledge; the second type is learning-by-doing, that is the development of knowledge or skills for a productive process as a by-product of practising that process; the last type is learning-by-using, that is the development of knowledge regarding a product (improvements, and so forth) joined to the use of that product.

Learning-by-doing or learning-by-using do not necessarily have a creative content. For example there is no creativity at all (in learning) when a worker 'learns' to perform a given productive action with a predetermined standard of accuracy and speed; neither can creativity be supposed when the practice of doing or using is only one of the means by which R&D receives feedback on the working of planned processes and products. Obviously, these cases are prevalent when the organisation of work is dominated by mass production and bureaucratic, top-down, relations (Kern and Schuman 1984; Piore and Sabel 1984; Best 1990).

In other cases, learning may have a creative content, more or less interdependent with R&D: for example, when the information which workers transmit to R&D is enriched by suggestions; or when new ideas spring directly from productive practice, and their development is sustained by technical education and/or by circulation and comparison of ideas among 'producers',[1] with the possible support of R&D. Then, it could be useful to identify these opportunities using a specific expression, for which I propose 'decentralised creativity'; 'decentralised' being meant to denote that the sources of the new knowledge are not concentrated in specialised divisions of a few isolated scientists, but also distributed among the crowd of producers. Here I will discuss in particular what I denote more precisely as decentralised industrial creativity (DIC); where 'industrial' is meant to exclude the cases of creativity associated with the activity of isolated craftsmen without formal technical education.

The building block of DIC is practical knowledge (experience). Specialised practice is the prerequisite of practical knowledge. Practice permits a broad sensory contact with reality; and the sensory data can be registered consciously and unconsciously by the agent in his/her routines of action and thought, which constitute practical knowledge. Specialisation of practice allows for reiteration, which helps the establishment of routines of action and thought (see, for example, Nelson and Winter (1982)). In comparison with formal knowledge, practical knowledge is less systematic in method and content, less articulated and thus more difficult to transmit in formal and general terms (Thrift 1985). The other side of the coin is that formal knowledge is separated, that is, 'it is removed in both time and space from the experiences and the events it describes' (ibid.). Now, not all the relevant circumstances of production and product-using are easily understandable by means of accepted systematic methods, nor are they easily communicable in formal and general terms (such as by means of textbooks, blueprints, written instructions, and so on). These circumstances can be economically grasped and accumulated as practical knowledge.

That part of practical knowledge which is not encompassed by formal knowledge may have economic value in itself,[2] and it is the specific advantage of DIC over separate R&D.[3] The producers may directly draw data from practical knowledge and combine them with personal endowments of flair, imagination, technical education, outer experience, and so forth. The combination may bring about new viewpoints and new hints, that is new approaches to circumstances of production and use of products.

One important constraint on the learning and creative effects of specialised practice is the degree of specialisation. A high degree of specialisation of labour, that is a very narrow definition of the scope of a given practice, limits the accumulation of meaningful and original approaches. Furthermore, there is a correlation between extreme specialisation of labour and Tayloristic-like organisations, in which the incentives to responsible reactions and creative actions are far removed from the majority of producers. Even apart from extreme specialisation, the fact that formal knowledge cannot cope adequately with all circumstances of time and space is not enough to imply that a useful practical knowledge is built upon such circumstances. How can such fragmented knowledge deal 'with the magnitude and complexity of modern industrial operations, and their intricate relations to and dependence on one another'? (Marshall [1919] 1927, p. 72).

Three very important conditions sustaining the learning and creative effects of specialised practice are the coexistence of several approaches; their mutual interaction; and the segmentation of the production system. First of all, 'the coexistence of different approaches creates the condition for a number of challenges in the formulation of any given problem' (Becattini 1990, p. 108). But coexistence can be useful only insofar as the different approaches, and the related experiences and personal endowments, do interact. Such interaction is restricted by feasibility and incentive problems, whose nature and solutions I will discuss later. Finally, the segmentation of the production system into partially autonomous production components makes room for single acts of DIC, within single components, even when the overall system is highly complex.[4] Then those acts may extend to other parts of the system. For example, they can generate tensions (disequilibrium effects) for some similar or connected components; and these tensions focus creative energies and mutual interactions towards useful generalisation and adaptation of specific solutions.[5] Another solution to the problem of complexity is the interplay of DIC and R&D (see next section).

When coexistence, mutual interaction, and decomposability are effectively reinforcing a large practical knowledge not encompassed by formal knowledge, the stage is set for a systematic manifestation of DIC. Like R&D, the systemic character of DIC denotes a regular promotion of innovation, even if, of course, no individual manifestation of creativity can be forecast. Unlike R&D, the systemic character does not extend to the quality of innovation. DIC's results have in themselves a bent for lack of generality, for variation and differentiation. The single manifestations of DIC have in general an incremental character; but their accumulation has possible major effects on economic performance.[6]

2. DECENTRALISED INDUSTRIAL CREATIVITY AND THE MARSHALLIAN INDUSTRIAL DISTRICT

According to some authors, what I call DIC plays an important role in the competitive capacity of some industrial organisations which escape the paradigm of the mass production bureaucratic firm (Rosenberg 1982, p. 122; Brusco 1986; Aoki 1988; Becattini 1990; Storper 1991). Among those organisations there are several types of local systems of small sized firms, one paradigmatic form of which is the Marshallian industrial district (MID). According to a definition by Giacomo Becattini the MID is:

> a socioeconomic entity which is characterised by the active coexistence of an open community of people and a segmented population of firms. Since the community of people and the population of firms live in the same geographical area, they will criss-cross one another. Production activities and daily life overlap. The community is open because the industrial nature of the district and the related problems of increasing returns imply incoming and outgoing flows of goods and people. The population of firms is segmented in the sense that different phases of the process of production are divided between the firms, each of which specialises in one or a few phases. (Becattini 1991, p. 111)

In the same paper, from which the preceding quotation is extracted, Becattini gives the foundations of the close relationship between DIC, which he calls spontaneous creativity, and the MID. I am going to re-sketch these foundations, trying to set the stage for the specific subject which finally I intend to discuss: that is the incentive problems connected to DIC within the MID form.

First of all, the segmented nature of the population of firms translates into a numerous population of entrepreneurs, more or less small and independent. The small independent entrepreneur is not far removed from the production and commercial divisions; often such a person has had direct practice in them. In any case such an entrepreneur is not separated from practical knowledge concerning production processes and use of products; and, as an entrepreneur, can use that experience creatively, both when the new ideas are his or her own, and when they are suggested by and in collaboration with employees.

Industrial relations within a small firm are not necessarily conducive to an intra-firm cooperation in creative processes. But some conditions within the scope of the MID form make for a proactive role of some employees. The overlapping of community and industry makes the formation of a local supply of a skilled workforce easier. This is a condition which supports, even if it does not necessarily imply, the planning of a qualified utilisation of (some) parts of the workforce by the entrepreneurs. And the productivity of such utilisation is higher for the production of customised and highly styled goods, than for standardised, mass-produced goods: it is higher, that is, for a type of production which is largely represented in the industrial districts.[7] Furthermore the existence of a large number of specialised firms, which supply all sorts of intermediate goods and services related to a given set of activities, facilitates the formation of spin-off firms, which absorb creative energies not accommodated within the incumbent firms in those activities.

The stage for DIC within the MID form is clearly set. But, the effective manifestation of DIC could be only occasional if the reinforcing conditions, referred to before, were lacking. Let us see how the MID is related to such conditions, that is the coexistence of different approaches, their mutual interaction, the decomposability of the production system.

The existence of different approaches, practical knowledge and personal endowments would appear severely restricted when a single industry dominates within an MID.[8] But the presence of a principal industry within a district is still consistent with the coexistence of subsidiary, complementary and secondary activities within the same district. And different phases of the principal industry are divided among different firms. Let us consider, for example, the textile industrial district centred on Prato, that is one of the most renowned Italian industrial districts, included in the lists referred to in note 8. Here the principal industry is traditionally defined as the production of woollen fabric; but it includes several phases with intermediate products made by different firms, and an important secondary activity, that is knitwear production. An important complementary industry is the manufacture of textile tools and machinery. Auxiliary industries are represented by the local supply of several types of services (such as specialised transportation services).

The coexistence of different sub-industries implies a differentiation of the specialised practices prevalent among the firms, thus promoting a differentiation of approaches. The mutual interaction of different approaches is directly sustained by two important defining properties of the MID: prox-imity, that is the fact that the population of firms is localised; and the overlapping of daily life and production activities. Generally speaking, face-to-face contacts are an effective means for the communication of practical knowledge and for the interaction of approaches.[9] Proximity facilitates a frequent and not strictly planned realisation of these contacts.[10] On the other hand, the socioeconomic overlapping promotes the formation of local traditions and standards of communication regarding those industries which characterise an individual MID;[11] and such formations further support the circulation of specific ideas within the district.

A case of circulation of ideas is represented by the processes of diffusion of innovation; here proximity works through the support of inter-firm mobility of workers and bandwagon effects and, more generally, through the intensification of informal contacts. One could object that imitation is outside the scope of creative processes and DIC. On the contrary imitation, when coupled with specific practical knowledge and differentiated market opportunities, allows for new creative stimulus, and that may bring about new variations.[12]

Another case of circulation of ideas is the interplay of DIC and R&D within an MID, which may occur in different forms: for example, in the form of local public and private joint ventures for the promotion of large research projects; or in the form of private R&D whose results are diffused and adapted, with some lag, within some subset of the firms of the district; or in the form of exchanges between manufacturers and private suppliers of knowledge services.[13] The last form is actually a case in point of the opportu-nities for DIC connected to the segmentation of the production system which is implied by the very definition of the MID.

Regarding incentives, innovation in general and DIC in particular are sup-ported by market conditions of active rivalry within the industry, and by the social acceptance of rules restricting the most harmful forms of rivalry. Two defining properties of MID are consistent with well developed rivalry: firstly, the localisation of an industry or a few industries, to which a population of several firms contributes, may bring about a high potential for competition by means of largely (if not perfectly) substitute products; secondly, proxim-ity aids the detection of different options for buyers both from the district and from the outside, and thus makes for effective competition.

The overlapping of industry and community supports the building of rules concerning typical transactions.[14] If rules restricting rivalry are rightly directed towards growth, and the rivalry within the rules is lively, then the incentives for a mobilising of individuals' creative energies are strong within the district: when such rules are set and accepted, their enforcement is sustained within the district by face-to-face contacts (which facilitate a quick assessment of moral attitudes); by the burden of social penalty (like exclusion from the community); and by the social reward for a rightful success.

But individuals' incentives are not enough for a systematic manifestation of DIC. What about mutual interaction? Ease of contact is, in itself, an incentive to the realisation of contacts and thus to the mutual interaction we are discussing. That is not enough. Actually, the incentives to interact present a fairly complex relation with conditions which sustain the individuals' propensity to innovate. In the next section I tackle this relation, taking advantage of an illustrative example concerning the customisation of software for some firms in a textile industrial district.

3. INCENTIVE-COMPATIBILITY PROBLEMS AND SOLUTIONS

The collaboration in creative processes between independent centres of responsibility and profit (such as firms) is subject to heavy problems of compatibility of incentives. Let us consider three examples. Firstly, an agent takes advantage of some information obtained during a joint-venture with another agent and, without any prior consensus, begins to compete directly against that agent or sells the information to one of that agent's competitors. Secondly, an agent refuses to give advice on common technological problems to another one, breaking opportunistically an agreement of reciprocal help. Lastly, an agent imitates another one outside the terms of any agreed joint-venture, and that drastically reduces the expected returns of the investment in innovation.[15]

Now it is possible to point out some mechanisms and conditions which circumvent the incentive-compatibility problems just discussed, or which limit their harmful effects. First of all, the social rules restricting rivalry might encompass also the more recurrent, manifest and disrupting forms of opportunistic behaviour in mutual interactions. But the scope of such action is generally limited by the difficulty of third-party assessment of the terms of exchange within a creative process based on mutual interaction.

In particular, it is not easy to assess the balance of negative and positive effects on DIC of rules which would restrict imitation too heavily. And the difficulty of assessment works against the formation and enforcement of such rules in growth-oriented MIDs. A rule which sometime sustains original creative efforts without hampering diffusion and variation is the award of social esteem and higher status to early innovators.

The incentive problems of direct cooperative efforts (as in the first and second examples) can be tackled by some combination of conditions connected to the nature of DIC and of the MID. Let us consider an instance concerning the development of customised software for the textile industry, which predominates in the industrial district of Prato.

Typically the 'final firm' in Prato is centred on the activity of a 'pure entrepreneur', who carries on the linking of external markets and production capabilities internal to the district – capabilities which in large part reside among a population of specialised local manufacturers.[16] The competitive advantage of the textile industry of Prato is traditionally based on customisation, fantasy, versatility in the production of woollen, usually combed, fabrics and yarns. The pure entrepreneurs 'incessantly design and redesign the product and, to a lesser extent, the process, according to the features of the external conjuncture and the internal situation of the district' (Becattini 1991, p. 112).

Prato's final firms have adopted and are adopting computers and software to support various internal functions: accounting, invoicing, design and development, monitoring of the stage of progress among the various specialised phases of batches of production, cost analysis, and so on. According to a case study based on interviews with some of Prato's leading entrepreneurs,[17] there is now a diffused demand for customisation of software, apart from that applied to routine administrative jobs. Some of the pure entrepreneurs interviewed have pointed out that their demand is met with the help of local software houses, in a process of close contacts (often face-to-face), supported also by the common reference to the textile tradition and by personal acquaintance. Interestingly, some of these entrepreneurs declare their awareness of and compliance with a strategy of the local software houses, which try, to some extent, to reduce the price of their service and to increase their market by adapting the customisation developed for a producer to other producers with similar needs.

Thus the development of software can be seen here as an example of the interplay of DIC and R&D in the form of interaction between producers (the pure entrepreneurs) and private suppliers of knowledge services (the software houses). On the other hand, the strategy of adaptation promoted by the software houses entails an indirect cooperation between producers in creative events.

The creative collaboration between a software house and a pure entrepreneur runs into incentive-compatibility problems of the type recalled before. A pure entrepreneur should be suspicious of the strategy of the software house, since that strategy could be to the advantage of some competitors, directly if the competitors buy customised software avoiding many of the uncertainties of the development stage, and indirectly if the software house obtains and passes on to the competitors some strategic information (such as on product innovation). The second eventuality can be held at bay if the pure entrepreneurs' competitive advantage lies effectively in their specific practice of the combinatorial and creative activity defined above. If this is the case, a single item of information stolen can represent a loss of profit opportunities, but the survival of the firm depends (in the absence of upheaval) on the possession of an evolving framework of knowledge, of which a single item of information is only a part. Thus, a risk of marginal loss can be rationally balanced against the advantages of reduced price of the software house's services.[18]

The other harmful eventuality previously referred to[19] is to be balanced against the effect of an extension of the relationship with the software house, beyond the event of the development of a single customisation. Such an extension is quite consistent with necessities of training, debugging, updating and upgrading. Then a pure entrepreneur, who has been involved in the development of an original customisation, may later on profit, through the long-term relation with the software house, from customisations developed elsewhere by the same software house.[20]

The working of this mechanism of indirect reciprocity might be threatened by the fear of opportunistic breaking-off of the long-term relation by the software house. But the advantages of such breaks in relations are reduced, or even nullified, by the fact that generally no big coups are at stake, and that a reiterated adoption of opportunistic conduct would be quickly registered among the agents of the district.[21]

Then, the case suggests that the incentive-compatibility problems connected with mutual interaction in creative processes can be overcome if a combination of conditions occurs:[22]

1. the creative outcome is constituted by a stream of incremental innovations, variations, adjustments;
2. no strategic information leaks out from the cooperative efforts;
3. there is a good number of agents who can be sequentially involved in the process, and they have some similar or connected exigencies;
4. reiterated opportunistic behaviour is punished.

A verification of the proposed interpretation is supplied by the doubts cast on the quality of the software houses' service by other Prato entrepreneurs: it happens that a case study reports a correlation between the manifestation of such doubts and the occurrence of some specific differences as to the traditional model of the Prato pure entrepreneur. Those who cast doubts on the collaboration with the software houses lead final firms which tend to be more vertically integrated, concerned with new textile products (such as synthetic leather) and with the creation of a stable market for them. Such final firms are a relatively small in number: which could represent protection against fierce rivalry. But since their competitive strength is in the market stabilisation of new products, they suffer more than their traditional counterparts from the leakage of information connected to their products. Furthermore, they are partially separated from the network of production traditions of the district. This condition and the small number of such a type of producer make it more difficult and uncertain for the software houses to extend and adapt a particular customisation: thus, *ceteris paribus*, the price of the service of customisation is higher for the non-traditional final firm than for the traditional one.

CONCLUDING REMARKS

Decentralised industrial creativity (DIC) denotes those sources of new knowledge, in production and products, which are distributed among large groups of producers. That part of producers' practical knowledge which is not encompassed by R&D's formal knowledge is the specific advantage of DIC over separate R&D. Such practical knowledge promotes original approaches to circumstances of production and use of products. The coexistence of several different approaches, their mutual interaction, and the segmentation of the production system, support the systematic manifestation of DIC.

The Marshallian industrial district (MID), as an idealised form of some important types of local systems of small firms, presents properties which are consistent with the regular working of DIC: in general, the proximity of the agents, the overlapping of community and industry, and the division of labour among a population of firms. This consistency has been analysed in particular with respect to the incentive-compatibility problems of cooperation in creative processes among independent agents. Here a combination of conditions is envisaged, whose occurrence allows for a solution to such incentive-compatibility problems: incremental innovation; no strategic leakage from cooperation; several agents involved sequentially; punishment of reiterated opportunism.

It is necessary to point out that these conditions are just particular manifestations both of the general defining properties of the MID and of the general conditions of feasibility of DIC. Thus, there is no apparent contradiction between our particular solution to incentive-compatibility and the general context of feasibility of DIC within the MID form. But this solution is by no means necessarily implied by such a general context. That is to say, it is possible perhaps to define different combinations of particular conditions that work; and, on the other side, it is possible to see how some combinations, within the same general context, may bring about a disruption of the compatibility of incentives in mutual interaction in some creative processes.

NOTES

1. The generic term 'producer' distinguishes here those in charge of the productive process or of the use of products from the researchers employed in separate R&D divisions.
2. According to Aoki (1988), the weight assigned to local information in the Japanese firm is an important factor in the competitive strength of this form of big firm.
3. R&D is, in itself, a separate activity, whose approach to economic events is based on formal knowledge. Richard Nelson (1980, p. 67) proposes that 'the degree of technique codification and the ability to learn through separate R&D, while logically independent variables, tend to go together empirically ... Research and development is limited to finding effective pieces of technique that can be replicated easily ... and which will likely have a positive impact on productivity regardless of the personal skills and organisational structure that must employ it'.
4. According to Simon ([1969] 1981, pp. 209–29) a general condition which facilitates copying with the complexity of a system is the eventual decomposing of the system itself into quasi autonomous components.
5. Such types of effects could be subsumed within various concepts referred to by some economists and historians as effective sequences, technological convergence, serendipity, creative symbiosis, and so forth.
6. See Russo (1989) for examples and references on this point.
7. See Becattini (1990) for a general assessment of that relation.
8. Sforzi (1990) has reported the existence of several industrial districts in Italy which show, according to an analysis of census data (years 1971 and 1981), a well defined principal industry. According to Porter (1990, pp. 155 and 443) a large part of Italy's industries with an international competitive advantage are centred in local clusters; the list of these clusters includes a good subset of the industrial districts reported by Sforzi.
9. See Brusco (1986, p. 188) for examples within some industrial districts.
10. Examples of informal contacts are the exchanges of ideas within social institutions, like families, clubs, and so on.
11. Alfred Marshall ([1919] 1927, p. 287) referred to effects like these when coining the term of 'industrial atmosphere'. For the interplay of market and community within industrial districts, see Trigilia (1990); Bianchi and Bellini (1991); Dei Ottati (Chapter 4 in this volume).
12. Marshall ([1890] 1986, p. 227) discussing processes of this kind wrote: 'if one man starts a new idea, it is taken up by others and combined with suggestions of their own: and thus it becomes the source of further ideas'. See Bellandi (1989) for a review of Marshall's thoughts on this matter.
13. See Russo (1989) and Brusco (1990). The interplay between DIC and R&D appears to work also, for example, within the Japanese paradigm of the big firm, according to Aoki (1988), and within some successful German corporations, according to Kern and Schuman (1984).
14. The local rules may find expression in custom or in formal regulation. The differences between the two types of rules are not considered explicitly in what follows.
15. For more on this sort of transactional problems, see Teece (1988).
16. The final firms have access to the final external markets; while the specialised manufacturers – or stage firms – realise intermediate or auxiliary goods or services for the final firms: see Brusco (1990). The final firms are identified in Prato as 'impannatori' and as 'lanifici incompleti'. The first ones are nearer to the ideal of a pure entrepreneur, who sees or creates market opportunities and tries to take advantage of them by developing products and realising their production through the organisation of a network of independent specialised suppliers. See Becattini (1990, p. 43).
17. See Bellandi and Trigilia (1992). The research was conducted during 1990.
18. Furthermore, temporary secrecy may allow for a satisfying lead time in the continuously variable markets in which a large part of Prato's pure entrepreneurs sell.

19. Connected to the fact that the competitors buy customised software, avoiding many of the uncertainties of the development stage.
20. Furthermore, a good software house may act as a centre for the accumulation and diffusion of ideas regarding new hardware and new standard packages.
21. We also see at work the creative effects induced by disequilibrium tensions: the software houses are stimulated by the particular requirements of some pure entrepreneurs; this stimulus helps in focussing the creative activity in software customisation. If good software is realised, it can be applied also to similar requirements. This possibility, eventually broadcast by the software house, provides a stimulus for other pure entrepreneurs, and that helps to focus their activity towards a creative collaboration for the adaptation of the software. And so on.
22. Actually, such a list of conditions is similar to that envisaged by Enric von Hippel (1990) as regards so called informal know-how trading.

REFERENCES

Aoki, M. (1988), *Information, Incentives and Bargaining in the Japanese Economy*, Cambridge: Cambridge University Press.
Becattini, G. (1990), 'The industrial district as a socio-economic concept', in F. Pike, G. Becattini and W. Sengenberger (eds), *Industrial Districts and Inter-Firm Cooperation in Italy*, Geneva: International Institute of Labour Studies, pp. 37–51.
Becattini, G. (1991), 'The industrial district as a creative milieu', in G. Benko and M. Dunford (eds), *Industrial Change and Regional Development*, London: Belhaven Press, pp. 102–14.
Bellandi, M. (1989), 'The industrial district in Marshall', in E. Goodman and J. Bamford (eds), *Small Firms and Industrial Districts in Italy*, London: Routledge, pp. 136–52.
Bellandi, M. and C. Trigilia (1992), 'Come cambia un distretto industriale: strategie di riaggiustamento e tecnologie informatiche nell'industria tessile di Prato', *Economia e politica industriale*, 70: 121–52.
Best, M. (1990), *The New Competition*, Cambridge: Polity Press.
Bianchi, P. and N. Bellini (1991), 'Public policies for local networks of innovators', *Research Policy*, 4.
Brusco, S. (1986), 'Small firms and industrial districts: the experience of Italy', in D. Keeble and E. Wever (eds), *New Firms and Regional Development*, London: Croom Helm.
Brusco, S. (1990), 'Small firms and the provision of real services', Paper presented at the *International Conference on Industrial Districts and Local Economic Regeneration*, Geneva, 18–19 October.
Kern, H. and M. Schuman (1984), *Das Ende der Arbeitsteilung? Rationalisterung der Industriellen Produktion*, Munich: Beck.
Hippel, E. von (1990), 'Cooperation between rivals: informal know-how trading', in B. Carlsson (ed.), *Industrial Dynamics*, Boston, MA: Kluwer Academic Publishers.
Marshall, A. (1919, reprinted 1927), *Industry and Trade*, London: Macmillan.
Marshall, A. (1890, reprint of the eighth edition, 1986), *Principles of Economics*, London: Macmillan.
Nelson, R. (1980), 'Production sets, technological knowledge, and R&D: fragile and overworked constructs for analysis of productivity growth', *American Economic Review*, 70: 62–7.

Nelson, R. and S. Winter (1982), *An Evolutionary Theory of the Firm*, Cambridge, MA: Harvard University Press.

Piore, M. and C. Sabel (1984), *The Second Industrial Divide*, New York: Basic Books.

Porter, M. (1990), *The Competitive Advantage of Nations*, London: Macmillan.

Rosenberg, N. (1982), *Inside the Black Box: Technology and Economics*, Cambridge: Cambridge University Press.

Russo, M. (1989), 'Technical change and the industrial district: the role of inter-firm relations in the growth and transformation of ceramic tile production in Italy', in E. Goodman and J. Bamford (eds), *Small Firms and Industrial Districts in Italy*, London: Routledge, pp. 198–222.

Sforzi, F. (1990), 'The quantitative importance of Marshallian industrial districts in the Italian economy', in F. Pike, G. Becattini and W. Sengenberger (eds), *Industrial Districts and Inter-Firm Cooperation in Italy*, Geneva: International Institute for Labour Studies, pp. 75–107.

Simon, H.A. (1969, reprinted 1981), *The Sciences of the Artificial*, Cambridge, MA: MIT Press.

Storper, M. (1991), 'Regional "worlds of production": conventions of learning and innovation in flexible production systems of France, Italy, and the USA', Paper presented at the *Annual Meeting of the Association of American Geographers*, Miami, 16 April.

Teece, D.J (1988), 'Technological change and the nature of the firm', in G. Dosi et al. (eds), *Technical Change and Economic Theory*, London: Pinter.

Thrift, N. (1985), 'Flies and germs: a geography of knowledge', in D. Gregory and J. Hurry (eds), *Social Relations and Spatial Structures*, London: Macmillan.

Trigilia, C. (1990), 'Work and politics in the Third Italy's industrial districts', in F. Pike, G. Becattini and W. Sengenberger (eds), *Industrial Districts and Inter-Firm Cooperation in Italy*, Geneva: International Institute for Labour Studies.

6. Trust, interlinking transactions and credit in the industrial district

Gabi Dei Ottati

'A most important portion of the *capital* ... has consisted of the knowledge which the contact of daily life has given them of those in whom they put their *trust*.'
(Marshall 1975, Vol. II, p. 367, my emphasis)

INTRODUCTION

In the now substantial literature on industrial districts, the issue of how development is financed does not seem to have attracted scholars' attention.[1] To date there has been little empirical or theoretical work in this area. As an attempt to redress the balance, this chapter deals with the issue of credit and, more exactly, with one specific form it assumes in the process of the rise and development of industrial districts.

The contents of this chapter are intended to refer more to an ideal-type of industrial district rather than any particular empirical case study. I should like to point out, however, that the remarks which follow are based not only on the numerous studies of industrial districts in Italy, but also on information accumulated during long and personal experience of empirical research. This research was carried out within the broad framework of studies dealing with the rise of the industrial district of Prato, between the end of the Second World War and the early 1950s (Becattini 1997). For the purposes of this research I consulted various sources including documents of entrepreneurial associations, trade unions, the proceedings of local government meetings, reports of the board of directors of the local bank, as well as the local press. The conclusion from consulting these sources, together with information gathered from interviews with local bank managers and entrepreneurs, was that informal credit, often linked to other transactions, in addition to self-financing, was very important in the formation of the Prato district. We can cite as an example of this the fact that in Prato, at the beginning of 1950, within a few months about 6000 workers, many of whom were weavers, set up a subcontracting system with machinery provided by their former employers. This machinery was then paid for in instalments by discounting the cost from the payment for work ordered by the lenders (Dei Ottati 1994).

As well as referring to the literature on the industrial district, I have also taken into account the economic literature on interlinking transactions. Previous studies in this area have focused mainly on credit in developing countries, and in particular on the interrelation between credit and land and/or labour markets in rural areas.[2] Despite the considerable differences between the agricultural situation in developing countries and the district form in industrialised countries, these studies highlight an essential aspect which is, paradoxically enough, common to both: namely, the spread of interlinking transactions and multiplex relations, that is, of joint economic exchanges in more than one market and of economic relations linked to social relations.[3]

The chapter is divided into three sections. The first section focuses on cooperation and trust in the industrial district. I then move on to look at interlinking transactions and to consider the economic implications of the interlinking of credit and subcontracting (section 2). In section 3, I take a brief look at direct financing and bank credit. A short conclusion follows.

1. COOPERATION AND TRUST IN THE INDUSTRIAL DISTRICT

1.1 Some Features of the Industrial District as a Socioeconomic System

Previous studies have highlighted some of the distinctive features of the industrial district as a model of socioeconomic organisation (Becattini 1987 and 1989; Brusco 1986 and 1992). I shall therefore confine myself to examining briefly those features which are useful for a better understanding of the subject of this chapter. The industrial district has been defined as 'a socio-territorial entity which is characterised by the active presence of both a community of people and a population of firms in one naturally and historically bounded area' (Becattini 1990, p. 38). Although in the industrial district people and firms tend to merge, for expository purposes I shall make a clear distinction between these and take into consideration firstly the outstanding features of the social environment and then those of the economic environment.

The social environment of the ideal-type industrial district presents the following principal features.

1. People, living in one naturally and historically bounded area, tend to have a common culture (values, ways of behaving, tastes, expectations, language, dialect, and so on). The reproduction of this culture is made easier by the tendency of these people to stay in the same area.
2. Because they live near to each other and share a common culture, the people who live in the district have frequent direct face-to-face relations which allow them to get to know and recognise each other.[4]
3. A decisive feature of the social culture of the people who live in the district is constituted by norms of reciprocity accompanied by relevant social sanctions, such as the withdrawal of reciprocity and expressions of approval/disapproval.
4. Another cultural feature of the population which is important for the economic dynamism of the industrial district is the practice of self-help, so that both individual initiative and the economic success which it may bring are generally approved, provided that they are obtained within the rules of reciprocity. The above elements point to a social environment which, in many aspects, resembles a community (Taylor 1982). However, the population of the industrial district is usually too large for the decentralised social control typical of a community to be completely effective; in addition, because of its industrial specialisation and the connected necessity of importing and exporting many different materials, the environment of the district cannot be as closed to the external world as a traditional community.

The economic environment of the district also has its own peculiar features. The first of these features is constituted by the fact that each of the numerous small firms is generally specialised in one, or very few, phases or functions of the same industry or in subsidiary industries, such as, for example, the manufacturing of textile machinery in a textile district (Marshall 1975, p. 197). In such an environment, the fact that the division of labour between firms prevails over the division of labour within firms (Tani 1987) strengthens the reciprocal interdependence of the firms in the district and favours the perception of local industry, and in particular of the human capital which it requires and develops, as if it were collective property. The second feature is constituted by the fact that there are usually several successive transactions between the same firms and individuals. This is also the consequence of specialisation and location in the same area, so that the possibilities of future business are usually protracted for a long even if unspecified period. A third element which is important for the economic organisation of the district (although it is dependent on the second of the above mentioned social features, that is the diffusion of direct personal relations) is the possibility for local agents to observe and remember the past behaviour of the people with whom they have had previous business relations. A fourth feature, also connected to the other features and distinctive of the industrial district, is the widespread possibility of punishing those who behave incorrectly, chiefly by withdrawing the willingness to conclude future transactions with them and by social disapproval.

1.2 The Custom of Reciprocal Cooperation and Trust as Collective Capital

Taking into account the community characteristics of the social environment typical of an industrial district, it is not surprising that economic relations are also influenced. In fact, as has been widely pointed out in the literature (Brusco and Sabel 1981; Piore and Sabel 1984; Pyke, Becattini and Sengenberger 1990; Dei Ottati 1991; Lorenz 1992), one of the distinctive elements of this kind of socioeconomic organisation is constituted by the reciprocal cooperation within it. The cooperative behaviour between the firms of the district, as widely noted in the research in this field, is therefore, at least in part, attributable to a local custom of reciprocal cooperation, directly connected to the more general norm of reciprocity, the real axis of the social culture of the district.[5] The custom of cooperation also has, however, important effects on trust within the district.

First of all, it increases the 'normal' level of trust, understood as correct expectations about the actions and characteristics of the local agents with whom transactions are conducted for the first time. Consequently, the custom of cooperation reduces the demand for substitutes for trust. In particular, it reduces the need to resort to various forms of monitoring which usually imply not only considerable direct costs, but also have the defect of reducing trust or even generating distrust (Leibenstein 1987). On the contrary, the custom of cooperation, being a self-enforcing implicit code of behaviour, does not have negative effects on trust. Thanks to this last characteristic, the custom of cooperation also has the advantage of making trust less fragile and easier to sustain, even in the case of deviations of limited nature and/or duration. However, just as the custom of reciprocal cooperation helps to reproduce trust, it also encourages its further growth within the district, trust being a good which up to a certain point increases with use (Hirschman 1984, p. 93). This in turn brings about a similar reduction in the degree of trust of its members towards people/firms outside the district.

The trust so far considered is based on custom and is not unlimited, but restricted within the boundaries defined by the implicit code of behaviour for each of the different contexts and types of transaction which are normally carried out in the district. Even if limited, trust based on the custom of cooperation constitutes a collective capital, available to all members of the district, and is of considerable economic importance. In fact, because of this trust there is less need to resort to costly safeguards and monitoring, which, in the absence of trust, would be necessary to conclude most transactions. But trust 'is extremely efficient' (Arrow 1974, p. 23) above all because it allows participants to obtain gains from transactions which, in its absence, would not be carried out. Thus, in the industrial district, trust as collective capital is largely a by-product of the common culture. And it is this culture which ensures the reproduction of this capital, at least in so far as decentralised social control remains effective. The social control which maintains the observance of the custom of mutual cooperation takes on an important role for the actual survival of the district as a model of socioeconomic organisation, since part of its dynamism depends on the collective capital of trust.

However, those decentralised social sanctions, which are effective in a small, homogeneous community, are usually not sufficient to guarantee conformity in a complex environment like an industrial district with a large population, a widely developed division of labour and an open local economic system. As a consequence, a whole series of local institutions complement social control in the industrial district to ensure conformity to the custom of mutual cooperation in support of the collective capital of trust. In this respect an important role is played both by institutions with general objectives, such as political parties and local government, and by economic institutions such as local entrepreneurial associations and trade unions (Trigilia 1986; Brusco and Righi 1989); in addition, trust is also occasionally provided by more specific institutions, possibly of a temporary kind, created especially to tackle certain problems, often economic ones, in the local community (Sabel and Zeitlin 1985; Dei Ottati 1994).

1.3 Reputation and Trust as Personal Capital

Besides favouring the maintenance of an important collective capital of trust (subsection 1.2), the socioeconomic context of the district (subsection 1.1) also promotes the building up of trust relations based on personal reputation. In fact, the small firms of the district, which are formally autonomous but economically interdependent since they are specialised in complementary activities, are involved in repeated exchanges with one another. In addition, the widespread development of direct contacts between agents living permanently in the same area, and generally sharing the same culture, makes it possible to observe, interpret and record, at least as far as those involved in the transaction are concerned, the behaviour of the people with whom they do business. Clearly, this is a context where the building up of a good reputation is stimulated by the prospect of future gains (Kreps and Wilson 1982). Even if information spreads with a certain ease within the district, because of its social structure, the dissemination is not perfect and the agreements between the contracting parties are necessarily incomplete: for example, as regards the quality of the goods exchanged and/or adaptation to unforeseen circumstances. Consequently, there are many transactions which can only be carried out if trust between contracting parties is not limited to respect of the custom of reciprocal cooperation, but is also based on a knowledge of the personal, moral and professional characteristics of the other party.

There are, therefore, incentives to invest in building up a reputation of particular trustworthiness, usually acquired through past behaviour. For example, if in several successive transactions with the same buyer a subcontractor supplies good quality products and shows that he is able to adapt himself to changing circumstances without taking advantage of variations of market power in his favour, he accumulates real personal capital by doing this. This can be considered as capital because it is obtained at a certain cost, above all by choosing to sacrifice immediate, certain economic gains, in favour of future advantages which may be uncertain. In addition, personal trust is capital because it can generate future yields through transactions which otherwise would never be carried out because they would be considered too risky.[6] This specific capital of trust, in fact, takes on a strategic importance for the conclusion of all those exchanges in which, owing to imperfect information, a person must take decisions whose outcome for that person depends most critically on the action and/or on the information of the other contracting party which the person cannot monitor, at least not at the moment of the decision. This happens, for example, when the content of the transaction is innovative, or when quality is of special importance, or when, being a matter of a deferred obligation, unforeseen contingencies can arise before accomplishment.

In all these cases, where there is considerable strategic uncertainty, the transaction is generally too risky to be concluded simply on the basis of the custom of cooperation. It is, therefore, in such cases that personal trustworthiness becomes a decisive element. Trust based on reputation, as distinct from trust based on custom, to which it is eventually added, is therefore personal capital with its own particular characteristics. In the first place, while this kind of trust is usually acquired gradually over time, it can be destroyed all at once (Dasgupta 1988, p. 62). Secondly, trust based on reputation is personal capital in the sense that it is part of the subject. Therefore, personal trustworthiness, as distinct from the reputation which a product may have and which can be advertised by means of a trademark, is not directly marketable.[7] In addition, the only people who know about it are those who have had the chance to do repeated good business with the person in question. It is therefore 'private knowledge' which circulates, at best, within a restricted group of agents of the district.

Consequently, trust based on personal reputation is also specific capital in a peculiar sense. In fact, as distinct from other cases of asset specificity, it can be used in different transactions, but only with those agents who, through direct or indirect experience, know about such a reputation. In short, it is specific capital to be used in business relations with a restricted number of subjects, rather than specific capital to be used in a narrow range of transactions. In addition, while transaction-specific capital allows a saving on production costs, personal-identity-specific capital reduces transaction costs.

2.   TRUST AND INTERLINKING TRANSACTIONS OF SUBCONTRACTING AND CREDIT

2.1   Trust as Personal Capital and Interlinking Transactions

As we saw above, the socioeconomic environment of the district very much favours the development of relations of trust within the district, because of the combined effect of social norms (subsection 1.2) and economic incentives (subsection 1.3). In particular, since the information is not perfect, trust based on reputation is personal strategic capital which can be used to effect transactions which pose measurement difficulties (Barzel 1982), such as non-standardised transactions, for example, or uncertain transactions such as those which, being carried out over a long period of time, need follow-on adjustments which are nearly always a source of conflict of interest. In fact, no one would conclude a transaction of this sort without knowing beforehand the specific trustworthiness of the other party, for fear of suffering great losses either as a consequence of 'adverse selection' or because of 'moral hazard'.[8] Trust based on reputation, as already noted, is particular specific capital, in the sense that to be productive it must be used with people who are familiar with the identity of its owner.

This usually implies that not only is it costly to build up personal trustworthiness, but it is also costly to look for agents who possess a specific trustworthiness. If, for example, a firm needs a component of a very high quality for its production, not only does it take time to find a supplier who can satisfy this need, but this can involve a loss if experimental orders have to be made (Leibenstein 1987, p. 603). Now, since both letting others know about one's personal, moral and professional characteristics, and getting to know the characteristics of others both involve some cost, it is obvious that when two or more agents have formed a relation of personal trust, this leads them to deal as much as possible with each other. In other words, the development of preferential economic relations, or 'particular markets' (Marshall 1923, p. 182), between subjects who make an investment specific to the business relations between them, is encouraged. As has been seen, this saves information costs and above all allows firms to benefit from transactions which otherwise would not have been carried out.

The formation of 'particular markets' has, however, a further effect: long-lasting personal relations and reciprocal cooperation in repeated transactions activate, in fact, a deep psychological and social process which tends to strengthen trust. This helps to explain why trust, as Albert Hirschman underlines, often grows with use.

We have thus seen that the industrial district is a favourable environment for the building up of relations of trust based on personal reputation, and therefore favours the development of preferential trading relations between agents who know each other. In this environment, in addition to repeated and protracted transactions between the same subjects, there is also a tendency for the development of so-called interlinking transactions. The term 'interlinking transactions' refers to transactions which are concluded by the same two parties in more than one market. They are essentially related in the sense that it would either not be possible, or it would at best be less convenient, for one or both parties to engage in separate transactions. In practice what we have here is a 'package' agreement in which the terms of the reciprocal double obligation are established jointly. Given the way in which production is organised, an important type of interlinking transaction in the industrial district is the one between subcontracting and credit. In such a case, for example, what matters is not solely the rate of interest and the amount borrowed or only the conditions of subcontracting, but all these factors together (Bell 1988, p. 797).[9]

The present chapter focuses mainly on this type of interlinkage. This is not to say, however, that the phenomenon of interlinking transactions is not to be found in other markets in the industrial district, such as the market in both new and secondhand machinery,[10] and raw materials. It should be noted that interlinking transactions between the sale of raw materials and credit play a role in the industrial district which is partially analogous to the one played by interlinking relations of subcontracting and credit. Whereas the latter promote the setting up and renewal of subcontractors, the former promote the establishment and reconversion of firms primarily concerned with the marketing of products. In fact, interlinking credit relations are often also responsible for the rise of such firms. They buy the raw materials on credit, have them transformed by existing subcontractors within the district and pay when the goods produced are sold. Interlinking relations of subcontracting and credit are important because they help to sustain existing small subcontractors and encourage their proliferation. In fact, for those who want to set up on their own at one of the different stages of the production process of the industry located in the district, or for the owners of existing small firms who want to buy new machinery, but who do not have sufficient financial means to do so, the way forward is clear. The simplest way for them to achieve these ends is through interlinking transactions of subcontracting and credit with entrepreneurs who know and trust them. In an industrial district like Prato, for example, these entrepreneurs often do not own a plant, but specialise in conceiving the business ideas and marketing the final product made in the industrial district.

Following Becattini (1990, p. 42), this type of entrepreneur will henceforth be referred to as the 'pure entrepreneur'. This is because direct knowledge and the generally informal procedure reduce both the costs and the time it takes to grant and manage credit. In addition, the fact that the lender is also a customer allows the subcontractor-borrower to repay the loan by discounting it from the payment for the work ordered by the lender. In fact, for example, this form of financing proved to be important in the formation of the textile industrial district of Prato, near Florence (Barbieri 1957; Lorenzoni 1980) and of the tanning district of Santa Croce, near Pisa (Bellandi 1990, pp. 51–2). On the one hand, entrepreneurs who know they can rely on their would be or actual subcontractors, because they have had previous business contact with them (through subcontracting or employment relations), can accept the double transaction, knowing that the risk of default is much reduced. The capital of trust based on reputation owned by the subcontractor-borrower represents a strategic resource for that person as it is this personal asset that enables them to turn to people who know them for help whenever the person needs it. On the other hand, those who do not possess such a personal asset do not find anyone prepared to give them credit.

2.2 Interlinking Transactions of Subcontracting and Credit, Implicit Partnerships and Market Uncertainty

Interlinking transactions of subcontracting and credit give rise to a type of informal organisation which is worth examining in more detail. By granting credit (in cash or in kind) for an investment, the entrepreneur-lender is taking a direct and personal share of the risk that such an investment will not repay itself. Interlinking relations of subcontracting and credit thus give rise to a type of organisation which can be considered as an implicit form of partnership between subcontractor and client. Before considering the advantages that this bilateral contracting relation presents in tackling the uncertainty due to market fluctuations, we shall briefly hint at the reasons which might lead local agents to prefer this type of informal organisation to an explicit partnership.

In the first place, we must keep in mind that the population of firms in the industrial district is made up for the most part of small enterprises (individual proprietorships or family concerns) and therefore joint-stock companies are relatively few. As a consequence, many firms in the district do not take advantage of the limited liability which the law provides for joint-stock companies. In practice, with interlinking credit a temporary quasi-partnership is established between the contracting parties, and if business goes badly, the one who has advanced part of the capital will risk at most losing only the amount lent. Interlinking credit is therefore a way of permitting small firms in the district to benefit partially from limited liability.

Considering the socioeconomic features of the industrial district and the decisive role which trust plays in it (subsections 1.2 and 1.3), we nevertheless believe that the main reason for preferring the implicit partnership to an explicit one is to be found in the changing nature of the relationship determined by passing from an informal to a formal organisation (Silva 1991, p. 275). In fact, if for example, the interlinking relation of subcontracting and credit between a subcontractor and a pure entrepreneur is transformed into a co-ownership, a former bilateral relationship becomes, at least in part, an authoritarian one (Coase 1937, p. 392). This is on account of property rights which consist precisely in the power of control and eventually of intervention in the management decisions of the subsidiary (Williamson 1985, pp. 145–6).

This kind of transformation, which in a different environment from the one considered here (section 1) could bring about a saving on transaction costs (Klein, Crawford and Alchian 1978), in the industrial district on the contrary would hamper the working of its delicate governance mechanism (see Chapter 4 in this volume) and even block it. In the first place, co-ownership reduces the importance of trust as personal capital. The power of control and of intervention connected to ownership make it less necessary to know the reputation of the other party, before concluding with them transactions which involve considerable strategic uncertainty (subsection 1.3). All this clearly weakens the need for trust as personal capital, and this, in turn, brings about a further reduction in its demand, since trust is a good which tends to decrease if not sufficiently used (Hirschman 1984).

Nevertheless, the negative consequences for trust caused by passing from an informal organisation to an explicit partnership do not imply only a lesser incentive to invest in personal reputation. They also imply a relationship of authority and monitoring – substitutes for trust which as already noted (subsection 1.2), can generate distrust. This is a serious threat to the custom of reciprocal cooperation which is at the base of trust as collective capital. In other words, if monitoring by authority prevails over self-control, peer monitoring (Arnott and Stiglitz 1991) and the reciprocal monitoring which are typical of bilateral relationships inside the district, not only is the incentive to produce trust as personal capital reduced, but the collective capital of trust can be eroded as well. In this way, however, the very possibility of reproduction of the industrial district as a specific model of socioeconomic organisation is jeopardised.

Interlinking transactions of subcontracting and credit create reciprocal obligations supported by credible commitments which, by encouraging the continuity of the relationship between the parties, provide a mutual insurance against market uncertainty: this affects both local subcontracting markets and partially also external markets for the district's products. As for local sub-contracting markets, even if the firms specialised in marketing the district's products tend to use subcontractors whose good reputation they know, this is not sufficient to assure the customer that the subcontractor will carry out his orders promptly even in periods of high demand. This is the case when the local market for subcontracting services is tight and it is difficult and/or very expensive for the pure entrepreneurs to find the available production capacity they need. Thus, in order to reduce the risk of having to give up good business precisely at a time when demand is high, it is in the pure entrepreneur's interest to create binding relationships with some subcontractors by offering them specific incentives in order to secure a dedicated production capacity. This happens particularly if there is considerable fluctuation and instability in the demand for the district's products.[11] On the other hand, if market conditions are unstable, it is also in the subcontractors' interest to create bonds with some pure entrepreneurs, so as to reduce the risk of remaining with excess capacity at a time of falling demand. Hence, interlinking credit granted on the basis of personal trust provides reciprocal insurance against the risks associated with the uncertainty of conditions in the local subcontracting market. With interlinking credit, in fact, if the pure entrepreneurs interrupt the flow of production orders when demand is slack and it is easier for them to find a substitute, not only do they risk losing a trustworthy subcontractor, but they also risk making a loss on the credit they had extended.

The situation is partly analogous if it is the subcontractors who break off the relationship when demand is high and their market power is on the increase. If they defect they will immediately lose their personal reputation with the other party and possibly, through communication, also with other pure entrepreneurs in the local business community. This double exposure of resources specific to the relationship between the two contracting parties thus helps to make credible the mutual commitment to continue such a relationship (Williamson 1983 and 1985, pp. 190–205). Interlinking credit is, therefore, a bilateral governance structure which allows the continuity of reciprocal exchanges between the parties to be safeguarded.

Despite the advantages already considered, the continuity of subcontracting relationships can be seen as an element of rigidity, and thus as an obstacle to the ability to face uncertainty in the 'state of nature', in particular changes in external market conditions. Let us now turn to a more detailed analysis of the implications of interlinking credit within the industrial district. Such a contractual device does indeed promote lasting economic relationships, but on the other hand it does not bind the parties to a contract which is rigidly defined once and for all. On the contrary, it constitutes a kind of 'blank agreement', in which the only obligation is to adapt one's behaviour fairly to changing conditions, so that the relationship can continue (Lorenz 1988, pp. 198–9).[12] However, as the interlinking of credit and subcontracting involves a reciprocal obligation to adapt to unforeseen circumstances, it becomes an incentive rather than a constraint to flexibility. Moreover, the continuity of the subcontracting relationship, plus the reciprocal interdependence it brings with it, tends to reinforce cooperation between the parties (Good 1988, pp. 44–5). The subcontractor will be more inclined to adapt to quantitative and qualitative variations in the orders commissioned, while the pure entrepreneur will be even more determined to think up and market new products and to establish contacts with new buyers in order not to lose the trustworthy subcontractors upon whose cooperation, at least in the medium term, the entrepreneur's profits depend. It must be borne in mind that in industrial districts pure entrepreneurs do not usually command their own production capacity, or if they do so, it is only to a limited extent. Thus, somewhat paradoxically, an organisational device which ensures the relative stability of relationships between contracting parties may also help those involved in tackling the uncertainty deriving from the external markets of the district. This is so to the extent to which it promotes productive flexibility and commercial enterprise, thus enhancing the dynamism of the local production system.[13]

2.3 Interlinking Transactions of Subcontracting and Credit, Vertical Mobility and Mobilisation of Resources

Given the way in which production is organised and exchange takes place in the industrial district, interlinking transactions also provide a viable path of upward mobility by developing the latent capabilities of a great number of people of middle and lower class origin. The moderate size of most firms within the industrial district reduces an employee's chances of a career within the firm. In fact, the management of a small firm is fairly narrowly circumscribed and is usually the province of the entrepreneur in person, perhaps with help from members of the family. In the industrial district, social and economic advancement is commonly obtained by becoming self-employed. Thus it is understandable that, for many of those who have been socialised in an industrial district, the desire for recognition and economic advancement tends to manifest itself in the aspiration to run their own business. In a different environment, this desire would tend to express itself in aspirations for a career in, for instance, the civil service or in a large firm.

As we have seen (subsection 1.3), the environment of the industrial district favours the building up of a personal capital of trust based on a good reputation; this capital is often decisive for those who intend to set up in business on their own. This is because, as Alfred Marshall already pointed out, it can be offered as 'personal security' (Marshall 1924, p. 82) to obtain the credit which is necessary to start a new business. We now have a partial answer to the questions why, and how, in an industrial district which functions normally, there are many people who are willing to set up their own business and are able to make investments on credit. However, this does not help us understand why some entrepreneurs are prepared to encourage their most capable and trustworthy employees to become self-employed. One explanation for this apparently strange behaviour may be in the greater flexibility and capacity to adapt to variations in the end market demands of a productive structure characterised by a division of labour between firms, rather than by a division of labour within a single vertically integrated large enterprise.

Nevertheless, this greater structural flexibility does not seem to be the only reason why several entrepreneurs in the industrial district are prepared to encourage their most trustworthy workers (or subcontractors) either to set up on their own or to develop their own business by, for example, granting them credit. Moreover, it is hard to imagine that the unlikelihood of making a career within the firm would be enough to make employees want to set up on their own, if it were too risky and if they did not think they could increase their expected income. There must, therefore, be some other reason that makes both parties prefer the subcontracting relationship, possibly interlinked with that of credit, to the employment relationship.

As we saw above, trust based on personal reputation is a necessary condition of interlinking credit. It is not, however, generally the only requirement. The owners of small firms, or those who aspire to become so, must have sufficiently developed professional skills to enable them to supervise production, even if such supervision is generally limited to a particular phase of the production process; they must not be risk averse; and they must have entrepreneurial skills. Apart from the attributes mentioned above, the owners of small firms, or those who intend to become so, often have other resources which are not easily marketable, like, for example, the opportunity to involve members of their family in the business. Not infrequently they are also able to use their own property, sometimes part of their own house, as a workshop. But some of the above mentioned resources, such as the ability to make entrepreneurial decisions and to supervise production, are not marketable because they are inextricably bound up with the activity of the person who owns them. Others, such as help from the family, are difficult to market because of various types of economic and social constraints. For these reasons, it is only possible to make full use of these resources by giving the person in possession of them the opportunity to use them in their own business.

The pure entrepreneurs of an industrial district have, therefore, another good reason to support the desire on the part of some of their trustworthy employees to set up their own small firms. They see it as an opportunity to share some of the benefits deriving from the full utilisation of their employees' potential. On the one hand, interlinking credit in the industrial district enables those wishing to set up on their own to exploit the resources in their possession, including the capital of trust based on personal reputation. On the other hand, it allows the pure entrepreneur-lenders to benefit from the externalities which the granting of credit has on the subcontracting relationship, precisely because of the utilisation of these resources.[14] This is because interlinking relationships provide a way of integrating the activity of the pure entrepreneur with that of the subcontractor, even if the integration is obtained through bilateral governance rather than a unified one within the firm (Williamson 1985, pp. 75–8). With interlinking credit, as with unified governance, it is possible to internalise both the economies which derive from the division of labour and those which relate to transaction costs.[15]

Interlinking credit and unified governance differ in two important respects. The first, as already noted (subsection 2.2), concerns the different nature of the contractual relationship: bilateral for interlinking credit and authoritarian in the other case. The second difference, which is connected to the preceding one, concerns the different distribution of property rights.[16] With interlinking credit the two parties remain autonomous and the subcontractor is the only residual claimant of his own business. This fact is a powerful incentive for the subcontractor to make full use of the resources at his disposal and, most importantly, to develop his latent capabilities.

3. DIRECT FINANCING AND BANK CREDIT

3.1 Interlinking Credit and Direct Financing

Up until now we have mainly considered the role of interlinking transactions of subcontracting and credit in the industrial district. We have said nothing, however, about how the lending firms, which are for the most part relatively small, can come to have sufficient financial resources to be able to make loans. First of all, it appears that it is only established entrepreneurs who are in a position to grant credit. Moreover, firms connected with the external markets in the industrial district tend to specialise in buying and selling, activities which do not generally require great freezing of fixed capital.[17] Nevertheless, they allow those involved to have a relatively high turnover. For the above reasons, interlinking credit seems to make entrepreneurs involved in the purchase of raw materials and/or the sale of products specialise in these activities, and grant credit to local subcontractors whom they trust rather than invest directly themselves. As far as the interlinking of subcontracting and credit is concerned, it is a necessary, but not sufficient, condition to make this double exchange profitable, that both parties behave honestly and be prepared to cooperate with each other. In addition, the investment project to be financed must also be commercially viable as well as technically sound. Knowledge of the quality of investment projects is usually considered 'inside' information (Leland and Pyle 1977). In the case of interlinking of subcontracting and credit in the industrial district, however, an important part of the information on the quality of projects, in particular the part concerning their suitability (in terms of quantity and quality) with regard to end market conditions, is held by the pure entrepreneur who is called upon to grant the loan.

Information on end market conditions on the one hand, and on conditions of production on the other, is usually controlled by different agents. Therefore the interlinking subcontracting and credit proves to be a device for screening projects according to their expected return, in that it involves the pure entrepreneur and the subcontractor in the appraisal of the investments to be financed. Now since subcontracting relations are widespread in the industrial district and the interlinking of subcontracting-credit has advantages not only as far as flexibility (subsection 2.2) and utilisation of resources (subsection 2.3) are concerned, but also regarding the choice of investment projects, it follows that direct financing is an important method of external funding in such a model of industrial organisation.[18] However, this does not mean that bank credit is of negligible importance for the development of the industrial district. Nor does it imply that the role of financial intermediation is marginal in this regard.

3.2 Trust as Personal Capital and Bank Credit

In the preceding section we maintained that in the industrial district entrepreneurs who specialise in buying and selling tend to grant credit to local subcontractors whom they know they can trust. However, even if we were to admit that marketing specialists are generally able to achieve a good return and that the funds thus made available could all be used in relations of interlinking credit, it is inconceivable that they would be sufficient to sustain high rates of economic development over a long period as, for example, has happened in several districts in Italy.[19] For such a development, bank credit is important, even if the characteristics of the industrial district tend to influence the way in which it is extended. As we have seen (subsection 1.3), the environment of the industrial district promotes the spread of trust relationships based on personal reputation; and this is true for every kind of exchange, including transactions with banks. Repeated personal relationship transactions between the managers of banks established in the industrial district and the local entrepreneurs who make the most use of the bank services develop profound mutual knowledge.[20] This often brings forth also a trust relationship, so that the usual banks' preference for giving credit to their best clients is definitely strengthened.

Now the best known clients of the bank in the industrial district tend to be those entrepreneurs who have contacts with external markets, as it is through them that the majority of local products are exported and frequently raw materials are imported. But if among the best known and trusted clients of the bank there are many pure entrepreneurs, it is simple to understand how they are able to obtain bank credit with relative ease. In fact, relationships of trust developed with the bank manager limit the risks for the bank deriving from adverse selection and moral hazard (subsections 1.3 and 2.1). This is because otherwise client-entrepreneurs would lose their capital of trust based on personal reputation – an asset which is of crucial importance for the continuation of their business. Furthermore, pure entrepreneurs often have economic interests in several types of business, although these are for the most part located within the industrial district. This also reduces the risks for the bank and thus further increases these agents' chances of obtaining credit from it. It now becomes clear that it is essentially through these agents that bank credit pours into the industrial district. For reasons which have been repeatedly underlined, bank managers prefer to give credit to agents whom they know and trust, either directly or indirectly through a guarantee.

3.3 Double Financial Intermediation and Credit in the Industrial District

The pure entrepreneurs of an industrial district who are trusted by the bank are thus in a position to become financial intermediaries themselves. The fact that they have repeated and personal business relationship transactions with both bank managers and subcontractors gives them the opportunity to lend trusted subcontractors funds received as a bank loan, at least partially on the basis of trust. As we saw above, it is clearly in these entrepreneurs' interests to make the most of this opportunity. In this way, since they have a trust relationship both with some local firms and with bank managers, pure entrepreneurs are in the unusual position of being at one and the same time entrepreneurs without a factory and lenders without money. In the industrial district, then, there are two sources of financial mediation: the banks on the one hand and the entrepreneurs who are trusted by the bank managers on the other.[21] The latter thus fuel a secondary market for bank loans, which is considered a rare phenomenon (Fama 1985, p. 37).

At this point we should ask ourselves what the consequences are of this double financial intermediation on the supply and allocation of credit, and hence on the development of the district. At first sight the system appears both anachronistic and inefficient; however, we have to bear in mind that this institutional mechanism helps overcome asymmetries in information. In fact, it is thanks to its role as a provider of information that this form of double intermediation seems able to reduce considerably the problems of adverse selection and moral hazard often associated with credit rationing (Jaffee and Russell 1976; Keeton 1979; Stiglitz and Weiss 1981). Moreover, this form of double intermediation also has advantages as far as the allocation of financial resources is concerned. It is clear, for example, that bank managers and pure entrepreneurs are not equally well informed as to both the reliability of the final borrowers and the quality of the projects to be financed.

Double financial intermediation allows the involvement of those with the greatest knowledge of the markets in the assessment of investments. For it is ultimately market conditions which determine their profitability. Once the screening of investment projects has been improved, the allocation of the available financial resources is also improved. On closer examination, double financial intermediation constitutes an organisational mechanism which, in normal circumstances, allows liquidity to flow into the many small firms of the industrial district. This allows the growth and vitality of the complex organism which is the industrial district as a whole to be limited as little as possible by shortage of financial resources, or by their misallocation.[22]

CONCLUDING REMARKS

As we have seen, credit plays a far from negligible role in the economic development of the industrial district. In such a model of organisation, however, the external financing of small firms tends to take on a different form from the financing of large vertically integrated firms. The external funding of small firms frequently takes less visible forms, such as inter-linking credit, for example. This does not mean that financial capital is a decisive factor in the formation and development of the industrial district. This is because in such an environment the economic activity of those involved is bound up with what, following Marshall, we have described as the 'capital of trust', more than with the availability of financial resources. In other words, the two resources which are crucial for economic development in the industrial district are the ability (in quantitative and qualitative terms) to work, and the possibility to know and trust one another.[23] In particular, it is relationships of trust between agents which make transactions such as informal credit possible. It is also thanks to the existence of such relationships that collateral seems to become less important, even for the granting of credit.

As we have seen, trust is a precondition for concluding transactions which are potentially profitable but subject to a high risk of opportunism. Therefore, trust seems to be more than an efficient lubricant of economic activity (Arrow 1974, p. 23). In particular, trust based on personal reputation assumes the features of a true although intangible capital, which is capable both of producing future gains and of fostering economic development. However, as has been emphasised, the scope for concluding agreements between people in order to realise implicit interests is connected with 'aspects of personal knowledge and of attitude towards others which refer to ways of social living, to the formal or informal, permanent or transitory structures which make of a group of individuals what we call a "society"' (Dardi 1990, p. 76).[24]

NOTES

1. Many of the most important studies on industrial districts may now be found in collections. See, for example, Becattini (1987), Bagnasco (1988), Brusco (1989); and in English, Goodman and Bamford (1989), Pyke, Becattini and Sengenberger (1990), and Pyke and Sengenberger (1992).
2. On interlinking transactions in an agrarian economy see, for example, Bardhan (1980 and 1989), Binswanger and Rosenzweig (1984), Braverman and Stiglitz (1982 and 1986), Braverman (1986); see also Bhaduri (1973).
3. Interlinking transactions and multiplex relations are related phenomena. Here an attempt is made to distinguish them. The term 'interlinking transactions' is taken to refer to joint economic exchanges, whereas the term 'multiplex relations' implies the superimposition of economic transactions and social obligations between the agents concerned. An example of multiplex relations might be employment relations in family businesses. In the present context we shall limit ourselves to considering some aspects of interlinking transactions in the industrial district.
4. The importance of frequent personal contact in overcoming difficulties in communication had already been pointed out by Marshall (cf. Bellandi 1989, pp. 140–41). On the role of face-to-face contacts in the innovation process in local systems of small firms, see Bellandi (Chapter 5 in this volume).
5. For evidence concerning north east and central Italy, see, for example: Brusco (1982); Fuà and Zacchia (1983); Lazerson (1990); Becattini (Chapter 1 in this volume). For evidence on other local systems of small firms, see Raveyère and Saglio (1984); Scott and Storper (1987); Lorenz (1988); Kristensen (1992).
6. The idea that personal trust based on knowledge constitutes capital is expressed by Alfred Marshall in the following passage: 'A producer, a wholesale dealer, or a shopkeeper who has built up a strong connection among purchasers of his goods, has a valuable property ... he expects to sell easily to them because they know and trust him and he does not sell at low prices in order to call attention to his business, as he often does in a market where he is little known' (1923, p. 182). It should be noted that Marshall recognised that the value of

trust depends on imperfect knowledge. On knowledge in Marshall's theory of economic progress, see Loasby (1986).

7. However, it should be noted that, even if it is not marketable, personal trust can, in a way, be lent on every occasion that a subject who is trusted acts as intermediary in a transaction, for example, where he becomes a guarantor (see Coleman 1990, pp. 180–85).

8. 'Moral hazard' is the term used in the literature on asymmetric information to refer to models with hidden action. In such models, whether or not it is in the uninformed party's (principal) interest to conclude a transaction depends upon the behaviour of the other more informed party (agent), behaviour which the principal cannot monitor. 'Adverse selection' is the term used to refer to models with precontractual hidden information (cf. Arrow 1985). In the literature on transaction costs, both adverse selection and moral hazard give rise to the possibility of opportunism. In this context, Williamson refers to ex ante and ex post opportunism respectively (Williamson 1985, p. 47).

9. It should be noted that as regards interlinking transactions in the industrial district and interlinking transactions in developing countries, the focus of much of the literature on interlinkage is, although similar in form, qualitatively different. In the industrial district, interlinking transactions are concluded when a relationship of trust has already developed between the parties and the moral hazard is consequently low. In the literature on developing countries, interlinkage is generally seen as a remedy in situations in which the risk of moral hazard is, on the other hand, considerable (see, for example, Sen 1981). A second difference is that in the industrial district the contracting party *cum* borrower generally has the freedom to choose whether or not to enter into relations of interlinking credit. This possibility is not open in situations of underdevelopment in which there are considerable and permanent asymmetries between the contracting parties as regards the resources endowments, access to information and substitutability concerning both the markets. These asymmetries give the contracting party-lender a power of monopoly, which is often reinforced by differences in caste (see, for example, Sarap 1990). A third difference concerns the type of credit: in the case of the industrial district, we are dealing with credit for investment and not for consumption as in developing countries. Moreover, the subcontractors in an industrial district are entrepreneurs and are thus not risk averse as it is generally supposed agricultural labourers-borrowers are in backward economies. Gangopadhyay and Sengupta (1986) show that if both contracting parties are risk neutral and the contracting party-borrower organises production, the rate of interest of interlinking credit does not differ from the market rate of interest on loans.

10. For evidence on the interlinkage between the sale of machinery and credit in the district of Prato, see Avigdor (1961, p. 143) and Marchi (1962, p. 211). For evidence concerning Emilia-Romagna, see Brusco and Solinas (1992).

11. On the economic importance of the ready availability of labour in periods of peak demand in agriculture, see Bardhan (1979).

12. The deliberate non-specification of the general agreement between pure entrepreneurs and subcontractors is confirmed by our own research conducted in the textile district of Prato in 1988. Most of the 284 firms we interviewed concluded agreements the details of which were sorted out as the orders came in.

13. The industrial district, like any other form of organisation, can give rise to inflexibility, despite its essentially flexible nature. This is primarily due to the accumulation of knowledge and experience and to the development of practices and routines which are specific to this form of organisation. Clearly these can constitute elements of inertia in case of radical change.

14. It should be pointed out that just as the interlinking of credit and subcontracting allows the potential subcontractor to make full use of resources which are not entirely marketable, such as the capacity to supervise production, the interlinking of credit and the sale of raw materials can allow the mobilisation of resources which the aspiring pure entrepreneurs have at their disposal. These would include a flair for business and contacts with clients.

15. Interlinking credit thus differs from simple trade credit, which provides a way of balancing the cash flow of the firm in a short period. Interlinking transactions including credit, in

fact, are kinds of micro-organisations thanks to which it is possible to internalise externalities (Braverman and Stiglitz 1982; Bardhan 1989, p. 239).

16. On how the distribution of property rights can influence, as well as be influenced by, the level and type of skills and in general the characteristics (more or less specific and more or less difficult to monitor) of the resources used in the economic process, see Pagano (1991).

17. It is however worth noting that the most important capital that pure entrepreneurs have is their personal knowledge of the local producers and their connections with the end markets of the products made in the district.

18. In order to appreciate the importance of direct finance in the industrial district, it is necessary to take account of all the interlinking exchanges which imply some form of credit, and not just the interlinking of subcontracting and credit (subsection 2.1).

19. One only needs to think of the sustained period of growth of various industrial districts in north east and central Italy in the postwar period (Fuà and Zacchia 1983). As far as the industrial district of Prato is concerned, from 1951 to 1981 the number of looms increased by 282 per cent, while the number of workers in the textile industry increased by 183 per cent (Dei Ottati 1990, p. 123).

20. For evidence concerning the tanning district of Santa Croce sull'Arno (Pisa), see ARPES (1982, p. 126).

21. It should be emphasised once again that just as interlinking credit is not limited to subcontracting relations, it is not only pure entrepreneurs who are trusted by the banks. Those who deal in raw materials, for example, or the manufacturers of and dealers in machinery may also be among them.

22. I do not assert that the mechanisms under consideration here are able to put the small firms of the industrial district on an equal footing with large holdings as far as access to external sources of finance is concerned. It should merely be noted that such mechanisms seem capable of reducing the drawbacks.

23. As Marshall puts it: 'In speaking of the difficulty that a working-man has in rising to a post in which he can turn his business ability to full account, the chief stress is commonly laid upon his want of capital: but this is not always his chief difficulty ... The real difficulty is to convince a sufficient number of those around [him] that [he has] these rare qualities: ... Firstly a *high order of business ability and probity*, and secondly, the *"personal capital" of a great reputation* among [his] fellows for these qualities' (Marshall 1932, pp. 173–4, my emphasis).

24. On the 'inextricable link between social, political and economic forces in determining how economies function', see Wilkinson (1983).

REFERENCES

Arnott, R. and J. Stiglitz (1991), 'Moral hazard and nonmarket institutions: dysfunctional crowding out of peer monitoring?', *American Economic Review*, March.

ARPES (1982), *Studio conoscitivo sul settore della concia, pelletteria e calzature*, Florence: Regione Toscana.

Arrow, K. (1974), *The Limits of Organization*, New York: Norton.

Arrow, K. (1985), 'The economics of agency', in J. Pratt and R. Zeckhauser (eds), *Principal and Agents: The Structures of Business*, Boston, MA: Harvard Business School Press.

Avigdor, E. (1961), *L'industria tessile a Prato*, Milan: Feltrinelli.

Bagnasco, A. (1988), *La costruzione sociale del mercato*, Bologna: Il Mulino.

Barbieri, G. (1957), 'Prato e la sua industria tessile', *Rivista geografica italiana*, 63(supplement).

Bardhan, P. (1979), 'Wages and unemployment in a poor agrarian economy: a theoretical and empirical analysis', *Journal of Political Economy*, 3.

Bardhan, P. (1980), 'Interlocking factor markets and agrarian development: a review of issues', *Oxford Economic Papers*, 32.
Bardhan, P. (ed.) (1989), *The Economic Theory of Agrarian Institutions*, Oxford: Clarendon Press.
Barzel, Y. (1982), 'Measurement cost and the organisation of markers', *Journal of Law and Economics*, 25, April.
Becattini, G. (ed.) (1987), *Mercato e forze locali: il distretto industriale*, Bologna: Il Mulino.
Becattini, G. (1989), 'Sectors and/or districts: some remarks on the conceptual foundations of industrial economics', in Goodman and Bamford (1989).
Becattini, G. (1990), 'The Marshallian industrial district as a socioeconomic notion', in F. Pyke, G. Becattini and W. Sengenberger (eds), *Industrial Districts and Inter-Firm Co-operation in Italy*, Geneva: International Institute for Labour Studies.
Becattini, G. (ed.) (1997), *Prato: storia di una città*, Vol. 4, Florence: Le Monnier.
Bell, C. (1988), 'Credit markers and interlinked transactions', in H. Chenery and T. Srinivasan (eds), *Handbook of Development Economics*, Vol. 1, Amsterdam: North Holland.
Bellandi, G. (1990), 'Subcontractor processing and expansion of minor companies in the tanning field', *International Studies of Management and Organization*, 4.
Bellandi, M. (1989), 'The industrial district in Marshall', in Goodman and Bamford (1989).
Bhaduri, A. (1973), 'Agricultural backwardness under semifeudalism', *Economic Journal*, 1.
Binswanger, H. and M. Rosenzweig (eds) (1984), *Contractual Arrangements, Employment and Wages in Rural Labor Markets in Asia*, New Haven, CT: Yale University Press.
Braverman, A. (1986), 'Rural credit markets and institutions in developing countries: lessons for policy analysis from practice and modern theory', *World Development*, 10–11.
Braverman, A. and J. Stiglitz (1982), 'Sharecropping and the interlinking of agrarian markets', *American Economic Review*, September.
Braverman, A. and J. Stiglitz (1986), 'Landlords, tenants and technological innovations', *Journal of Development Economics*, 2.
Brusco, S. (1982), 'The Emilian model: productive decentralisation and social integration', *Cambridge Journal of Economics*, 6(2).
Brusco, S. (1986), 'Small firms and industrial districts: the experience of Italy', in D. Keeble and E. Wever (eds), *New Firms and Regional Development in Europe*, London: Croom Helm.
Brusco, S. (1989), *Piccole imprese e distretti industriali*, Turin: Rosenberg & Sellier.
Brusco, S. (1992), 'Small firms and the provision of real services', in F. Pyke and W. Sengenberger (eds), *Industrial Districts and Local Economic Regeneration*, Geneva: International Institute for Labour Studies.
Brusco, S. and E. Righi (1989), 'Local government, industrial policy and social consensus: the case of Modena (Italy)', *Economy and Society*, 4.
Brusco, S. and C. Sabel (1981), 'Artisan production and economic growth', in F. Wilkinson (ed.), *The Dynamics of Labour Market Segmentation*, London: Academic Press.
Brusco, S. and G. Solinas (1992), 'I processi di formazione delle nuove imprese in Emilia Romagna', Bologna: Regione Emilia Romagna.
Coase, R. (1937), 'The nature of the firm', *Economica*, November.

Coleman, J. (1990), *Foundations of Social Theory*, Cambridge, MA: Harvard University Press.
Dardi, M. (1990), 'Il mercato nell'analisi economica contemporanea', in G. Becattini (ed.), *Il pensiero economico: temi, problemi e scuole*, Turin: UTET.
Dasgupta, P. (1988), 'Trust as a commodity', in D. Gambetta (ed.), *Trust: Making and Breaking Cooperative Relations*, Oxford: Basil Blackwell.
Dei Ottati, G. (1990), 'L'agricoltura nel distretto pratese: da sostegno dello sviluppo industriale ad attività di "consumo"', *La questione agraria*, 38.
Dei Ottati, G. (1994), 'The metamorphosis of a localised industry: the rise of the Prato industrial district', in R.Y. Leonardi and R. Nanetti (eds), *Regional Development in a Modern European Economy: The Case of Tuscany*, London: Pinter Publishers.
Fama, E. (1985), 'What's different about banks?', *Journal of Monetary Economics*, 15.
Fuà, G. and C. Zacchia (eds) (1983), *Industrializzazione senza fratture*, Bologna: Il Mulino.
Gangopadhyay, S. and K. Sengupta (1986), 'Interlinkages in rural markets', *Oxford Economic Papers*, 1.
Good, D. (1988), 'Individuals, interpersonal relations and trust', in D. Gambetta (ed.), *Trust: Making and Breaking Cooperative Relations*, Oxford: Basil Blackwell.
Goodman, E. and J. Bamford (eds) (1989), *Small Firms and Industrial Districts in Italy*, London: Routledge.
Hirschman, A. (1984), 'Against parsimony: three easy ways of complicating some categories of economic discourse', *American Economic Review*, 2.
Jaffee, D. and T. Russell (1976), 'Imperfect information, uncertainty and credit rationing', *Quarterly Journal of Economics*, 90.
Keeton, W. (1979), *Equilibrium Credit Rationing*, New York: Garland Press.
Klein, B., R. Crawford and A. Alchian (1978), 'Vertical integration, appropriable rents and the competitive contracting process', *Journal of Law and Economics*, October.
Kreps, D. and R. Wilson (1982), 'Reputation and imperfect information', *Journal of Economic Theory*, August.
Kristensen, P. (1992), 'Industrial districts in West Jutland, Denmark', in Pyke and Sengenberger (1992).
Lazerson, M. (1990), 'Subcontracting in the Modena knitwear industry', in Pyke, Becattini and Sengenberger (1990).
Leibenstein, H. (1987), 'On some economic aspects of a fragile input: trust', in G. Feiwel (ed.), *Arrow and the Foundations of the Theory of Economic Policy*, London: Macmillan.
Leland, H. and D. Pyle (1977), 'Informational asymmetries, financial structure and financial intermediation', *Journal of Finance*, May.
Loasby, B.J. (1986), 'Marshall's economics of progress', *Journal of Economic Studies*, 5.
Lorenz, E. (1988), 'Neither friends nor strangers: informal networks of subcontracting in French industry', in D. Gambetta (ed.), *Trust: Making and Breaking Cooperative Relations*, Oxford: Basil Blackwell.
Lorenz, E. (1992), 'Trust, community and cooperation: toward a theory of industrial districts', in M. Storper and A. Scott (eds), *Pathways to Industrialization and Regional Development*, London: Routledge.
Lorenzoni, G. (1980), 'Lo sviluppo industriale di Prato', in *Storia di Prato*, Prato: Cassa di Risparmi e Depositi.

Marchi, R. (1962), *Storia economica di Prato*, Milan: Giuffré.

Marshall, A. (1923), *Industry and Trade*, London: Macmillan.

Marshall, A. (1924), *Money, Credit and Commerce*, London: Macmillan.

Marshall, A. (1932), *Elements of Economics of Industry*, London: Macmillan.

Marshall, A. (1975), *The Early Economic Writings of Alfred Marshall 1867–1890*, edited by J. Whitaker, London: Macmillan.

Pagano, U. (1991), 'Property rights, equilibria and institutional stability', *Economic Notes*, 2.

Piore, M. and C. Sabel (1984), *The Second Industrial Divide*, New York: Basic Books.

Pyke, F., G. Becattini and W. Sengenberger (eds) (1990), *Industrial Districts and Inter-Firm Co-operation in Italy*, Geneva: International Institute for Labour Studies.

Pyke, F. and W. Sengenberger (eds) (1992), *Industrial Districts and Local Economic Regeneration*, Geneva: International Institute for Labour Studies.

Raveyère, M.-F. and J. Saglio (1984), 'Les systèmes industriels localisés: éléments pour une analyse sociologique des ensembles de PMEs industriels', *Sociologie du travail*, 2.

Sabel, C. and J. Zeilin (1985), 'Historical alternatives to mass production: politics, markets and technology in nineteenth century industrialization', *Past and Present*, August.

Sarap, K. (1990), 'Interest rates in backward agriculture: the role of economic and extra-economic control', *Cambridge Journal of Economics*, 14(1).

Scott, A. and M. Storper (1987), 'High technology, industry and regional development: a theoretical critique and reconstruction', *International Social Science Journal*, 112.

Sen, A. (1981), 'Market failure and control of labour power: towards an explanation of "structure" and change in Indian agriculture', part 1 and part 2, *Cambridge Journal of Economics*, 5(3–4).

Silva, F. (1991), 'La dimensione dell'impresa: tecnologia, contratti, organizzazione', in S. Zamagni (ed.), *Imprese e mercati*, Turin: UTET.

Stiglitz, J. and A. Weiss (1981), 'Credit rationing in markets with imperfect information', *American Economic Review*, June.

Tani, P. (1987), 'La decomponibilità del processo produttivo', in Becattini (1987).

Taylor, M. (1982), *Community, Anarchy and Liberty*, Cambridge: Cambridge University Press.

Trigilia, C. (1986), 'Small-firm development and political subcultures in Italy', *European Sociological Review*, 3.

Wilkinson, F. (1983), 'Productive systems', *Cambridge Journal of Economics*, 7(3–4).

Williamson, O. (1983), 'Credible commitments: using hostages to support exchange', *American Economic Review*, 73(4).

Williamson, O. (1985), *The Economic Institutions of Capitalism*, New York: Free Press.

7. On entrepreneurship, region and the constitution of scale and scope economies

Marco Bellandi

INTRODUCTION

In contemporary industrial economies the majority of products are made with the help and the contribution of several specialised production activities. We shall call a 'production system' a set of activities for the production of a limited group of similar or complementary goods, constrained by an endowment of not (easily) 'transferable' productive assets, concerning skills, equipment, attitudes, and rules.[1]

A production system may include, among others, one or more activities characterised to some extent by economies of scale or by economies of scope. The definition of this situation implies some plain questions, which currently, however, do not have plain answers. Does a relationship exist between such economies and division of labour among firms in the production system? What happens if new economies appear? How does the regional dimension affect the constitution of new economies; and vice versa, how are regions shaped by such processes?

I here propose a framework for analysing such questions. The framework is built upon three bases: Pagano's concept of techno-organisational equilibrium; Salais and Storper's classification of the worlds of contemporary industry; and Silver's model of entrepreneurial vertical integration.

The four worlds of contemporary industry are a proper reference for defining, at a general level, the manifestation of economies of scale and scope as tied to the prevalence of different combinations of organisations, technologies, and regional characters. The concept of techno-organisational equilibrium allows an analytical definition of worlds of production as ideal-types. Then the definition is used in order to draw the starting points and points of temporary arrival of paths of transition concerning the techno-organisational configuration of a production system. In particular, the process of constitution of new sources for (large) economies of scale and scope is seen as an aspect of a transition from an equilibrium to another non-neighbouring equilibrium. Taking advantage of some variations on the model of entrepreneurial vertical integration, the capacity to overcome possible discontinuities of such transition is understood as the result of the interplay between incremental and systemic entrepreneurship.

1. THE PRODUCTION SYSTEM

Let us define:

1. a production system's organisation in terms of coordination and incentive solutions for the integration of its complementary activities;
2. a production system's technique in terms of location (in space, time, and so on) of capacities of technical capitals, know-how of human capitals, and their reciprocal degrees of 'specialisation' and 'specificity';[2]
3. a techno-organisational configuration in terms of the composition of an organisation and a technique.

Different models of techno-organisational configuration can be distinguished more or less coarsely, on the basis of the combination of a few aggregate components (Storper and Harrison 1991): for example, on the basis of the extension and quality of the division of labour among firms,[3] and of the territorial relationships among them.[4]

'Feasibility' depends on the endowment of strategic non-transferable factors. In particular, organisational feasibility depends upon the pool of entrepreneurial attitudes, organisational skills, and transactional rules which is implied (directly or indirectly) by such an endowment; technical feasibility depends upon the possibility to satisfy, by means of available technical and human capitals, the needs of specialisation and differentiation in the different activities of the system for the realisation of its typical final products; feasibility of a configuration depends, furthermore, upon compatibility constraints between organisational and technical solutions.[5]

In a world of perfect transferability different production systems would not exist: we would have just a global all-inclusive one. Conditions of non-perfect sectoral and territorial mobility are instead widespread, even in the presence of contemporary progress in flexible manufacturing, transportation, and communication systems.

According to the experience of contemporary Italian industrial districts, for example, regional traditions of civism, small farming property, artisan creativity, and trade with non-local markets have at first helped the growth of their localised industries. Then, attitudes towards entrepreneurship, civic rules, trade, learning of basic technical notions, and circulation of new ideas on businesses, have been reproduced within each industrial district, supported by stable relations between its population of small specialised firms and a local community which share some experience connected to the economic prevalence of the localised industry.[6] It is the so-called 'industrial atmosphere', taking on a celebrated expression of Alfred Marshall's.

Other conditions of non-perfect transferability, in non-district cases, can be found in the resources tied to the specific corporate culture of large companies. And so on.

The meaning of non-transferability in terms of time, space, companies' identities, and so forth, may vary. In any case, the availability and size of a set of non-transferable resources identify a production system's borders, and determine – both as a constraint and an opportunity – the feasibility of techno-organisational configurations; while non-specific (easily transferable) resources, which are to be combined with the internal endowment in order to realise a class of products, can be acquired as far as they are needed. The dynamical aspects of these relations will be considered in the next sections.

2. THE TECHNO-ORGANISATIONAL EQUILIBRIUM

We shall say that a feasible techno-organisational configuration of a production system is 'viable' in face of certain external conditions (external markets, legal environment, and so on) if it guarantees the long-run reproduction of the endowment of non-transferable assets of the system.

Let us now suppose that:

1. starting from every given configuration, there are adjustment costs for changing the configuration: costs of transaction, but also costs of acquiring technical and organisational knowledge belonging to the new configuration;
2. the adjustment costs are low within a small neighbourhood of any given configuration, and they are very high instead if the new configuration is outside such neighbourhood;
3. there are, within the system's endowment, 'incremental' entrepreneurs who are able to adopt the most efficient industrial configuration within each given neighbourhood – here efficiency may be defined in terms of aggregate profit, after the owners of the technical and human non-transferable assets are rewarded according to the necessity of reproduction;

4. once a new configuration has been reached, the neighbourhood of possible low cost adjustments may be redefined.

A configuration which, given a certain mix of external conditions and internal endowment, has gained the position of a local maximum in each of the sets of low cost adjustments in which it may be included is (if it does exist) a techno-organisational equilibrium with respect to the given combination of internal and external conditions.

By 'incremental' entrepreneur here we mean any economic agent who has the possibility to make choices directly affecting the techno-organisational configuration of the system, but who limits their decision set to choices somewhat tied to the current and operational experience, and in any case to the available set of non-transferable resources.

Abstract examples of incremental entrepreneurs are the 'partial' entrepreneurs referred to by Ugo Pagano or the managers in a multi-division company referred to by Paul Milgron and John Roberts (Milgron and Roberts 1992, pp. 108–13; Pagano and Rowthorn 1993, p. 254). They define equilibria in which: (1) manufacturing entrepreneurs or production managers choose the technology that maximises profits, given the existing property right system or the existing choices of marketing managers; (2) on the other side, 'financiers' or marketing managers arrange transactions that maximise profits given the existing technology.[7]

The collectivity of incremental entrepreneurs who operate in the system may not be able to fix the techno-organisational configuration within the viability constraint, and this for various reasons. First of all, the organisation of the system at a certain moment may not rule out a short term profitable exploitation of owners of strategic assets by the entrepreneurs.

Secondly, even ruling out the short term exploitation problem, the intersection of feasible and viable configurations could be empty at a certain moment, because of the economic incompatibility between external conditions and the internal endowment of non-transferable factors.

Thirdly, even ruling out the two above mentioned explanations, the system could be trapped in a local maximum which is not above the line of viability, even though other non-neighbouring configurations exist which are both feasible and viable. In what follows we will allow only for this third reason for non-viability.[8]

3. WORLDS OF CONTEMPORARY INDUSTRY

The viability of the configurations of a production system depends, generally speaking, on how external conditions and the internal endowment of strategic factors are combined.

In order to define a manageable framework of viable configurations (including possible equilibria) it is necessary to simplify; here we will focus analytically on some combinations of qualitative characteristics of the external final markets and types of non-transferable resources, in particular those concerning the knowledge utilised by the producers of the system. Following a classification proposed by Robert Salais and Michael Storper (1992):

1. with regard to markets, we shall distinguish production systems characterised by generic products, that is, directed towards markets which tend to be undifferentiated and of limited variability, from systems characterised by personalised products, that is, directed towards markets which tend to be fragmented and variable;
2. with regard to knowledge, we shall distinguish production systems characterised by a widespread employment of relatively standardised and communicable technologies kept together by the specific knowledge of a few system specialists (for example, top management, R&D directors, and so on), from production systems in which knowledge is more differentiated, being rooted in 'communities of specialists'.

The combination of the two distinctions suggests four ideal-types, which in the interpretation of Salais and Storper represent the 'worlds of contemporary industry': the 'industrial world', in other words, mass production, characterised by standardised technologies and vast, stable, and homogeneous markets; the 'world of the market networks', with still relatively standardised technologies, but with relatively variable and fragmented markets; the 'world of Marshallian markets', in other words, flexible specialisation, with technologies which are 'local' – that is restricted to communities of specialists – and with markets which are variable and fragmented; and the 'world of innovation', with local technologies and potentially non-personalised products but with narrow markets due to their newness.

In order to illustrate the link with the concept of techno-organisational equilibrium presented in the preceding section, let us consider an oversimplified representation of a production system with only two production activities: the upstream one supplies the principal input to the downstream, which keeps contacts with the final markets. Let us now assume that, as regards the upstream activity, the contribution of two groups of assets would be necessary: one (R) dedicated to manufacturing and commercial routines; and the other (X) setting up adjustments in those routines, in order to face variations in the demands of the downstream activity (and/or in the supplies of inputs).

We may now consider the following stylised representation of the worlds of production, in terms of the characteristics of the (R,X) sets in the upstream activity.

In the innovation world the upstream activity is divided in groups of units of R and X, groups adapted internally and with respect to specific requirements inside the downstream activity, for the development of new products.

In the mass production world, R and X are standardised to respond to the uniform necessities of the downstream activity, which are derived from the mass demand of the final markets; standardisation in the upstream activity is attained by means of a widespread adoption of a model of rigidly and highly adapted groups of assets (R,X). Here, the high degree of specificity is converted to standardisation because just one type of specific solution is largely adopted throughout the production system.

In the market network world, R is standardised according to some common characteristic of the derived demand of the downstream activity; but here the final markets are also the field of differentiation phenomena, and these are accommodated, as regards the upstream activity, by a capacity of adjustment of X less rigidly defined than in the case of mass production.

In the flexible specialisation world, the R assets are differentiated and the X units have convergent characteristics, in terms of a general capacity of adjustment to the necessities of the downstream activity. Here, generality does not necessarily mean lack of specialisation, since the investments in general capacity may be widespread and convergent towards types which are highly specialised for the purpose.[9]

Such a stylised representation brings, in its turn, some suggestions on the nature of the viable techno-organisational configurations which include equilibria typical of each world.

In the innovation world, a high degree of vertical integration for relatively small businesses is consistent both with the high level of specificity which characterises new lines of products and the small extent of young markets.[10]

In the world of mass production the high degree of standardisation and the potential for large economies of scale in the upstream activity would seem to be coherent with a high degree of business specialisation. This possibility, in fact, should not be excluded. Nevertheless the high level of uniformity reduces the diseconomies of internal coordination. Furthermore the coherence between technological standardisation and a high level of market uniformity may be favoured by the centralised control inside an integrated firm of large size, which consequently takes advantage of large internal economies of scale.

In the flexible specialisation world the general capacity of X reduces the degree of transactional specificity between businesses specialised in the upstream and downstream activities. Furthermore, the convergence of the investments in X towards assets with a general capacity is the basis for the realisation of various types of economies of scale. These, applied to the different capacities of R, eventually translate into economies of scope at the aggregate level of the upstream activity. The differences in R involve peculiarities of technical knowledge which push specialised producers with capacities centred on R to integrate adaptation capacities belonging to X, and therefore to maintain active relationships with a plurality of buyers.

In the case of more standardised technical knowledge, instead, the capacities of adaptation of X may be more easily separated from R. In this way R may characterise the activity of manufacturing and easily interchangeable producers, possibly as subcontractors. X may characterise the activity of specialised intermediaries, or may fall under the control of firms which integrate X and the downstream activity. The reference to the latter solution, seen as typical, justifies the expression of (worlds of) 'market networks'.

Adding up more qualifications on external and internal conditions allows a more articulate definition of the characters of techno-organisational equilibria. For example, a flexible specialisation production system featuring an industrial district has a localised set of strategic non-transferable technical resources, which allows the manifestation of potential economies of scope as agglomeration economies.[11] Then, the realisation of such economies as external economies can be supported by specific organisational resources.

Let us focus in the next section on some qualifications concerning precisely the character of economies of scale or scope and the availability of specific organisational resources.

4.   ECONOMIES OF SCALE AND SCOPE AND COLLECTIVE GOODS

In mass production, economies of scale are tied to conditions of consistency between market uniformity and technological standardisation. In the same way, in flexible specialisation economies of scope are tied to the convergence of investments in general capacities of adaptation.

In general terms the economies of scale (and of scope) go together with problems of consistency of the organisational design, which call for a convergent conduct on the part of a collectivity of production units.[12] When these economies involve a correct design of large parts of the overall system, the convergence at the base of their realisation is a collective good; more precisely it is a set of collective goods, since convergence is usually comprised of a set of different aspects.

The regulation by pure market transactions (among the agents of the production system) of a collective good is subject to failures resulting from the difficulties of bargaining the formation and management of large coalitions, with which may then be associated, in various ways, problems of definition of property rights, imperfection of information, and specificity (Inman 1987, Section 2). The costs of setting up and using markets are plausibly very high, and such as to block an internalisation (of the external effect connected to the collective good) pursued 'simply' through a more complete structure of the markets (Casson 1982, p. 189; Newberry 1989).

Another route to internalisation of the collective good, in particular of investment convergence, is business integration. This is exemplified by the mass production equilibrium discussed above. Here convergence is secured by hierarchically centralised governance, while conditions of market uniformity and technological standardisation reduce the influence costs typical of this solution (Milgron and Roberts 1992, pp. 272–3).

In the same way, in flexible specialisation the conditions of convergence and generality bring about systemic coordination and incentive problems, which imply high costs for a regulation based purely on the price system. However, in this case, the variability of the market imposes higher costs on a hierarchically centralised solution.

A potentially more promising type of solution lies in the definition of the convergence conditions in the form of 'market rules' set up by the collective action of the agents of the production system, and included within institutions of various kinds: collective contracts, conventions, and social customs.[13] Institutions of different types may operate jointly, with stratifications which also include, possibly, focused types of public intervention:[14] such as when public bodies for formal training sustain the production of new competencies inside the system according to some standard.[15] In such a case the economies of scale and of scope manifest themselves as economies partially external to the single firm, but internal to the given production system with its endowment of rules and institutions.[16]

In realistic conditions of positive transaction costs, economies of scale/scope involve – as such and contrary to Williamson's view – organisational problems. Their manifestation is interwoven with technical, organisational, and marketing factors.[17]

5. EQUILIBRIUM, ORGANIC PATH OF CHANGE, AND TRANSITION

What is the empirical importance of the techno-organisational equilibria? Of course, change of external conditions and internal endowments is the normal situation, at least in contemporary industry, but it may be sensible to distinguish among three different cases.

In the first case change is very slow and the stationary state, with an unchanging combination of external (market) and internal (endowment) conditions, is a good first approximation. In the second case change is steady, following a regular growth of the size and productivity of the set of specific resources; the incremental variations do not modify – or do so slowly – most of the general features of the prevailing techno-organisational configuration. In the third case change is discontinuous.

For an example of the last case, consider a steep decline in the principal markets for the typical products of a production system, which could be faced by producing classes of goods not so far from the typical ones (in technological terms), but nonetheless requiring a widespread adaptation of manufacturing and transaction standards and market channels, the disappearance of some of the traditional specialised manufacturing activities and resources, and the constitution of new local specialised activities and resources.[18]

The answer to the above question on empirical importance is thus twofold. From a strictly formal point of view, the only appropriate empirical application of a techno-organisational equilibrium is an approximated stationary state. From a more partial but sometimes useful point of view, it is possible to refer the equilibrium also to conditions of steady state.

By definition most of the general features of a techno-organisational configuration do not change in steady state; while the incremental adjustments in the other features may be seen as realised by the same incremental entrepreneurship whose reactions to small random shocks make for the stability of the stationary state. So, as far as the unchanging features are concerned, it is possible to describe the configuration of a steady state by means of a techno-organisational equilibrium, redesigned with respect to some stable logic of development of internal endowments in presence of growing opportunities in external markets. For example, this is the typical setting for the analyses of Italian industrial districts which took, as empirical reference, periods of pretty stable growth observed during the 1960s and 1970s.[19]

A path of change resulting from adjustments by incremental entrepreneurship – which I call an 'organic (or Marshallian) path' – may be a steady state for somewhat prolonged periods of time, possibly interposed with shorter periods of transition in which some of the main and generally stable features also change, even if incrementally all the same. The result of a process of transition is the constitution of a new equilibrium; which may be characterised, in general terms, by new sources of economies of scale or scope.[20]

Here we meet the problem of the multiplicity of possible maxima, given the set of feasible configurations. In traditional price theory a technology with increasing returns allows for a multiplicity of local maxima (in terms of a firm's profits). A similar result applies here for techno-organisational configuration in a production system, when (large) economies of scale/scope are assigned to some configurations within the feasible set.[21]

The problem with multiplicity is that the organic path may be trapped at a low level (in terms of aggregate profit, and consequently bad in terms of long run viability) maximum. This is so even if there are higher level but non-neighbouring equilibria, with superior potentialities for the constitution or re-constitution of economies of scale and/or scope.

Assuming the point of view of evolutionary economics, this inertia would help to explain the demography of production systems.

I here propose to consider the possibility that, within the endowment of strategic factors, there exist mechanisms and agents of adjustment which, in certain conditions, may allow the production system a higher degree of flexibility, that is a divergence from the organic path and thus the transition to a superior end-equilibrium.

In order to study the characteristics and the conditions of such solutions I think it useful to reconsider a model of entrepreneurial vertical integration proposed by Morris Silver (1984).

6. ENTREPRENEURIAL VERTICAL INTEGRATION: SILVER'S MODEL

The central theme of Silver's model concerns the solution to the incentive problems connected to innovative ideas whose realisation would imply an extended cooperation. The root of these problems, according to Silver, is that it is difficult for the entrepreneur to explain their idea to the producers of the specialised activities which contribute to the realisation of the project.

Silver refers to the conditions which block an effective communication of the innovative idea as 'information impactedness' – an expression publicised by Oliver Williamson. These conditions have a double meaning for the action of the entrepreneur. On one hand, they constitute a barrier to a quick entry of competing entrepreneurs (or to an excessive number of these), which may be a necessary condition for the existence of an incentive to action.

On the other hand, in conditions of information impactedness it may be difficult to obtain productive and commercial contributions from other agents, when these contributions require of such other agents investments with uncertain returns: that is, investments conditioned by the success of the entrepreneurial project. The entrepreneur is ready to bet on the quality of the idea; but may not be able, without an excessive effort, to persuade other producers characterised by different experiences. It follows that independent producers may not be inclined to make the necessary investments.

An important solution to this problem, according to Silver, lies in vertical integration, seen as a typical (but not unique) expression of centralisation, that is of asymmetrical distribution of decision making power in the organisation of production.

By vertical integration Silver intends the stipulation of employment contracts and the renting or the property of a set of complementary capital goods, all inside the entrepreneur's business. Employees' consensus is encouraged by a fact which often accompanies, for obvious reasons, the relationships of command, namely the decrease in value of the investments which weigh upon the employees themselves.

However, the integration of specialised activities within the central control of the entrepreneur presents some disadvantages as opposed to more decentralised organisations.

The direction of the activities absorbs the decision making capacities of the entrepreneur. These, even if vast, are nonetheless limited. The different operations are characterised by different bases of knowledge, more or less 'dissimilar' from those which the entrepreneur dominates with greater confidence and which often incorporate the new idea.[22] As the similarity diminishes, the average productivity of the employment of the entrepreneurial resources also diminishes. This explains a greater employment of other inputs than that carried out by specialised producers. The ensuing difference of cost will grow with the growth of the dissimilarity of the integrated activities with respect the entrepreneur's know-how.

Instead, in the absence of general reasons for assuming differently, the marginal reduction of cost of information transmission, which stems from the integration of an activity instead of entrusting it to a specialised producer, is given as a constant.

Given the time and context, to which we will return later, the equilibrium level of vertical integration is defined by a set including the more similar activities, and in which the marginal activity, that is the more dissimilar in the set, has a marginal cost of vertical integration almost equal to the benefits (savings on information transmission costs). Correspondingly, each activity in the complementary set is more dissimilar than those included in the integrated set and would imply, if integrated, marginal costs superior to the benefits.

As time passes and if the enterprise succeeds, the difficulties of transmission of the new idea to complementary producers tend to decrease. Nothing is as successful as success, at least in demonstrating the economic feasibility of the innovation. Other things being equal, the ensuing reduction of the costs of communication to independent producers would imply a reduction of the equilibrium level of vertical integration.

On the other hand, the learning and the setting up of routines within the entrepreneur's firm mean, in the absence of other factors of change and adaptation after the original one (represented by the innovation with integration), the reduction of the difference between the internal production costs of the entrepreneur's firm and the specialised producers' costs. And this may reduce the extension of vertical dis-integration within the entrepreneur's firm. However, new firms which enter the industry drawn by the success of the incumbent entrepreneur will not benefit, at first, from such learning effects, and will show the lower level of vertical integration.[23]

Other changes possibly follow from learning effects within the new-comers' and within the independent producers' firms, which however do not modify in general the result of the model: that is that the extension of vertical integration in one or more industries tends to increase in correspondence with the introduction of large scale innovative ideas; while it tends to decrease in correspondence with the success and the diffusion of the same ideas.[24]

7. VARIATIONS ON SILVER'S THEME

Let us now try to make explicit an element of generalisation which does not contradict the results of Silver's model. Such an element concerns the hypothesis on the initial endowment – in the production system in which the innovative entrepreneur operates – of skills, communication structures, and collaboration routines between firms and/or within firms.

Starting with skill endowment, note that Silver imagines a situation in which the specialised skills are available and adequate; the entrepreneur must only explain the type of intermediate goods or services required and the producers are able to correspond adequately. However such a hypothesis of 'absence (of need) of training (of skills)' may prove severely limiting. The introduction of training needs reduces the homogeneity of the conditions of the Silver model but does not bring about major changes in the analytic picture. Other things being equal, a need for training brings about an increase of the level of the differential costs of transmission of the information to independent producers, and a reduction of the difference of internal produc-tion costs. The result is the strengthening of vertical integration.

The dynamic predictions may also be maintained, at least if we accept the interpretative picture proposed by Paul Auerbach, when he declares that the diffusion, over time, of a growing level of technical and managerial skilfulness creates 'an infrastructure which makes market solutions possible and therefore acts against the forces of vertical integration' (Auerbach 1988, pp. 222–4).

In a similar vein we can enlarge the implications of other variables of the Silver model. Let us therefore consider the case of information impactedness. In certain situations communication costs tend to be higher and in other situations the same costs tend to be lower. For example, a typical characteristic of production systems in many Italian industrial districts (and not only Italian) is represented by the practice of face-to-face contacts, of personal acquaintance, and circulation and discussion of new ideas. We may hypothesise that these characteristics, if present in the initial situation from which an entrepreneurial project of transition starts, decrease communication costs and therefore decrease, other things being equal, the extension of vertical integration.

A last premise regarding the set of possible organisations may be usefully articulated. Silver, in describing his model, adopts one variable to define organisational solutions: the extension of vertical integration. But the same author, in the application of the model, takes account of the possibility of intermediate solutions, between vertical integration and market transactions. Among these are the collaboration (cooperation) mechanisms based on the acceptance between independent contracting parties of some degree of obligation – and therefore of a certain degree of insurance – regarding future conduct (Richardson 1972), and more generally based on the recognition of common rules between agents (in the same production system).

If the entrepreneurial project implies specific investments for suppliers, however, the possibility of collaboration does not modify Silver's picture: if the project fails and with this also the entrepreneur's firm fails, the capacity of the same to fulfil economic commitments decreases drastically.

The picture changes if instead the collaboration permits the identification of contexts in which suppliers' risks are reduced. For example, investments may be oriented so that they are not strictly tied to the entrepreneur's project, but they can be applied to a larger set of different projects.

In this case, the vertical control of the entrepreneur will remain important, within the relationship of collaboration with specialised producers, so as to ensure the coordination of supplies, the adaptation of skills, and the reduction of risks in investments for specialised production.

Nevertheless, such vertical control can be carried out even in the absence of vertical integration: as with the quasi-vertical integration in which highly specific machinery used by specialised suppliers is owned by the commissioning firm; or in the case of the relationships between the big Japanese firm and its suppliers, and in the case of input-output relationships among firms within the industrial district; or in the relationship of franchising. Communication costs of collaboration might not be negligible. However, they are limited by traditions of inter-firm collaboration; eventually connected to practices of face-to-face contacts, personal acquaintance, and so forth, such as those recalled above in relation to the industrial district.

8. SYSTEMIC ENTREPRENEURSHIP AND PATHS OF NON-ORGANIC TRANSITION

The variations proposed in Section 7 help to draw a linkage between Silver's model and the analysis of paths of transition implying the constitution of potentialities of new economies of scale/scope.

According to William Lazonick it is precisely the strategy of setting up integrated complexes of skills which permits the constitution of new opportunities of economies of scale and economies of scope. Such opportunities are not subjected for a certain time to the potential competition of firms which have not developed the same skills, and which are not able to gain them rapidly on the market, since – for a certain time – such skills are tied to the innovative firm by the peculiarity of the ways in which these skills have been formed and put together (Lazonick 1991, Chapter 3).

Rephrasing Lazonick's model in terms of the above defined relation between economies of scale and collective goods: an innovative idea which implies the constitution of potentialities of new economies at the production system level also implies a web of new collective goods which does not have (or not easily) an appropriate governance solution by way of the existing structure of markets, market rules and public policies. Here the distinction made by David Teece between 'autonomous innovation' and 'systemic innovation' can be properly applied.[25]

Who is the entrepreneur able to take responsibility for such complexities? Their identity should not correspond to that of the incremental entrepreneurs defined above. But among the 'crowd' there can be a few who have the mental and economic power necessary for supporting the hazards of a systemic trial. I would call a 'systemic entrepreneur' one whose project implies, for a production system, a variation in several aspects of the techno-organisational configuration and of the mechanisms of reproduction of the internal endowment of strategic resources.

A potentially successful systemic entrepreneur has a wide if not necessarily very accurate perception of the web, in relation to their innovative idea and its potentialities of economies of scale/scope. This complexity will add to the difficulties of communication to independent producers, while the uncertainties surrounding a partially or obscurely perceived need for new collective goods will add to the risks perceived by potential independent suppliers.

Coordination and incentive problems of the Silver type have, in these conditions, a large ground of manifestation. The entrepreneurial project should include, on the organisational side, a relatively large extension of various forms of vertical control, which constrain the choices and rewards of a relatively large set of incremental entrepreneurs.

The eventual success of the project brings about a reduction in the advantages of vertical control through the potential reduction of communication costs to independent producers. The push towards vertical disintegration is also strengthened by the possible delimitation of economies of scale at the level of a single activity, which demand a large size of the latter. Large savings of the entrepreneur's decision-making power may be achieved by outsourcing dissimilar activities characterised by large economies of scale.[26]

However, the realisation of these disintegration effects is conditioned by the type of world of production which the entrepreneur's project is aiming at, and by other factors: the presence and quality of other systemic entrepreneurial projects; the initial endowment of strategic resources diffused among the agents of the production system; and finally, the organisational solutions adopted in the entrepreneurial project, involving particular organising skills which remain incorporated in the system for a while.

Summing up, the result of the above analytical hints is the outline of a possible framework for the study of 'non-organic' paths of transition in a production system. Systemic entrepreneurship, promoting the constitution of potentialities of new scale or scope economies, is at the core of adjustment mechanisms which enlarge the capacity of a production system to cope with important variations in the relations between external conditions and the internal endowment of strategic productive factors, and thus in its space of competitive advantage.

9. DISCONTINUOUS CHANGE IN INDUSTRIAL DISTRICTS

We have seen in Section 4 that the realisation of large potential external economies within a flexible specialisation equilibrium calls for the availability of collective goods, as market rules and products of focused public intervention, complementing market relations among the specialised firms of a production system. We are now able to investigate some aspects of the constitution of these conditions.

We will consider just two cases: (1) the transition from a flexible specialisation equilibrium to a non-neighbouring new flexible specialisation equilibrium; and (2) the transition from a mass production equilibrium to a flexible specialisation equilibrium.[27]

In a previous paper of mine (Bellandi 1996) the principal results of the transitional model are applied, together with other models, to a reflection on possible paths of non-organic transition in production systems featuring industrial districts when they meet conditions of discontinuous change.

The production system which is the main industry of an industrial district may be defined as a type whose internal endowment of non-transferable factors is tied to the socioeconomic relationships developing within the set of localities constituting the district, and whose possible techno-organisational configurations share some features. They are: (1) on the technical side, a large vertical specialisation and a relatively low level of specificity among subsets of horizontally specialised assets localised in a relatively limited territory; and (2) on the organisational side, a large division of labour among specialised firms and a complex, not fixed, mix of competition and cooperation among them.

Flexible specialisation equilibria, like those defined previously, are largely consistent with such a type of production system.[28]

The situation of discontinuous change discussed in that paper concerns the transition from an old flexible specialisation equilibrium to a possible new flexible specialisation equilibrium, still consistent with the district form.

The general problem which arises there is that, if a successful systemic project is realised by means of a very high degree of vertical integration, then this tends to wipe out from the district a large part of any previous experience of diffused incremental entrepreneurship and internal market relations. This situation tends, even after the success of the innovative idea, to hold up the entry of independent specialised suppliers, the entry of newcomers competing with the incumbent firm of the systemic entrepreneur, and an appropriate constitution of market rules.

The discussion goes on to show that other forms of organisational solution to transition exist which can allow for the coexistence of an appropriate degree of systemic orientation of investments and the survival, within the endowment of factors of the production system, of a rich enough fabric of experience in market relations.

Two solutions are discussed in particular: (1) 'community leadership', constituted by a set of interlinked unions, business associations, universities, and political leaders, aiming at the constitution of collective real services and training centres; and (2) 'business leadership', constituted by a few more structured firms working within the district, who are able to support partly systemic projects with some extension of vertical control and integration, but who also break the ice for a larger population of followers.[29]

10.   THE CONSTITUTION OF EXTERNAL ECONOMIES

We come now to the second case. I here propose another application of the transitional model, consisting in re-reading the choice of productive decentralisation in a production system characterised by the dominance of mass production and vertically integrated firms. Stories consistent with the following model are presented for example by Gabi Dei Ottati (1994), referring to the metamorphosis in the structure of Prato's textile industry which brought about the birth of Prato's industrial district in the early 1950s; and by Michael Storper (1989), referring to the metamorphosis of Hollywood's movie industry in the mid-1940s.

Let us consider a situation of increase in unpredictability of demand, with consequences in terms of conflict and dismissals in the labour markets within the production system. Such deterioration may be the result of various influences, which we will pass over. The crisis is prolonged. A systemic entrepreneurial project is conceived: a restructuring project which accepts, as a medium term fact, some turbulence in product markets and recognises in the labour conflicts, and in the existence of a mass of laid-off employees with various qualifications, the opportunity to resort (at least temporarily) to 'production decentralisation'. That is, to stop carrying out some activities inside and to acquire their products or services from small specialised suppliers. Part of the fixed costs of the integrated firm become variable costs.

However, the solution is not automatic. The entrepreneur must persuade some of his technicians to start an independent activity as suppliers, carrying out some of the specialised activities of the integrated firm.[30] Communication costs are, however, high since the technicians are aware that product markets are unstable and are not sure that the proposal might not turn out to be useless and unworkable.

Then we may expect the constitution of relations of vertical control: for example, relationships of financial and technical assistance designed to reduce the amount of risk weighing on suppliers' investments.

If in this case the project is carried out and starts meeting with success, the other vertically integrated firms will follow suit. And because the very success of the new strategy depresses the market still further for firms sticking to the old strategy, the set of specialised suppliers may easily grow.

Note that the organisational solution for the transition entails a reduction in the extension of vertical integration, in favour of a vertical control in the sphere of a relationship of asymmetric collaboration. This is not the final result at which the entrepreneur aims, but just a transitional solution. The entrepreneur wants to decrease fixed costs, widening the sphere of their suppliers; this is the final aim (in the medium term). But the entrepreneur cannot bring about this change directly; they must pass through a solution of vertical control – that is of greater centralisation with respect to the aim – which decreases the risks for specialised producers.

Furthermore, if supplier relations continue along the same lines, the skills of specialised firms will tend to grow, and this will make the return to a high degree of vertical integration less profitable.[31] The end result can be either a market network equilibrium or a flexible specialisation equilibrium, if the new configuration of the production system does not allow the recovery of a high degree of stability and homogeneity on final markets.

In both cases the new configuration is characterised by sets of complementary specialised firms realising external economies of scale and scope; but in the first case the economies are largely internal to the networks led by a few entrepreneurs, in the second case the economies are partly external also to single networks but largely internal to the production system.

We may wonder what the conditions are that make the first or the second result relatively more probable. The transitional mechanism described just above is of the 'business leadership' type. I would maintain that a decisive role is played here by characteristics of the endowment of factors of the production system which are not directly affected by the working of such a mechanism.

In particular, referring to the above mentioned historical cases, the local availability of a multiplicity of specialised capacities connected with the principal industry, and a supporting collective action by local or regional, private or public, organisations seem to favour a flexible specialisation result with strong local characteristics. Instead, the capacity of the systemic entrepreneur to tap global reserves of standard subcontracting capacity, and to coordinate extended networks, should favour the market network solution.

It should be clear, lastly, that the mental and economic power of a systemic entrepreneur does not always make for a successful transition. And even when a systemic project supports an effective transition, allowing a new lease of life for a large part of the internal resources of a production system, the characteristics of the end-equilibrium may be very different from what was in the entrepreneur's mind.

CONCLUSIONS

In industrial economics it is usual to find two conceptions of the relationship between economies of scale and dynamics. The first highlights the presence of economies of scale inside functions of research and development directed to the acceleration of economic progress. The second conception draws attention to how the realisation of economies of scale demands an adaptation process of the economic structures.

In the picture developed in this chapter it becomes difficult to retain a clear distinction between the aspects at the centre of the two conceptions. It follows that the combination of potential extent of the market – and therefore also of production system size – with elements of resource endowment and transitional organisation, according to the knowledge that the entrepreneur more easily controls, guides the constitution of economies appropriate to that size.

Similarly, the terms of Edith Penrose's distinction between economies of growth and economies of scale tend to fade. According to this distinction the economies of growth inside the firm, tied to the possibility of developing new activities and lines of business making full use of under-utilised productive capacities, do not necessarily translate into economies of scale. When a new activity is established, the totality of the resources (in the first place, skills) which permit the reproduction of such an activity may turn out to be not strictly dependent upon the central abilities which have sustained its development in the firm. In such a case the new activity may be detached from the parent firm without loss of efficiency.

However, in our framework of dynamic analysis, the techno-organisational solutions of the end-equilibria reveal themselves as partially (but always) conditioned by the centralised solutions of transition. That is because these involve particular organising skills, which remain incorporated in the system even after the transition.

Nevertheless, this does not always and necessarily translate into internal economies of scale. In the first place, this is because some dynamic (transitional) contexts of constitution of economies of scale/scope are compatible with different forms, not necessarily internal, of centralisation of the investment decision making. In the second place, it is because in such contexts the advantages of business specialisation when large potentials for economies of scale or scope are constituted show themselves as a strong push towards decentralisation.

A final consideration concerns the role of face-to-face contacts, personal ties, and attitudes to the local circulation of new approaches to production and trade, which we have met in some sections above. They are characteristic, if not exclusive, of production systems with a regional (or sub-regional) territorial basis. They tend to decrease (not to cancel out) the need of transitional centralisation for the implementation of systemic projects and to embed them within the local or the regional context. Such a relationship is an enduring force behind regions in the midst of change. The constitution of new scale and scope economies as agglomeration economies is supported by regional centralisation as a partial substitute for entrepreneurial centralisation, and vice versa.

NOTES

1. Transferability here means, in the case of human capital assets, the possibility of moving their application by means of emigration/immigration flows; in the case of technical assets it means the possibility of trading them on general external markets. According to

Antonelli (1995, p. 103), the coexistence of different paths of technological change on global markets is also explained by the diversity of the starting point connected to particularities of national factor markets. We will come back to non-transferability later.

2. (Vertical) specialisation here mean that, within a complex production process, different phases (that is, activities) are distinguished, and attributed as the task of different sets of human and technical assets. The degree of specificity is here defined as an aggregate index which depends upon how much the productivity of human and technical assets can be potentially increased by means of differentiation, that is 'horizontal specialisation': a partition of the assets within each activity, such that each subset is 'specifically' adapted to the characteristics of other particular subsets in the other activities. The increase of productivity is only potential because the under-utilisation of the capacity of the horizontally differentiated assets is not excluded. The concept of specificity is at the centre of the development of Williamson's transaction cost theory during the 1980s. See Williamson (1989). The concept which I adopt presently is designed, as in Seravalli (1993, p. 25), to distinguish between (vertical) specialisation and asset specificity.

3. These range from the type centred on the large vertically integrated firm, in which that division of labour is almost absent, to the networks led by large diversified firms, to systems of small businesses featuring many Italian industrial districts, where no firm has a dominant position in the system.

4. Here we could distinguish systems in which the location of firms is more or less agglomerated.

5. An example of unfeasibility is an abstract configuration combining specialisation among agents and autarchy of each agent.

6. So the firm-family relations are at the base of the reproduction of the fabric of many working and entrepreneurial attitudes; and local organisations of various types play a supporting role to the activities of local small firms, supplying essential collective goods like, for example, basic technical education, local standards for manufacturing and transacting, general information on external markets, fiscal law, and so forth, and specific infrastructure (collective industrial purifiers, and so on).

7. The hypothesis which attributes to a population of entrepreneurs an ability to locally maximise aggregate profits may seem particularly heroic. It must however be considered that what counts, in the model under examination, are the differences of profit among the configurations within reach; and these configurations constitute a set bound in various ways. First of all, as we have seen, there is the neighbourhood limitation. Secondly, there is the limitation implicit in the assumption of the production system as the unit of analysis.

8. The first reason for non-viability may be excluded, for example, by the conditions of institutionalised potential conflict between the workforce and the entrepreneurs within the firms, which limit the short term instability connected to attempts at exploitation of the workers, and which Brusco (1982) attributes to the production systems typical of the 'Emilian model'. For other examples, explicitly applied to a production system context, see Dei Ottati (1994).

9. See also, on generality of capacity, Pagano (1991).

10. This is a way to recover Stigler's intuition of a relation between small and young markets and vertical integration. See Stigler (1951).

11. For examples, economies of pooled reserves, when similar firms of the upstream phases constitute a virtual collective warehouse of production capacities for demands of a certain type coming from the downstream phases, are supported by the proximity of the firms, which makes easier adaptation of supplying networks through face-to-face contacts and reduces the transport costs for quick supplies.

12. According to Milgron and Roberts (1992, pp. 91–3) they are 'design problems': 'These are problems in which (1) there is a great deal of a priori information about the form of the optimal solution, that is, about how the variables should be related, and (2) failing to achieve the right relationship among the variables is generally more costly than are other kinds of errors, including slight miss-specifications of the overall pattern, as long as the individual pieces fit.' Size is not enough; the design nature of economies of scale/scope comes from the need to use selectively large capacities in productive services.

13. See Piore and Sabel (1984); Becattini (1990, p. 42); Salais and Storper (1992). Such institutions are not necessarily the result of conscious action.
14. Public intervention has high costs in these cases, when it is conceived in a centralised form, and translates into regulations imposed from above on market situations which present a large variety of cases.
15. See, for example, Brusco (1982). In the case of market networks, the institutional role is played firstly by the leading firms.
16. This is a variation on a well known, if not largely appreciated, Marshallian theme. See Becattini (1989).
17. In a model criticised by Williamson (1975, pp. 17–19), Stigler (1951) suggests the importance of this interweaving, but he gives an explicit analysis of only few and selected relations, in which organisational aspects are only implicitly accounted for. I would refer to Bellandi (1995, Chapters 2–5) for some considerations of mine on this theme of Stigler. See Dietrich (1994, p. 138) and Jacquemin (1987, Chapter V) for some general statements on the interweaving of production and transaction costs.
18. Empirical situations of discontinuous change are described, for example, in Crevoisier (1993) and Cooke and Morgan (1994).
19. Becattini (1990). See Bellandi and Russo (1994) for some reflections on the definition of the steady state logic sustaining the stability of production systems featuring industrial districts. Of course, it is possible to define different mechanisms of growth. See Penrose (1980) on the steady state logic sustaining configurations centred in a large diversified firm.
20. 'Sourcing' in the sense that, as in Marshall, the realisation of economies of scale is evolving through time with the accumulation of experience and ideas in a certain context of technical and organisational problems.
21. Let us again consider the stylised (R, A) representation of the worlds of production. The absence of (large) economies of scale/scope would imply the possibility of reproducing on a very small scale the overall features of different configurations. Thus it would fall within the span of action of each single incremental entrepreneur to adopt – for their own single concern, or for single parts of it – one or another among the different feasible configurations. In that case there would be only one equilibrium at the level of the production system, corresponding to the sum of the configurations chosen by the single entrepreneurs. In sections 3, 4 above the definition of techno-organisational equilibria has been implicitly referred to a situation in which a proper realisation of economies of scale/scope typical of each world demands the cooperation of large parts of a production system.
22. On the concept of similarity and dissimilarity see Richardson (1972).
23. Let us note that this is a case of 'internal vertical equilibrium' in an industry according to the definition of Perry (1989, p. 232): a vertical equilibrium in that 'no firm would alter its choice of the stages in which it operates', an internal one since firms with different degrees of vertical integration coexist.
24. It is interesting to notice how coordination and incentive problems are wedded in the Silver model. The reduction in communication costs which accompanies the success of the entrepreneurial project may be interpreted not only in terms of a decreasing effort of persuasion, but also in terms of the easier constitution of market rules and standards which facilitate the workings of the price system: with success certain problems which were not routine become recurrent. On the other hand, the diversity in the degree of integration, between incumbents and newcomers, is to be interpreted, also in Silver's terms, by the fact that the first have had time to develop (as a joint product of experience) internal routines, which guide the internal decentralisation of coordination problems, permitting the reduction of the internal costs of coordination. Some more considerations on the subject are in Bellandi (1995, Chapter 6).
25. See Teece (1988, p. 26). Cooke and Morgan (1994, p. 94), talking of what I would define as a situation of discontinuous change for some production systems centred in Baden-Wurttemberg, describe the systemic content of a possible discontinuous transition: '... what the "lean" message was pointing to was the need for "systems integration" of many of the discrete managerial and production innovations perceived as being Japanese in

152   *Inside the district*

origin. The key point here is that in isolation they seldom lead to major quality or productivity improvements'. Obviously here we also borrow a Schumpeterian theme.
26. Here Silver (1984, p. 134) meets Stigler (1951) and his idea of a push towards division of labour among firms implied by large economies of scale in specialised activities.
27. The second case is, almost by definition, a case of non-organic transition. The first one is a case of non-organic transition since we suppose that the new flexible specialisation equilibrium corresponds to a configuration which dominates the old equilibrium but which escapes the capacity of adjustment by pure incremental entrepreneurship. That is, there are multiple non-neighbouring local maxima and the system, if led only by incremental entrepreneurs, is trapped in a low level local maximum. Another relevant case of constitution of new large external economies is the transition from an innovation equilibrium to a market network or to a flexible specialisation equilibrium. For this last case see Langlois (1992). For more on the overall question, see Bellandi (1995, Chapters 6 and 7).
28. But of course, there are both flexible specialisation equilibria not consistent, and equilibria of other worlds of production which could be consistent with such a type.
29. Brusco (1990); Asheim (1994); Cooke and Morgan (1994). The theory of leadership by F. Perroux could also be applied here. See Russo (1996).
30. The activities will be chosen from among those less tied to the productive core of the same firm. In some models of productive decentralisation the decentralised activities are the more dirty and labour intensive. For a review, see Brusco (1990).
31. Here the dynamic effects may play a role unexpected by the entrepreneur, but consistent with the previsions of the model. The entrepreneur could have a vision, according to which the instability of the market will cease or decrease in the long run. The entrepreneur could also connect this to the recovering of a high degree of vertical integration after the crisis.

REFERENCES

Antonelli, C. (1995), *The Economics of Localized Technological Change and Industrial Dynamics*, Dordrecht: Kluwer Academic.
Asheim, B. (1994), 'Industrial districts, inter-firm co-operation and endogenous technological development: the experience of developed countries', in Unctad and Deutches Zentrum fur Entwicklungstechnologien (eds), *Technological Dynamism in Industrial Districts: an Alternative Approach to Industrialization in Developing Countries?*, New York and Geneva: United Nations, pp. 91–142.
Auerbach, P. (1988), *Competition: The Economics of Industrial Change*, Oxford: Basil Blackwell.
Becattini, G. (1989), 'Sectors and/or districts: some remarks on the conceptual foundations of industrial economics', in E. Goodman and G. Bamford (eds), *Small Firms and Industrial Districts in Italy*, London: Routledge, pp. 123–35.
Becattini, G. (1990), 'The Marshallian industrial district as a socio-economic notion', in F. Pyke, G. Becattini and W. Sengenberger (eds), *Industrial Districts and Inter-Firm Cooperation in Italy*, Geneva: International Institute for Labour Studies, pp. 37–51.
Bellandi, M. (1995), *Economie di scala e organizzazione industriale*, Milan: Franco Angeli.
Bellandi, M. (1996), 'Innovation and change in the Marshallian industrial district', *European Planning Studies*, 4: 353–64.
Bellandi, M. and M. Russo (eds) (1994), *Distretti industriali e cambiamento economico locale*, Turin: Rosenberg & Sellier.

Brusco, S. (1982), 'The Emilian model: productive decentralization and social integration', *Cambridge Journal of Economics*, 6: 167–84.

Brusco, S. (1990), 'The idea of the industrial district: its genesis', in F. Pyke, G. Becattini and W. Sengenberger (eds), *Industrial Districts and Inter-Firm Cooperation in Italy*, Geneva: International Institute for Labour Studies, pp. 10–19.

Casson, M. (1982), *The Entrepreneur: An Economic Theory*, Oxford: Martin Robertson.

Cooke, P. and K. Morgan (1994), 'Growth regions under duress: renewal strategies in Baden Wurttemberg and Emilia Romagna', in A. Amin and N. Thrift (eds), *Globalization, Institutions, and Regional Development in Europe*, Oxford: Oxford University Press.

Crevoisier, O. (1993), 'Spatial shifts and the emergence of innovative milieux', *Environment and Planning*, 11: 419–30.

Dei Ottati, G. (1994), 'Prato and its evolution in a European context', in R. Leonardi and R.Y. Nanetti (eds), *Regional Development in a Modern European Economy: The Case of Tuscany*, London: Pinter.

Dietrich, M. (1994), *Transaction Cost Economics and Beyond*, London: Routledge.

Inman, R.P. (1987), 'Markets, government and the "new" political economy', in A.J. Auerbach and M. Feldstein (eds), *Handbook of Public Economics*, Amsterdam: North Holland, pp. 647–77.

Jacquemin, A. (1987), *The New Industrial Organisation*, Oxford: Clarendon Press.

Langlois, R.N. (1992), 'External economies and economic progress: the case of the microcomputer industry', *Business History Review*, 66: 1–50.

Lazonick, W. (1991), *Business Organisation and The Myth of the Market Economy*, Cambridge: Cambridge University Press.

Milgron, P. and J. Roberts (1992), *Economics, Organisation, and Management*, Englewood Cliffs, NJ: Prentice-Hall International.

Newberry, D.M. (1989), 'Missing markets: consequences and remedies', in F. Hahn (ed.), *The Economics of Missing Markets, Information, and Games*, Oxford: Clarendon Press, pp. 211–42.

Pagano, U. (1991), 'Property rights equilibria and institutional stability', *Economic Notes*, 2: 189–228.

Pagano, U. and R. Rowthorn (1993), 'Economic democracy in a world of self-sustaining institutions', Paper given at the International School of Economic Research: Economics and Politics, Certosa di Pontignano, Siena (Italy), 4–10 July.

Penrose, E.T. (1980), *The Theory of the Growth of the Firm*, second edition, Oxford: Basil Blackwell.

Perry, M.K. (1989), 'Vertical integration: determinants and effects', in R. Schmalensee and R.D. Willig (eds), *Handbook of Industrial Organisation*, Amsterdam: Elsevier, Vol. 1, pp. 183–255.

Piore, M. and C. Sabel (1984), *The Second Industrial Divide. Possibilities for Prosperity*, New York: Basic Books.

Richardson, G.B. (1972), 'The organisation of industry', *Economic Journal*, September: 883–96.

Russo, M. (1996), 'Units of investigation for local economic development policies', *Economie appliquée*, 1: 85–118.

Salais, R. and M. Storper (1992), 'The four "worlds" of contemporary industry', *Cambridge Journal of Economics*, 16: 169–93.

Seravalli, G. (1993), 'L'organizzazione dei rapporti di subfornitura: profili teorici', Paper presented to the *International Seminar on Small Business and Local Development*, Parma, 28–30 September, pp. 1–23.

Silver, M. (1984), *Enterprise and the Scope of the Firm: The Role of Vertical Integration*, Oxford: Martin Robertson.

Stigler, G.J. (1951), 'The division of labour is limited by the extent of the market', *Journal of Political Economy*, June: 185–93.

Storper, M. (1989), 'The transition to flexible specialisation in the US film industry: external economies, the division of labour, and the crossing of industrial divides', *Cambridge Journal of Economics*, 13: 273–305.

Storper, M. and B. Harrison (1991), 'Flexibility, hierarchy and regional development: the changing structure of industrial production systems and their forms of governance in the 1990s', *Research Policy*, 20: 407–22.

Teece, D.J. (1988), 'Technological change and the nature of the firm', in G. Dosi, C. Freeman, R. Nelson and G. Silvenberg (eds), *Technological Change and Economic Theory*, London: Pinter, pp. 256–81.

Williamson, O.E. (1975), *Markets and Hierarchies: Analysis and Antitrust Implications*, New York: Free Press.

Williamson, O.E. (1989), 'Transaction cost economics', in R. Schmalensee and R.D. Willig (eds), *Handbook of Industrial Organisation*, Amsterdam: Elsevier, Vol. 1, pp. 136–82.

PART III

Towards Local Development

8. Local development in the experience of Italian industrial districts

Fabio Sforzi

INTRODUCTION

Italy has gained a reputation as a country of small firms. True enough, there are more small companies in Italy than in other industrialised nations (Table 8.1). However, studying a country's economic structure through the size of its industries is not a purely statistical, neutral and objective approach, but a distinct choice of perspective that pinpoints the business as a suitable unit of analysis for studying the national economic system. If one is not aware of this, one commits a serious error without even realising it. The practical implications that arise from this approach involve the specific features of the national economy, as well as the industrial policy measures such features can suggest or compel.

In my view, the company – be it a small business or a large factory – should always be viewed as part of its socio-geographical context. The economic and geographical literature, both theoretical and applied, usually accepts this perspective for small companies, but does not extend it to other firms. This is an anachronistic attitude, especially in today's post-Fordist world, when even the largest firms are focusing ever more frequently on vertical dis-integration and on searching for local-external economies by finding other companies with which to share the major phases of manufacturing and service provision.

Of course, this focus on the local business community applies automatically to small companies, since they seek and achieve economies in production outside their own walls, within the local system where production takes place and interacts with the social environment. The source of the gains in productivity and innovation shifts from the individual company to its local system, which becomes, to all intents, the real unit of production.

Therefore, a country's economy can be described by means of its local systems of firms (Sforzi 1996), some of which will be manufacturers while others will be, say, tourist or agro-industrial concerns. Some will be *industrial districts* (made up of small and medium-sized enterprises), and others will be *industrial poles* because they consist of large firms that dominate the productive fabric and lead the local economy (Figure 8.1).

What really sets the Italian economy apart from those of other nations is its high number of industrial districts, with respect to its manufacturing local systems as a whole.

Table 8.1   Employment shares by enterprise size, manufacturing industries, 1990s (percentage values)

Enterprise size	Italy	Germany	France	UK	Spain	USA	Japan
	1991	1992	1992	1993	1991	1991	1991
Up to 250	71.4	37.5[b]	47.0	44.5	67.8	36.6[e]	74.1[g]
From 1 to 9	23.3	7.4	8.1	7.2	18.3	3.0[d]	5.0[d]
From 10 to 49	29.2	14.3	17.7	15.6	29.1	n/a	n/a
From 50 to 249	18.9	15.8[a]	21.2	21.7	20.4	n/a	n/a
More than 250	28.6	62.5[c]	53.0	55.5	32.2	63.4[f]	25.9[h]
Total	100.0	100.0	100.0	100.0	100.0	100.0	100.0

Notes:
(a) From 50 to 199.
(b) Less than 200.
(c) More than 200.
(d) From 1 to 10.
(e) Less than 500.
(f) More than 500.
(g) Less than 300.
(h) More than 300.

Source: Brusco and Paba (1997)

1.   THE MAIN FEATURES OF INDUSTRIAL DISTRICTS

Industrial districts are local systems with an active co-presence of people and of a primary industry consisting of small, independent firms specialised in the different phases of a single production process.

'Active co-presence' means that the community plays an independent role in organising the production activity, which arises from its social culture. A system of values and rules – dominated by a spirit of initiative and widely shared in terms of the main aspects of life, such as work, consumption, saving, and attitudes toward uncertainty – creates a cultural environment that fosters business ventures and has an influence on industrial relations and local government decisions. The high aptitude and enthusiasm of individuals and families for self-employment – be it working at home, practising a craft or trade, running a small business or working freelance – favour the development and diffusion of organisational skills, creativity, pragmatism and individual and group capabilities.

Meanwhile, the production setup created through independent small and medium-sized firms, each of which tends to cover an individual phase of production, and which are connected by specialised transaction networks and coordinated by more or less explicit forms of cooperation, is made possible by the fact that the production process is technically divisible and profits from local-external economies as well as internal economies of scale.

This division of labour among the firms results from an increase in the demand for goods which is not standardised, but rather highly fragmented in terms of the quality and timing required. The localised industry of the district is highly adaptable and can easily meet the needs for elasticity (posed by quantitative changes in demand) and flexibility (requiring qualitative changes in output) thanks to the practical skills of its workers and the specificity of the production formula.

Organisational intelligence, experimental and practical skills, creative and inventive talent, craftsmanship, technical abilities and a capacity for innovation are what make the district dynamic, and what give it its strength in the realm of international competition.

The district's primary industry – together with the auxiliary industries and the many services it needs to function – tends to pervade the community, providing jobs to practically every layer of the population: youths, adults and elderly people, men and women alike. The result is a local community dominated by small business owners and self-employed workers, employees, and the widespread participation in the business by young people and married women, while the extended family is the typical household structure. It is easy to understand why the population of a district tends to be community-oriented, rather than firm-oriented as in the case of industrial poles overshadowed by large corporations.

As for creating the knowledge needed to pursue the business, a vital role is played in industrial districts by tacit rather than codified knowledge. While the latter is tied in with technical progress and transferability mechanisms that act through the market, tacit knowledge is a form of ability that depends on the specific sociocultural environment where production takes place, and which is rooted in the actions of the economic agents belonging to that

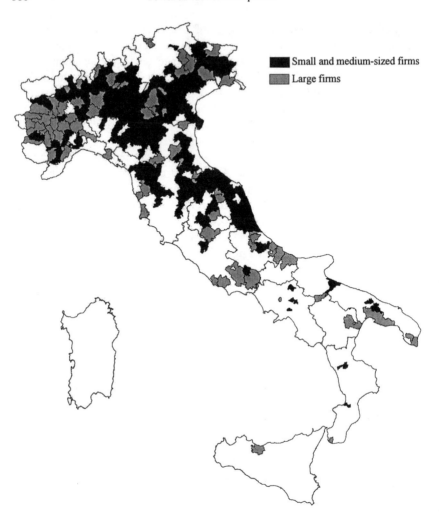

Figure 8.1 The manufacturing local systems by firm size, 1990s

Source: Compiled by the author

environment. It spreads throughout the local production community mainly by means of personal, direct contact, and is based on untraded interdependencies associated with the daily business routine, rather than on traded interdependencies involving input and output relationships. Therefore, it is both human and social capital, in other words *individual production know-how* (human capital) consisting in the accumulated learning of each person, mainly through education, training and experience, and *collective production know-how* (social capital) consisting in the learning amassed through the relational structures between individuals. The latter consists essentially of common knowledge that is created and propagated within the community, collective abilities as regards stimulation, coordination and regulation, and, in general, the set of institutions that fosters organisation and helps reduce transaction costs. In this sense, the district is both a place to accumulate business and life experiences and a place to collect new production knowledge, and these are the crucial resources in contemporary capitalist development.

Of course, the district's capacity for innovation does not depend simply on its wealth of tacit knowledge, but on its ability to integrate that with codified knowledge. In other words, it has to be able to appropriate and internalise codified knowledge, that is, to adapt it to and absorb it into the local production process. This triggers an expansion of knowledge and generates a steady flow of *new* tacit knowledge, which is socialised through the sharing of experiences. For a district, the ability to maintain its competitive advantage over time depends on how well it integrates the two forms of knowledge in order to produce and socialise new tacit knowledge, thus feeding the cognitive circuit.

A mechanism of generating knowledge and organising production like that found in the district can benefit from technological advances (in microelectronics, computers or information technology) that reduce the limitations of company size. This is because the corresponding socio-economic organisation puts the district in a position to oversee economic processes which develop through the increasing delegation of production phases to specialised firms, a trend which requires entrepreneurial skills and forges closer links among the companies involved in production. The differentiation and integration of functions, within the district or outside it (but among districts or productive places belonging to the same network), are hallmarks of the organism's growth and evolution. Indeed, the same evolutionary mechanism is at work whether the differentiation and integration take place within the district (in other words, the achievement of economies in production requires social/geographical proximity) or outside it (the achievement of such economies requires de-localisation).

If the geographical allocation of production phases works selectively enough (maintaining an appropriate ratio between companies specialised in the manufacture of goods, on which the functioning of the district hinges in its connotation as a production and social machine, and companies specialised in the provision of services, which unite the district internally and connect it to the end markets), then the district evolves in its canonical form. On the other hand, if the competitive advantage of the district's firms depends on their roots in the community and on the system of regulations and customs that connects them to local institutional entities, it is hard to imagine that de-localisation can involve phases other than those for which labour costs are the primary concern. The strategic phases, such as product design, prototype or sample production, order collection, marketing of the finished product, and after-sales service – all of which require abundant production knowledge and professional skills, as well as familiarity with local facilities that have a 'cultural' orientation toward these activities and thus make it easier to achieve them – are unlikely to be de-localised. Of course, if time proves the prevalence of the current tendency to shift all or most of the production phases 'in the factory' until they virtually disappear from the district, and to develop the commercial phases until the area turns into a 'mercantile community', then the industrial district will become something different from what we mean by that name today (Becattini 1990).

2.   THE HISTORICAL, SOCIAL AND ECONOMIC PROCESSES THAT LED TO ITALY'S DISTRICT STRUCTURE

Industrial districts represent a pathway to industrialisation with strong roots in Italian economic history. Despite what is still believed in many academic and operational circles, districts are not a product of post-Fordism. However, few studies have been conducted in this field and there have been few attempts to reliably determine the historical conditions that favoured the birth and development of industrial districts in Italy (Brusco and Paba 1997; Galimberti and Paolazzi 1998). The problem of identifying them empirically, and giving them a documented place in the history of Italian industrialisation, must be approached through the explicit acceptance of a district-based model (as outlined in the introduction), rather than through a search for the origins of individual industrial districts. This means looking at economic processes within the specific geographical contexts in which they take place, in relation to the social environment. The idea is to understand the limitations and opportunities that arise or are derived from the intertwining of the community's technical/productive and sociocultural capabilities, or from the input from outside of technical/productive capabilities, and which explain the evolution and durability of industrial districts over time.[1]

It may be that once this way of interpreting a country's economic development becomes commonplace, or is simply adopted, it is of no help at all in identifying district-type situations outside Italy. However, the fact that no systematic attempts in this direction have been conducted in other countries has led to the notion that industrial districts are a purely Italian feature. Nevertheless, until there is proof to the contrary, one can assert that the failure to pinpoint industrial districts in other developed countries is due to the limitations of the analytical approaches used, rather than an actual absence of the phenomenon.

While it's true that industrial districts are not the product of post-Fordism, the decline of Fordism has helped the district model take root in social and economic reality. This does not mean that the decline of the production system based on the large, vertically-integrated firm and on mass production actually generated industrial districts, but that it fostered the growth of a fragmented, variable demand for goods which boosted market opportunities for existing industrial districts and those that were latent, which flowered thanks to the change in the international context. Otherwise, there would be no explanation for the fact that the district model is fundamental to interpreting the socioeconomic development of one Italian region, Tuscany in the 1950s and 1960s, in a study conducted in 1969 (Becattini 1969). For the record, that study lies at the very origin of empirical research on industrial districts in Italy (Conti and Sforzi 1997).

It should be noted too that the changes in the production organisation of large firms have also fostered the spread of 'processes of districtisation' (the gradual division of labour, the creation of local markets and other institutions, the integration between tacit and codified knowledge, the emergence of professional figures and institutions that connect the various phases of production, and the creation of entrepreneurship) in large-firm communities where there was already an extensive fabric of small and medium-sized enterprises, while those polarised onto one or two large firms, as manufacturing cities are, have witnessed gradual industrial decline.[2]

Geographical concentrations of small and medium-sized firms are a defining trait of Italian economic history. However, historians have not studied the issue systematically from the perspective of industrial districts, simply because the perspective has emerged too recently in this scientific community to have produced a view of Italy as a whole (Fontana 1998). Not even geographers can claim to have a tradition in the subject, although there are local and regional studies that could help reconstruct the processes of district-based industrialisation throughout the various stages of history (Milone 1937 and 1961).

What we do know about local situations suggests that the 'embryos' of many of today's districts were conceived between the late 19th century and the beginning of the 20th (Galimberti and Paolazzi 1998, pp. 25–7). At that time Veneto was already producing frames in Cadore, hiking boots in Montebelluna, footwear in the Riviera del Brenta, and brooms and wooden articles in Viadana; Friuli-Venezia Giulia was specialised in chairs from Manzano and knives from Maniago; Lombardy was known for cutlery and water taps (Lumezzane) and household goods (Omegna); the Marche was producing slippers and footwear in Fermo and Macerata, leather goods in Tolentino and barrel organs in Castelfidardo; and Emilia-Romagna had made a name for itself with its straw hats produced in Carpi. Even older manufacturing places include Biella, with its textiles and woollen goods (Piedmont), and the Tuscan towns of Prato, specialised in carded fabrics obtained from rags, and Santa Croce sull'Arno, with its leather tanning industry.

The districts gained momentum between the two World Wars. 'Goods such as nylon hosiery, period furniture, boots and ceramic tiles animated the production activity of the industrial districts, expanding those in existence and giving birth to new ones' (Galimberti and Paolazzi 1998, pp. 95–7). Veneto became known for fine furniture made in Bassano del Grappa and mock-antique furniture made in Cerea and Bovolone; in the clothing industry, Lombardy produced women's hosiery in Castelgoffredo while ski and mountain boot companies proliferated in Montebelluna (Veneto); ceramic tile production took root in Sassuolo (Emilia-Romagna); and Civita Castellana, in Lazio, prospered from the production of ceramic dishes and bathroom fixtures. Some manufacturing places began to diversify: Carpi moved from straw hats to knitwear, Viadana from brooms to paintbrushes, and a pattern-making school was opened in the Riviera del Brenta.

Today, these 'manufacturing places' are industrial districts recognised by economic and geographical research, economic policy and public institutions.

Recently, a survey based on economic census data from the years since World War Two (covering the period from 1951 to the present) provided an overview of industrial district dynamics (Brusco and Paba 1997). According to the survey, in 1951 about 15 per cent of all local productive systems had the characteristics of a district, and provided employment for a total of 360 000 people. Twenty years later, the proportion of districts was roughly the same, but employment had risen to just over a million workers. In 1991, districts accounted for 25 per cent of local productive systems and employed over two million workers.

The only way to gain a clear picture of the processes that made Italian industrial districts what they are today is to examine the socioeconomic background of each one. It is crucial to understand how that background enabled the district to take advantage of the opportunities lent by the broader community, which each interpreted first according to the possibilities of its sociocultural environment, and only secondarily according to those of its technical and economic structure.[3] The 'broader community' includes such aspects as national regulations; the role of intermediate institutional bodies lying between the local scale and the nation-state (such as the municipal, provincial and regional authorities, or chambers of commerce), which offer public aid in the form of tax breaks or low-cost land for the construction of factories; the networks that connect one district to other districts or productive places, in order to share political strategies (such as lobbying) or development goals (as in the case of the textile districts) or to establish complementary client/supplier arrangements (for example, one district that makes leather sofas, and another specialised in leather preparation that supplies the first with raw materials); and the domestic or international markets where a district sells its products.

Italy has come up with a series of special laws that have influenced small enterprise. According to some, the laws limit such companies' growth, while others say they provide an incentive to stay small. Italy's retail distribution structure, which is fairly dispersed, has helped keep production on a small scale and protected the design capabilities of the companies, which have managed on their own to place their goods on the international markets when the time seemed right.

I have already discussed the growth prospects for districts that have opened up (and largely been realised) with the transition from a worldwide demand for standardised goods to a demand for personalised goods. Likewise, I have mentioned the large firms' change in organisational strategy, as they break up into independent businesses, seek to involve small suppliers in the design phase, as well as entrusting them with production, while urging them to have direct relations with the market as well.

What remains to be said is that for an understanding of the Italian district experience, one needs to reflect on the fact that Italy's production structure has historically consisted of a multitude of geographically concentrated businesses, where crafts and trades and the various forms of self-employment (from home industry to small-farm ownership and sharecropping) have prospered for decades. These geographical concentrations have been anchored to a close-knit network of small (but not tiny) and medium-sized towns, which make up residential and production fabrics that are neither fragmented nor scattered, but rather integrated and compact, somewhere between the large cities and the deep countryside. This socioeconomic and geographical structure is the habitat where industrial districts have developed and flourished. It is still a defining feature of the Italian industrial landscape, but it has never described it completely. The South has not been a part of this illustration, and only in the last few years has it shown signs of industrialisation and urbanisation that are generating this intermediate industrial/residential structure. It is no coincidence that, in the South, the new industrialisation of small and medium-sized enterprise is taking place mainly outside the large metropolitan cities.

One can argue, therefore, that most of Italy's production structure never became Fordist, and that in Italy there have always been two pathways to industrialisation: the classic, Fordist pathway, which obtains production economies from internal economies, and an 'anomalous', district-based pathway, which derives its economies from local-external ones and which allows geographical concentrations of small, specialised firms to survive and advance in the market. The decline of Fordism and the growing opportunities offered by the globalisation of production and the markets have made the district-based pathway to industrialisation the very model of Italian development.

3. THE ROLE OF INDUSTRIAL DISTRICTS IN THE ITALIAN ECONOMY

3.1 General Framework

Industrial districts make up 25.4 per cent of Italy's local productive systems and 71.3 per cent of its local manufacturing systems. The districts are home to 24.2 per cent of the Italian population (13.7 million people) and employ 32.2 per cent of the workforce (2.2 million). They account for 44.8 per cent of Italy's manufacturing jobs, and 43.3 per cent of its manufacturing exports. These figures, which refer to 1996, give an idea of the extent and importance of industrial districts in Italy.

From 1981 to 1991, when large firms were cutting jobs, the districts were creating them. In the 1990s as well – from 1991 to 1996 – the districts employed growing numbers of manufacturing workers. If we set 1991 at 100, the manufacturing employment rate in 1996 was 105.

3.2 Geographical Localisation

The industrial districts are found almost exclusively in central and northern Italy, and are divided quite evenly between those two areas (Figure 8.2). The highest concentration of districts is in the North East (32.7%), followed by the centre (30.2%) and the North West (29.6%), while the South accounts for 7.5 per cent of the total. The distribution is different in terms of employment: 41.5 per cent of industrial district jobs are in the North West, 37.6 per cent in the North East, 18.3 per cent in the centre and 2.7 per cent in the South. The different weights the areas assume when it comes to employment are explained by variations in the size of the businesses. The north-western districts usually

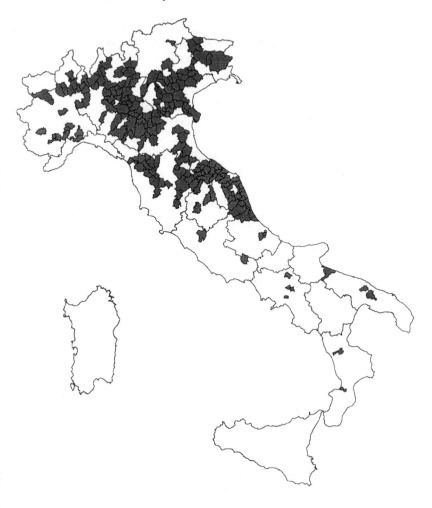

Figure 8.2 The industrial districts, 1990s

Source: Compiled by the author

have medium-sized businesses (a high proportion employ 51 to 250 people), those in the centre feature small businesses (up to 50 workers), and the north-eastern districts have a more balanced size structure.

The regions play a variety of roles. Lombardy is the region with the highest number of industrial districts (42 or 21.1% of the total), followed by Veneto and the Marche (both with 34 or 17.1%). More than half of Italy's industrial districts are concentrated in these three regions. Other regions with a large share of industrial districts are Emilia-Romagna (24, or 12.1%), Tuscany (19, or 9.5%) and Piedmont (16, or 8%).

These six regions account for 85 per cent of all of Italy's districts. Their importance in terms of manufacturing jobs does not change their national ranking, with the exception of the Marche: despite that region's high number of districts, it accounts for just 7.6 per cent of Italy's industrial district employment.

This is because its districts are smaller, with a lower average workforce, than those in the other mentioned regions. Nevertheless, the Marche is the region where districts employ the highest percentage of the population (offering 83 per cent of the region's manufacturing jobs). Next in line are Veneto (72.5%), Lombardy (61.0%), Emilia-Romagna (59.0%) and Tuscany (53.2%) (Tables 8.2 and 8.3).

In the remaining regions of central and northern Italy there is but a modest presence of industrial districts. Liguria has just one, while there are four in Trentino-Alto Adige, three in Friuli Venezia-Giulia and two in Lazio.

In the South, the most important region in this regard is Abruzzo, with six industrial districts. The businesses there are small and medium-sized, and account for 1.2 per cent of total employment. Actually, Abruzzo is considered part of the South by mere statistical convention; it has become a true industrialised region with growth traits similar to those in central/north-eastern Italy, and together with Emilia-Romagna and the Marche it defines the 'Adriatic belt' of development. Although there are gaps along the way, this manufacturing belt now extends as far as Puglia.

Industrial districts are few and far between in the other regions of the South. There are just nine in all, and most of the regions (Molise, Basilicata, Sicily and Sardinia) have none. In any case, there are four districts in Campania, accounting for just 0.3 per cent of all jobs; Puglia has three (one per cent of employment), and Calabria has two.

The main reason for this paucity is the difference in industrialisation between the regions of central/northern and southern Italy, so a nationwide analysis does not reveal latent district-type industrialisation patterns in the South.[4]

Table 8.2 Industrial districts by their dominant manufacturing industries, 1991 (number of districts – absolute values)

Region	Textile and clothing	Leather, leather goods and footwear	Wooden furniture, ceramic goods	Mechanical engineering	Metal goods	Rubber and plastics	Paper, printing and publishing	Food industries	Jewellery, musical instruments	Total
Piedmont	5	–	3	5	–	–	1	2	–	16
Valle d'Aosta	–	–	–	–	–	–	–	–	–	–
Lombardy	19	–	3	12	1	4	–	3	–	42
Trentino-Alto Adige	1	–	1	2	–	–	–	–	–	4
Veneto	15	3	10	5	–	–	–	–	1	34
Friuli-Venezia Giulia	–	–	2	1	–	–	–	–	–	3
Liguria	–	–	–	–	–	–	1	1	–	1
Emilia-Romagna	4	1	5	6	–	–	1	7	1	24
Tuscany	6	4	4	1	–	–	2	1	1	19
Umbria	2	–	2	–	–	–	1	–	–	5
Marche	11	14	6	–	–	–	–	1	2	34
Lazio	–	–	1	–	–	–	1	–	–	2
Abruzzo	3	2	1	–	–	–	–	–	–	6
Molise	–	–	–	–	–	–	–	–	–	–
Campania	1	2	1	–	–	–	–	–	–	4
Puglia	2	1	–	–	–	–	–	–	–	3
Basilicata	–	–	–	–	–	–	–	–	–	–
Calabria	–	–	–	–	–	–	–	2	–	2
Sicily	–	–	–	–	–	–	–	–	–	–
Sardinia	–	–	–	–	–	–	–	–	–	–
Italy	69	27	39	32	1	4	6	17	4	199
North West	24	–	6	17	1	4	1	6	–	59
North East	20	4	18	14	–	–	1	7	1	65
Centre	19	18	13	1	–	–	4	2	3	60
South	6	5	2	–	–	–	–	2	–	15

Source: ISTAT (1996)

Table 8.3 *Industrial districts by their employment in manufacturing industries, 1996*

Region	Number of districts		Employment of districts		Employment of region	
	Absolute values	%	Absolute values	%	Absolute values	%
Piedmont	16	8.0	99,136	4.6	530,153	18.7
Valle d'Aosta	–	–	–	–	6,515	–
Liguria	1	0.5	1,017	–	78,427	1.3
Lombardy	42	21.1	784,676	36.1	1,286,976	61.0
North West	59	29.6	884,829	40.7	1,902,071	46.5
Veneto	34	17.1	469,326	21.6	647,350	72.5
Trentino-Alto Adige	4	2.0	16,016	0.7	72,179	22.2
Friuli-Venezia Giulia	3	1.5	47,519	2.2	124,636	38.1
Emilia-Romagna	24	12.1	299,856	13.8	508,163	59.0
North East	65	32.7	832,717	38.3	1,352,328	61.6
Tuscany	19	9.5	203,545	9.4	382,538	53.2
Umbria	5	2.5	20,755	1.0	66,755	31.1
Marche	34	17.1	165,902	7.6	199,458	83.2
Lazio	2	1.0	9,431	0.4	217,385	4.3
Centre	60	30.2	399,633	18.4	866,136	46.1
Abruzzo	6	3.0	28,465	1.3	96,763	29.4
Molise	–	–	–	–	16,913	–
Campania	4	2.0	7,024	0.3	214,270	3.3
Puglia	3	1.5	20,339	0.9	181,320	11.2
Basilicata	–	–	–	–	25,703	–
Calabria	2	1.0	794	–	35,395	2.2
Sicily	–	–	–	–	115,106	–
Sardinia	–	–	–	–	50,998	–
South	15	7.5	56,622	2.6	736,468	7.7
Italy	199	100.0	2,173,801	100.0	4,857,003	44.8
North West	59	29.6	884,829	40.7	1,902,071	46.5
North East	65	32.7	832,717	38.3	1,352,328	61.6
Centre	60	30.2	399,633	18.4	866,136	46.1
South	15	7.5	56,622	2.6	736,468	7.7

Source: ISTAT (1996)

3.3 Employment

In 1996 (the year of the intermediate economic census), industrial districts accounted for a higher percentage of Italian employment (32.2%) than of the country's population (24.2%), and an even higher percentage of the nation's manufacturing jobs (44.8%). In industrial districts, manufacturing jobs amounted to 48.9 per cent of total employment, compared with just 28.7 per cent in Italy's other local systems and a national average of 35.2 per cent.

Industrial districts claim 15.8 workers and 1.7 manufacturing businesses for every 100 inhabitants compared with 6.2 workers and 0.8 businesses in the rest of Italy. The size category of district manufacturing firms that encompasses the highest number of jobs (with respect to other local systems) is that with 16–19 workers (54.8% of jobs).

The other size categories that account for more than half of the jobs all fall between 10 and 99 workers. More specifically, the category mentioned above is followed by those with 10–15 workers (52.3%), 20–49 workers (52.6%) and 50–99 workers (52.1%) (Table 8.4).

Large firms are rather scarce in industrial districts. This is consistent with the production model, which is based on a high division of labour, a multitude of companies specialised in the various productive phases, products and parts, and a weak hierarchy among the firms, although they work for each other under subcontracting organisation. Indeed, a subcontractor works for several firms, and there are specific 'phase markets' for the various stages of processing. On the other hand, a single district may have a dual production circuit: a main one, consisting of the district's specialisation (the primary industry), which orientates the local economy and society; and a secondary one, with firms from industries other than the primary industry. Some industrial districts contain branches of multinational groups, both Italian and foreign, although no systematic research has been conducted on the relationships between such entities and the small firms localised inside the districts.[5]

Although there is no doubt that the main business of industrial districts is manufacturing, we must not ignore the importance of business services – especially in light of the strong customer orientation that distinguishes the district-based system. Production programmes are generally based on orders, so marketing constitutes the startup phase of the manufacturing cycle. In many cases the firm has to sell the customer an idea, in other words a product design rather than a product, and the task of its salespeople (be they representatives, agents on commission or buying agents) is to convince customers that the article they want can be made in the district. The key step in the production process is therefore product research and development, rather than just the satisfaction of orders received. Depending on conditions,

Table 8.4   Employment shares by plant size in industrial districts and other local systems, manufacturing industries, 1996

Plant size	Industrial districts	Other local systems
1	3.2	5.4
2	3.6	4.6
3–5	8.7	9.3
6–9	9.7	8.2
From 1 to 9	25.2	27.5
10–15	12.0	8.9
16–19	6.7	4.5
20–49	20.1	14.7
From 10 to 49	38.8	28.1
50–99	12.0	9.0
100–199	10.2	8.7
200–250	2.9	2.6
From 50 to 250	25.1	20.3
251–499	5.9	7.3
500–999	3.1	6.5
1000 and over	1.9	10.3
From 251 and over	10.9	24.1
Total	100.0	100.0

Source: Calculated by the author from ISTAT data

this phase may take place outside the district, at least to a certain extent. One consequence of this style of production is that relationships between the businesspeople in the district and their clients are close and constant, because contact must be maintained until the order is filled, and the result is daily business relations instead of an ordinary exchange of information. All this helps create specialised services skills that wind up in service companies, rather than internal departments of the firm, since the district model – being a production model with practically no vertical integration – favours a (nearly) continuous proliferation of autonomous or semiautonomous businesses that conduct such activities.

Therefore, it should come as no surprise that many industrial districts associate a manufacturing specialty with a focus on business services.[6] This shift to services within Italian districts began in the early 1980s. From 1981 to 1991, business service jobs in industrial districts increased by 64.4 per cent compared with 38.5 per cent in the rest of Italy. At that time, districts made up 66 per cent of the local systems with a geographical concentration of business services higher than the national average, and 25 per cent of those with a high concentration of information-handling services. In 1996 the shift to services was still under way, and there was a stronger relative focus on information-handling rather than goods-handling services.

This does not mean that industrial districts are self-sufficient, or that they have no need for the specialised services offered by cities like Milan, Florence and Bologna. However, that interaction amounts to major trade fairs, services that can be procured online, and those that do not require personal, direct contact except on occasion. What is more, there are many district-based firms that use the exhibition services of major European cities (Paris and Frankfurt, for example) to make or maintain contact with international customers.

Other services, those of everyday interest or which require ongoing face-to-face contact – that is, those that imply geographical proximity for the sake of smooth operations – proliferate and take root where production takes place. This is partly because such services have to suit the specific nature of the district. Obviously, services that work for the textile/silk-weaving district of Como will not be appropriate for the textile/knitting district of Prato.

In passing, it should be noted that there are many districts which combine a manufacturing specialty with a focus on tourist and consumer services, proving that this type of industrialisation has less of an environmental impact than large industry. This confirms the fact that the model has traditionally taken root in semi-urban areas, where small manufacturing cities are integrated into the surrounding countryside, creating that typical setup of the Italian industrial landscape for which the term 'urbanised countryside' was coined long ago (Becattini, Chapter 1 in this volume; Sforzi, Chapter 2 in this volume).

3.4 Manufacturing Specialisation

Industrial districts produce a bit of everything, but they focus on personal goods (textiles and clothing, leather and footwear, jewellery, and so forth) and household goods (wooden furniture, tiles and other glass and ceramic items), as well as machines for such industries, instrument engineering, machinery, and equipment in general (Figure 8.3).

The districts specialised in textiles and clothing are the most numerous (34.7%), followed by those specialised in household goods (19.6%), engineering (16.1%), leather and footwear (13.6%). There are others with a focus on the food industry (8.5%), paper products and printing (3.0%), jewellery (2.0%), rubber products and plastics (2.0%), and even metallurgy (0.5%). In practice, industrial districts are specialised in all sectors of manufacturing industry except means of transport (Table 8.5).

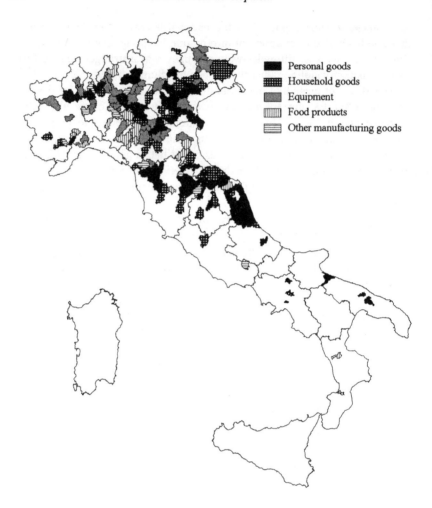

Figure 8.3 The industrial districts, according to manufacturing specialisation, 1990s

Source: Compiled by the author

There are manufacturing industries that concentrate such a high proportion of the nation's jobs within districts that they can be classified as true
'districted industries'. The prime example are the leather (tanning and goods)
and footwear industries, which concentrates 66 per cent of their jobs in
industrial districts. Others are textiles and clothing (61.9%); jewellery,
sporting goods and musical instruments (51.8%); household goods (47.8%);
and engineering (41.4%). Chemicals and manmade fibres (32.4%), food
(32.0%), paper and printing (30.8%) and metallurgy (24.8%) follow these.

Means of transport is the sector with the lowest number of jobs in districts
(17.0%), but again, there are no districts specialised in this industry. There
are, however, industrial districts in which the furniture and furnishings
sectors have generated production chains whose end products are means of
transport. For example, the Poggibonsi district in Tuscany also produces
caravans and motor homes.

The numbers of people districts employ in their various industries – the
primary ones, which define the sector of specialisation, and the complementary ones, which exploit the local-external economies generated by the
primary industries – give us a pretty accurate idea of how much of the Italian
manufacturing structure they constitute. On that basis, it can be safely said that
the industrial district is the main industrialisation model of contemporary Italy.

3.5 Exports

This last statement is confirmed by the extent to which industrial districts
contribute to Italian manufacturing exports. In 1996, exports by manufacturing and trading companies in districts came to 43.3 per cent of the national
total (ISTAT 1999).

Some categories of product, chiefly those from the *made in Italy* industries and specialised mechanics, accounted for an even higher percentage
of the nation's exports. They include wooden furniture (67.4%), leather (tanning and goods) and footwear (67.4%), textile products (67.3%), products
from the manufacturing of non-metallic minerals (58.1%), clothing (54.5%),
metal goods (54.0%), mechanical engineering (46.9%) and electrical engineering (44.5%) (Table 8.6).

If we look at exported goods in greater product detail, that is, in relation to
the 95 groups listed in the classification of manufacturing-related businesses,
the contribution of districts to national exports is above 50 per cent for 35
product groups. For the following groups, district-made products account for
more than two thirds of the nation's exports: sporting goods (93.5%), leather
and leather goods (84.2%), ceramic tiles and freestone (82.0%), jewellery
(74.6%), musical instruments (72.0%), agricultural machinery (71.5%),

Table 8.5   Industrial districts by their dominant manufacturing industries, 1991 (number of districts – percentage values)

Region	Textile and clothing	Leather, leather goods and footwear	Wooden furniture, ceramic goods	Mechanical engineering	Metal goods	Rubber and plastics	Paper, printing and publishing	Food industries	Jewellery, musical instruments	Total
Piedmont	7.2	–	7.7	15.6	–	–	16.6	11.8	–	8.0
Valle d'Aosta	–	–	–	–	–	–	–	–	–	–
Lombardy	27.5	–	7.7	37.5	100.0	–	–	17.6	–	21.1
Trentino-Alto Adige	1.4	–	2.6	6.3	–	100.0	–	–	–	2.0
Veneto	21.7	11.1	25.6	15.6	–	–	–	–	25.0	17.1
Friuli-Venezia Giulia	–	–	5.1	3.1	–	–	–	–	–	1.5
Liguria	–	–	–	–	–	–	–	5.9	–	0.5
Emilia-Romagna	5.8	3.7	12.8	18.8	–	–	16.7	41.2	–	12.1
Tuscany	8.7	14.8	10.3	3.1	–	–	33.3	5.9	25.0	9.5
Umbria	2.9	–	5.1	–	–	–	16.7	–	–	2.5
Marche	15.9	51.9	15.4	–	–	–	–	5.9	50.0	17.1
Lazio	–	–	2.6	–	–	–	16.7	–	–	1.0
Abruzzo	4.3	7.4	2.6	–	–	–	–	–	–	3.0
Molise	–	–	–	–	–	–	–	–	–	–
Campania	1.4	7.4	2.6	–	–	–	–	–	–	2.0
Puglia	2.9	3.7	–	–	–	–	–	–	–	1.5
Basilicata	–	–	–	–	–	–	–	–	–	–
Calabria	–	–	–	–	–	–	–	–	–	–
Sicily	–	–	–	–	–	–	–	11.8	–	1.0
Sardinia	–	–	–	–	–	–	–	–	–	–
Italy	100.0	100.0	100.0	100.0	100.0	100.0	100.0	100.0	100.0	100.0
North West	34.8	–	15.4	53.1	100.0	100.0	16.7	35.3	100.0	29.6
North East	29.0	14.8	46.2	43.8	–	–	16.7	41.2	25.0	32.7
Centre	27.5	66.7	33.3	3.1	–	–	66.7	11.8	75.0	30.2
South	8.7	18.5	5.1	–	–	–	–	11.8	–	7.5
Italy	100.0	100.0	100.0	100.0	100.0	100.0	100.0	100.0	100.0	100.0
Italy	34.7	13.6	19.6	16.1	0.5	2.0	3.0	8.5	2.0	100.0

Source: ISTAT (1996)

knitted goods (71.1%), footwear (69.0%) and woven textiles (66.9%). These others weigh in at half to two thirds of total exports: furniture (65.8%), metal cisterns, tanks and containers (65.4%), textile fibre yarns (64.3%), knitwear products (62.0%), leather clothing (61.8%), cutlery, utensils and finished metal products (58.6%), meat and meat-based products (56.2%), machine tools (51.5%) and machinery for special use (50.5%).

Table 8.6   The manufacturing exports of industrial districts, 1996
(percentage of Italian manufacturing exports – Italy = 100.0)

Products	%
Wooden furniture	67.4
Leather, leather goods and footwear	67.4
Textiles	67.3
Manufacture of non-metallic mineral products	58.1
Clothing	54.5
Timber, cork and wooden articles (except furniture)	54.1
Metal goods	54.0
Mechanical engineering	46.9
Electrical engineering	44.5
Pulp and paper	40.9
Metal manufacturing	38.4
Processing of rubber and plastics	38.1
Instrument engineering	35.9
Food and drink	31.3
Printing and publishing	24.5
Motor vehicles and parts thereof	23.2
Chemical products and man-made fibres	21.7
Other transport equipment	19.7
Tobacco industry	18.8
Office machinery and data processing	13.2
Electronic equipment	8.4
Mineral oil processing and nuclear fuel production	0.8
Total	43.3

Source: ISTAT (1999)

The districts specialised in textiles and clothing account for 42.6 per cent of Italian exports in this industry (the Tuscan district of Prato contributes 10.8% on its own). Those specialised in leather (tanning and goods) and footwear contribute 47.4 per cent of the sector total (with the Tuscan district of Santa Croce sull'Arno contributing 8.0% on its own). The districts producing household goods account for 37.9 per cent of the sector total, with Sassuolo, in Emilia-Romagna, representing 9.3 per cent. Those specialised in jewellery, musical instruments and so on contribute 39.6 per cent (alone, the district of Arezzo in Tuscany accounts for 25.5%); and those known for engineering contribute 18.1 per cent of the total.

4. PROSPECTS FOR THE FUTURE

In general, there is no reason to believe that local-external economies – external to the company but internal to the district, the true production unit – lose importance with the passing of time, if one takes into account that the trend in the organisation of production is moving in the direction of a strengthening of their importance to the detriment of economies of scale internal to the individual company. Furthermore, if we consider that the districts prosper in industries where economies of scale in production are in any case limited, the variety of products is high and industrial concentration low, the district formula seems capable of maintaining its effectiveness over time (Brusco and Paba 1997).

Nonetheless, one often wonders if the industrial districts will remain a cornerstone of the Italian economy in the future. The question hides two different aspects: the first concerns the goods that the district produces, in other words the specialisation in durable consumer goods (for people and household) and the related instrumental goods and services to produce them; the second concerns the district production formula.

The first aspect goes back to the problem of the *Italian model of specialisation* and is part of the discussion that opens periodically in Italy on our limited industrial variety, in particular on the low level of high-tech or capital-intensive sectors in the country's manufacturing structure. This is certainly true, and it is right that public policies pose the problem of developing, locally or by attracting foreign companies, those industries in which Italy does not manifest world leadership. But our cultural and scientific background will not allow us, at present, to succeed in these sectors other than occasionally, considering the advantage accumulated by other industrialised countries and their partner newly industrialised countries.

Thus, as long as the Italian manufacturing structure is dominated by industries that produce clusters of consumer durable goods with a high content of know-how, design and creativity, the production of which is organised in industrial districts, one can reasonably predict that the districts will remain one of the cornerstones of the Italian economy in the future. This conviction is reinforced by the fact that these clusters of products guarantee Italy a world leadership and that, as we have seen before, they are the backbone of our balance of trade. It would therefore be senseless not to support them through appropriate public policies for the districts and their individual components, to ensure that the production process, as well as producing goods – adapting them to changes in the market, in other words to consumer tastes, and obviously, also guiding them – constantly and deliberately also reproduces the material and human conditions (values, knowledge and institutions) required by production and which help the production process to last over time.

The problem of expanding sectoral variety in the manufacturing structure is part of the question of whether in Italian society and in its social and geographical variety – industry's immense and decisive background – there are the technical, production and especially sociocultural conditions that make it 'ready and open' to this type of development that would lead it away from its sectoral specificity (Becattini 1995–96). I underline *sectoral specificity*, because also in capital intensive, high-tech and R&D intensive sectors (electronic components, aerospace industry and so forth), many different from the Italian model of sectoral specialisation, in the countries where they have established themselves, the industrialisation model is getting close to, if not actually identifying with, the industrial district in line with the specific characteristics of the local society rather than the industrial pole. This means that the way in which these industries organise production is comprised of numerous elementary processes of districtisation. These include, for example, cooperation between companies; entrepreneurial networks; the diffusion of ideas and innovation through person-to-person contacts; the circulation of knowledge (production know-how) through informal and formal channels and so on, that occurs locally and in the local/global exchange. This realisation entails the need for public 'local system' policies rather than ones for companies or sectors, aimed at strengthening the latent conditions that are present in the various local systems – or to ensure 'contextual' local conditions, such as public order in many areas of the Mezzogiorno[7] – so as to make these local systems capable of pursuing a pathway to industrialisation focused on the production of the goods we mentioned (capital intensive, high-tech, R&D intensive and so on) and which break with the Italian tradition.

The second aspect – concerning the 'tenacity' over time of the district production formula – is usually posed in terms of company size, calling attention to the fact that Italian companies are smaller than those in the main industrialised countries. In the introduction to this chapter we have already clarified that examination of the Italian model of industrialisation in terms of companies instead of using the theoretical district approach, hinders understanding of the true nature of Italian industrialisation. The district is the theoretical framework that allows us to explain how the productivity and innovative capacity of small and medium-sized enterprises does not depend just on the capital and technical progress used by each of them individually, but above all on the capacity of the local community:

1. to provide the production systems with a regular supply of economic agents (entrepreneurs, self-employed workers and employees) ready to put into practice the wealth of typical knowledge and behaviour developed in the district, in line with the changing conditions of the market of the goods produced;
2. to produce, at the same time, local institutions (economic, educational, research, cultural, political and so on) suitable and adapted to the needs of the portion of the external market, and its changes, on which the district depends (Becattini 1999).

One could object that not all small companies are part of a district. And that, as a consequence, not all are included in a production process so intimately tied to the life of the local community that allows a relationship between resources inside the individual company and external district resources greater than that of companies in local social-territorial contexts that are not districts. But this only confirms the existence of a district effect – empirically measured by numerous studies (Signorini 1994; Bagella, Becchetti and Sacchi 1998; Fabiani et al. 1998; Casavola, Pellegrini and Romagnano 1999) – that brings a competitive advantage to the companies that are part of it and are able to exploit it. This seems an argument in favour of the maintenance over time of the effectiveness of the district production formula, at least for the competitiveness of small companies.

In addition, as has been said before, there is a general trend towards districtisation even by major companies. This is not only an Italian phenomenon but also a global one, which has been emerging in recent years.[8] Neither the large local company, nor the great global corporation now ignore the diversity of places – whether they be the place of origin or the place where they decide to localise their own branch-plants – and no longer do they see the world economy as a space without local-geographical variety or irrelevant to its own economic strategy. They too are searching for tacit (contextual) knowledge and target growing integration between their own codified knowledge and their own internal economies of scale and the tacit knowledge and local-external economies that they can extract from the places where they locate, seeking out competitive advantages (Vaccà 1994 and 1995). This seems to me an argument in favour of the diffusion of the district production formula even outside the industrial districts, within industrial poles that were first Fordist and that are now, or are becoming, post-Fordist. The exception is continuous flow production (such as in the chemical industry), where technically it is not possible to break down the production process into phases that are run autonomously by individual production units. Instead, the companies in industries where the production process can be broken down draw further advantage in implementing vertical disintegration strategies from the technical change linked to the diffusion of flexible and microelectronic manufacturing systems.

In the end, it appears capital and technical progress are no longer enough to compete in global markets, and to ensure productivity and innovative capacity, not even for large corporations. If it is necessary instead to integrate the individual capacities of the company with the active involvement of the local society where it is located, as happens with the industrial districts, to appropriate the human and social capital, that something *extra* that makes the difference between a non-districted company and a districted one, then the district model is destined to spread even more than at present in Italy. And it will be the task of politics and policies to create the district effect in local systems where it is insufficient or missing.

NOTES

1. I am not alone in this view. From a completely different background, even economists like Michael Porter have long wondered whether the nation-state is an appropriate unit of analysis: 'The importance of geographic concentration raises interesting questions whether the nation is a relevant unit of analysis. The conditions that underlie competitive advantage are indeed often localised within a nation, though at different locations for different industries. Indeed, the reasons why a particular city or region is successful in a particular industry are captured by the same consideration embodied in the "diamond"; for example, the location of the most sophisticated buyers, possession of unique factor-creating mechanisms, and well-developed local supplier base. The theory can be readily extended to explain why some cities or regions are more successful than others are. The London region is prospering in the United Kingdom, for example, because of its advanced demand for many goods and services, its clusters of supporting industries, and the presence of highly skilled labor pools, among other considerations' (Porter 1990, pp. 157–8).
2. As G. Becattini argues, if 'the flowering of the small manufacturing firm expresses post-Fordist capitalism's acute need to extract from its immense social base the resources of creativity and versatility that are necessary to keep expanding and differentiating the global market – a need that has always existed, but which post-Fordism has brought to a pitch – then the return of industrial districts expresses the immanent need of capitalism (viewed as a social as well as productive machine) to mould suitable people to a formula that produces well-being, and not just GDP, only if the flesh-and-blood individuals are led by their own life circumstances to interiorise behaviours which guarantee both the competitiveness of the supply source of goods for which they work (this is always a set of companies within a social context) and the satisfactory reproducibility of their community in all its dimensions (naturalistic, ethical, political, etc.)' (Becattini 2000, p. 37).
3. Today, the most representative work covering the evolution of an industrial district is the study on Prato (Becattini 1997).
4. An exercise conducted by ISTAT (the National Institute of Statistics) in order to highlight the latent industrial districts in the South – by basing calculations on the average for southern regions, rather than the national average – identified 60 local manufacturing systems of the 'district type'. This is four times the number obtained on a national scale, when only 15 were identified. Among southern regions the number of districts increased in

182 *Towards local development*

Campania (from four to 19), Puglia (from three to 16), Abruzzo (from six to nine), Calabria (from two to three) and Sardinia (from zero to five), while the other regions (Basilicata and Sicily) were left with none (ISTAT 1996).
5. Multinational groups inside industrial districts amount to 108 corporations with a total of 116 plants and 54 registered offices (Tessieri 2000).
6. Readers may not be aware that in 1991, the industrial district of Prato came first in a national classification of local systems that combined both manufacturing industries and business services (Lorenzini 1997).
7. It is well known that there are situations in the South of Italy where the main obstacle to direct investment from the rest of the country is represented by crime. There, 'local context' actions aimed at guaranteeing public order would be a preliminary condition to encourage investment in local systems characterised by the presence of a young, educated population that could easily be encouraged to acquire new knowledge for production, very distant from that of local tradition.
8. The dual convergence between small and large companies within the model of flexible specialisation underlined in 1988 by Sabel (*Flexible Specialisation and the Re-emergence of Regional Economies*) fits into the framework of theoretical thinking on the districts that sees the identification of the local system as an integrated production unit (Sforzi 1996).

REFERENCES

Bagella, M., L. Becchetti and S. Sacchi (1998), 'Agglomerazione geografica delle imprese e performance dell'export: un'analisi empirica sui microdati per l'Italia', *Sviluppo locale*, 5(8): 122–48.
Becattini, G. (1969), 'Lo sviluppo economico della Toscana: un'ipotesi di lavoro', *Il Ponte*, 25(11–12): 4–32.
Becattini, G. (1990), 'The Marshallian industrial district as a socio-economic notion', in F. Pyke, G. Becattini and W. Sengenberger (eds), *Industrial Districts and Inter-Firm Co-operation in Italy*, Geneva: International Institute for Labour Studies, pp. 37–51.
Becattini, G. (1995–96), 'I sistemi locali nello sviluppo economico italiano e nella sua interpretazione', *Sviluppo locale*, 2–3(2–3): 5–25.
Becattini, G. (ed.) (1997), *Prato: storia di una città*, Vol. IV – *Il distretto industriale*, Florence: Le Monnier.
Becattini, G. (1999), 'Più piccole, più competitive', *Il Sole-24 Ore*, 14 September.
Becattini, G. (2000), 'La fioritura della piccola impresa e il ritorno dei distretti industriali', in G. Becattini, *Il distretto industriale*, Turin: Rosenberg & Sellier, pp. 25–37.
Brusco, S. and S. Paba (1997), 'Per una storia dei distretti industriali italiani dal secondo dopoguerra agli anni novanta', in F. Barca (ed.), *Storia del capitalismo italiano dal dopoguerra a oggi*, Rome: Donzelli, pp. 265–333.
Casavola, P., G. Pellegrini and E. Romagnano (1999), 'Imprese e mercato del lavoro nei distretti industriali italiani', *Sviluppo locale*, 6(10): 41–59.
Conti, S. and F. Sforzi (1997), 'Il sistema produttivo italiano', in P. Coppola (ed.), *Geografia politica delle regioni italiane*, Turin: Einaudi, pp. 278–336.
Fabiani, S., G. Pellegrini, E. Romagnano and L.F. Signorini (1998), 'L'efficienza delle imprese nei distretti industriali italiani', *Sviluppo locale*, 5(9): 42–72.
Fontana, G.L. (ed.) (1998), *100 anni di industria calzaturiera nella riviera del Brenta*, Venice: ACRiB, Grafiche Editoriali La Press.

Galimberti, F. and L. Paolazzi (1998), *Il volo del calabrone: breve storia dell'economia italiana del Novecento*, Florence: Le Monnier.

ISTAT (1996), *Rapporto annuale: la situazione del Paese nel 1995*, Rome: Istituto poligrafico e Zecca dello Stato.

ISTAT (1999), *Rapporto annuale: la situazione del Paese nel 1998*, Rome: Istituto poligrafico e Zecca dello Stato.

Lorenzini, F. (1997), 'Il cambiamento industriale e lo spostamento verso i servizi', in ISTAT, *I sistemi locali del lavoro 1991*, edited by F. Sforzi, Rome: Istituto Poligrafico e Zecca dello Stato, pp. 177–207.

Milone, F. (ed.) (1937), *La localizzazione delle industrie in Italia*, Rome: Anonima romana editoriale.

Milone, F. (ed.) (1961), *Le Regioni d'Italia*, Turin: Utet.

Porter, M.E. (1990), *The Competitive Advantage of Nations*, New York: Free Press.

Sforzi, F. (1996), 'Italy-local systems of small and medium sized firm and industrial changes', in OECD, *Networks of Enterprises and Local Development*, Paris, pp. 99–113.

Signorini, L.F. (1994), 'Una verifica quantitativa dell'effetto distretto', *Sviluppo locale*, 1(1): 31–70.

Tessieri, N. (2000), 'Multinazionali e sistemi locali in Italia', *Sviluppo locale*, 7(13): 17–99.

Vaccà, S. (1994), 'Sviluppo locale e mercato globale: tra passato e futuro: incontri pratesi sullo sviluppo locale', Paper presented at a conference on *Sviluppo locale e mercato globale*, Artimino, 12–17 September.

Vaccà, S. (1995), 'Impresa locale distrettuale e transnazionale', Workshop on *Localizzazione e radicamento dell'impresa*, Faculty of Economics, Urbino, 17 May.

9. Local governance and industrial districts' competitive advantage

Gabi Dei Ottati

INTRODUCTION

The industrial district is a complex, inextricably economic and social form of organisation which contains within itself the essential factors of its own formation and development. This is why it is reasonably stable over time.[1] As a matter of fact, an industrial district will rise and flourish only when its productive apparatus is able to offer goods and services which are competitive in their outlet markets.

A fundamental condition for the existence of an industrial district, therefore, is that the firms within it should be able to acquire and maintain enduring competitive advantage from their edge in productivity, and above all in variety, compared to other supply sources (Becattini 2000a, pp. 28–30).

The economic factors responsible for this extra productivity (localised external economies) are treated in the literature, to which the reader is referred (Becattini 1984; Bellandi 1989). It is my conviction, however, that at the basis of the relative stability of the competitive advantage of districts there also lies social and institutional factors that have to date been little investigated. It is therefore on these factors that I shall focus in what follows.

A district's competitive advantage, especially as regards innovation – by which is meant principally the ability to adapt production to the changing demands of the market – depends to a significant extent on the characteristics of the social context in which production is embedded. Indeed, contrary to what happens in the case of radical innovation, the ability to differentiate the range of products and services supplied, as well as to find new markets, depends less on investments in research and development than on the willingness of skilled workers (employed and self-employed) and entrepreneurs (subcontractors and commissioning) to cooperate in devoting their different expertises to constant improvement and variation in products and processes, so as to satisfy ever more diverse and variable demand.[2]

This active and sometimes creative participation of many different workers and firms in the economic process cannot be obtained merely by means of bureaucratic controls, or even monetary incentives. It instead requires genuinely shared objectives, as well as a satisfactory distribution of income among the parties involved.

Thus, a second condition for the existence of an industrial district, one which is complementary to competitive advantage, is the building and maintaining of (a) good internal social cohesion, and (b) consensus among the main local interest groups on a shared development project. This consensus feeds, and is fed by, the formation and development of a widespread sense of belonging to the local community and its production system.

1. THE ESSENTIAL COMPONENTS OF THE INDUSTRIAL DISTRICT

If the attaining, and especially the maintaining, of a competitive advantage by the localised industry depends on collaboration among the different categories in the district, then we must first identify these categories, and then consider how they can achieve a viable compromise among their distinct interests.

As regards the first point, and taking account of the (vertical and horizontal) division of labour among firms distinctive of industrial districts, there are at least three economic and social categories indispensable to its existence. The first category is made up by the workers (employed or self-employed), since they possess the codified and above all contextual skills[3] essential for the competitiveness of the localised industry. The second consists of the phase firms, each of them specialised in one or a few phases of the local industry's production process, and in the activities subsidiary to it. Phase firms are important because they are the repositories of a large part of production know-how, and of the capacity to use it in a versatile and innovative manner. The third category is comprised of the final firms specialised in the design and marketing of the district's products. These too are crucial, because they ensure relatively stable links between the local production system and its outlet markets.[4]

In addition to these three categories – roughly represented respectively by the workers' unions, the artisans' associations and the employers' associations – there are various other collective actors who can be grouped under the heading of 'local establishment'. By this is meant a composite set of intermediate institutions which usually differ among districts but have local government as their core. These intermediate institutions may be private or public agencies, such as service centres, chambers of commerce, banks, training agencies and so forth of importance to the local economy. Local government is crucial for two reasons. Firstly, the public administrators, as the official representatives of the local community, are in a better position to mediate among the interests of the various categories in the district. Secondly, as a permanent body endowed with regulatory powers (such as planning for urban and industrial land use, licenses for business startups, and so on), and money to spend on infrastructures (roads, depolluting plants, and so on) and on public services (public transport, technical education, and so on), local government is able to intervene on behalf of one or other category in order to find a viable compromise between the interests at stake.

2. SOCIAL PACT, INTEGRATION AND COMPETITIVENESS

Unlike in the so-called National Fordist model of social concertation, where there are two main collective actors (employed labour and capitalist entrepreneurs), there are at least three in an industrial district, as we have just seen: employed labour, phase entrepreneurs and final entrepreneurs. Interest groups are more articulated in industrial districts, but at the same time they are culturally more homogeneous, compared to a nation-state, which is typical of Fordism. These features of industrial districts make them culturally and structurally suited both to the diffusion of market transactions within them (high work and capital mobility, good sharing of information and innovation), and to the thickening of social and institutional relations.

Contrary to what is often believed, the greater social cohesion at the basis of the extra adaptability which fuels the continuous regeneration of the district's competitive advantage is not an entirely spontaneous outcome[5] of shared rules and values inherited from the past. Quite the opposite, in fact. This cohesion is typically the result of conscious concerted action among the different categories that contribute to local development. The ensuing social pact may initially be implicit,[6] but it usually comes about through mediation by local government. This is because local government is a credible guarantor by virtue of its powers of intervention, and of its organic concern with local development. This is important, of course, because it implies that the formation of industrial districts can be encouraged by appropriate policies.

Not only the collective actors but also the contents of the social pact for local development are different and more complex than those of a mere income distribution agreement, which is normally the subject matter of national-level concertation in the Fordist model. Firstly, in industrial districts the agreement is not concerned solely with the distribution of income among the different categories (employed and self-employed workers, phase firms, final firms and service firms), even though such distribution is still essential. The aim is a more general agreement which, in the medium- to long-term, ensures that the various sections of local society will have a living standard that, on the whole, they consider satisfactory. This is necessary to enable the reproduction over time of the various categories essential to local development. It also implies distribution of the costs, as well as the benefits, deriving from the continual adjustment of individuals and firms to external changes (market, technological and organisational). Furthermore, this distribution should be perceived as 'historically equitable'. As a consequence, one of the most important elements of the local social pact is definition of rules of behaviour that discourage the spread of destructive forms of competition (see section 10).

Such rules should instead promote cooperation among the local individuals and institutions so as to facilitate learning and innovation. These are the indispensable preconditions for maintenance of the competitive advantage typically enjoyed by district firms.

3. MAIN TYPES OF DISTRICT FIRMS

Having outlined the essential features of the district microcosm which enable its definition as a small 'social market economy' (Becattini 2000b, pp. 221–4), we may now turn to analysis of the distinctive characteristics of its firms.

Because of the marked division of labour characteristic of an industrial district, a first important distinction to be drawn is between final firms and phase firms. Final firms specialise, mainly or exclusively, in the design and marketing of the products which they typically contract out to other local firms. A distinctive feature of an industrial district is that there are many such firms within it. In this it differs from an industrial pole, for example, where there may be just one, or at most only a few.[7] This creates a real local market for the design and marketing services offered by such firms. Final firms are therefore essential for the vitality of industrial districts because they provide the local production system with stable links with its external sources of supply and, most importantly, with its sale markets.

Phase firms typically specialise in one or a few phases of the production process of the district's principal industry. Therefore, firms specialised in different phases differ not only in their minimum efficient scale but also in the skills and the intensity and quality of the capital required. In this case too, there are numerous firms specialising in each phase, and this gives rise to a complex system of interconnected local phase markets. It is the wealth of skills and production expertise accumulated by the mix of different populations of phase firms[8] that accounts for a large part of the variety and continuous change of district products and processes.

This distinction between final and phase firms, which derives from an important feature of districts' production structure, must always be borne in mind, in particular when comparing firms belonging to the same sector but only partly organised in districts as regards, for example, exporting capability, capital intensity, or size.

A third type of district firm consists of firms specialised in subsidiary industries (Marshall 1975, Vol. 2, p. 197), that is, in activities that belong to the main district *filière* (Montfort 1983) but not to the main localised industry, to which however they are linked by buyer-supplier relationships. Significant examples are manufacturers of machinery used in the localised industry's production process, or firms specialising in transportation, accounting or financial services, or other types of producer services.

Firms belonging to this third type, which may be broadly called service firms, constitute a relatively small composite aggregate, at least in recently formed districts. However, their number and variety tend to increase with the growth of the district, and therefore with the spread of both phase and final firms. This in turn may cause some of the subsidiary activities to expand to such an extent that the respective firms can place their products on external markets as well, and activate their own social division of labour.[9]

4. DISTRICT FIRMS AND HUMAN CAPITAL

This multiplicity of types of firms combines with a complexity peculiar to district firms, clarification of which requires a distinction between two different ideal types of firms: the 'project-firm' and the 'nucleolus-firm'.[10]

'Project-firms' are those whose main aim is the accomplishment of a life project on the part of one or more agents who have decided to start up a business for various reasons, among whom one often finds the full utilisation and further development of previously acquired business relations and skills.[11] An important consequence of this set of motivations is that evaluation of the performance of such firms is not confined to the maximisation of returns on the money capital invested in them. Revenue, at least in the middle term, must exceed expenditure, but the sum of economic and non-economic yield judged satisfactory by the owners is only roughly related to the average return on the money invested.

'Nucleolus-firms' are those whose main aim is the maximisation of the financial capital invested in them. In contrast to project-firms, in nucleolus-firms the people involved, from managers to unskilled workers, are all instrumental to the accumulation of capital.

Obviously, real firms are always a combination of the two ideal types just outlined. However, district firms (phase, final or service) are normally closer to 'project-firms' than to nuclei of money capital seeking to increase itself rapidly. And this is not due just to the presence of such a large number of artisans and of small family firms;[12] it is also because of their genesis and the importance for them of human capital.

Firms in which the 'life project' component prevails, unlike 'nucleolus-firms', are born in an endeavour to develop human capital. Within districts, an important component of the human capital necessary for the birth of a firm is the skill, especially contextual, possessed by the (present or would be) entrepreneurs. Such skill is more technical in the case of phase firms, and more marketing-related in that of final firms.

An important consequence of this feature is that the capital that really matters to start up a business is human capital. It is therefore not surprising to find that one of the aims of these firms is the full utilisation of the skills and business connections possessed by their owners. Indeed, it is the accumulation of such human capital, during the very realisation of district production, that powers the twofold process of social mobility and division of labour, the true engine of local dynamics.

5. FORMATION AND CONSOLIDATION OF DISTRICT FIRMS

The prevalent 'life-project' nature of a representative district firm influences not only its aims but more generally its evolution from birth to consolidation, and also the way in which it reacts when faced with difficulties.

Indeed, the majority of district firms spring from the natural aspiration for economic and social improvement of individuals possessing either production or trade knowledge, usually acquired within the district itself (Accornero 1999). However, these people are often short of money capital. Or at most they have an amount barely sufficient to buy an item of secondhand machinery or a single batch of raw materials. It is not rare, therefore, for district firms to start up with finances directly or indirectly advanced by their business partners. Depending on the circumstances, these partners may be final firms, machinery suppliers, raw materials wholesalers, or even purchasers of the finished goods.[13] The frequent initial shortage of cash of new district firms increases their mortality rate during the first years of their lives (Solinas 1996), when the professional and work stamina qualities of the new entrepreneur (and of their family members) are severely tested. It should be noted, however, that even failures provide useful experience with which to reduce the risk that other local initiatives will be unsuccessful in the future.

Nevertheless, once a district firm has managed to acquire an adequate amount of fixed capital and to build its goodwill, it will consolidate through a twofold process: on the one hand by developing and increasing its specialised knowledge; on the other by carefully selecting the firms with which to establish recurrent exchange relations. The aim of this selection is to single out other specialised firms that, by virtue of their expertise and reliability, enable the selecting firm to produce goods in some way different (in quality, innovation or service) from those offered by its close competitors. The firm is thus able to make the most of its capital, which, as repeatedly stressed, is made up mainly of production skills and trust relations.

In conclusion, because of the process of horizontal and vertical division of labour characteristic of the district, once a firm has reached an efficient scale it does not grow internally but displays a tendency to remain focused on its core business, and to aggregate with other firms specialising in complementary activities. This method of consolidation gives rise to district teams and groups of firms.[14] However, district teams are only partly formed through the establishment of business relations among existing firms. They are also formed through the creation of new enterprises by ex-workers (or relatives of the entrepreneur) from already consolidated firms; a creation process which is fostered (through orders, technical assistance and even financial help) by these consolidated firms.

At this point it seems appropriate to ask why is it that district firms do not grow internally but aggregate with others, or even encourage the formation of new enterprises. A significant role in this process is played by the cultural conditioning exerted by the previous experiences of many district entrepreneurs on the firms' behaviour. But there are other reasons as well.

Firstly, district firms are of moderate size because they are highly specialised (in a phase, a product, a function or a service). Hence, in order to achieve economies of specialisation, they tend to aggregate with other firms specialised in complementary activities. They are thus able to keep their organisation lean, reducing internal coordination costs and so-called X-inefficiency (Leibenstein 1966).

Secondly, district firms tend to foster the birth of new enterprises mainly to secure business partners on whom they can rely as regards professional competence, morality, and willingness to adapt to their requirements, thereby lowering the costs of external coordination. On closer scrutiny therefore, the distinctive process by which district firms consolidate through the formation of teams of enterprises, more or less closely linked by financial ties, proves to be economically efficient. Indeed, the extra adaptive and innovative capacity of district firms depends to a large extent on the spread and variety of production knowledge, and on its full exploitation through entrepreneurial activity, for this allows the distribution of economic, social and psychological incentives among a great number of people. And these incentives favour learning and the development of latent capabilities.[15]

6. THE PRODUCTION EMBEDDEDNESS AND THE CONTINUUM BETWEEN EMPLOYED WORK AND SMALL BUSINESS

The features of district firms outlined in the previous section make the local system an environment comprising a large variety of enterprises but which at the same time is relatively homogeneous, as regards both its production knowledge and the nature of its firms. I now turn to the so-called district labour market.

One of the distinctive features of the district labour market and production system is their embeddedness in local society. The presence of numerous different production forms (from cottage industry to artisan workshops, from the small factory to the medium-sized family firm) is a manifestation of the interlinking economic and social relations typical of a district. Such interlinking is pervasive, even if differentiated, being usually closer in cottage and artisan enterprises than in medium-sized firms.

As pointed out elsewhere (Becattini 2001), this embeddedness of economic activities in the everyday life of communities rich in artisan traditions has enabled many Italian districts to achieve a kind of industrialisation largely based on the adaptation and development of knowledge and institutions inherited from the past.

However, here I wish to underline the fact that the intermingling of production and everyday life gives rise to an exceptional expansion of the labour market. Indeed, the type of work normally supplied and demanded in a district is not just dependent employment. On the contrary, there are many different types of work: for instance, work carried out at home and part-time work, on the one hand, and a wide spectrum of self-employed activities on the other.[16] The labour market therefore expands to such an extent that it becomes an incubator of entrepreneurship. This is because workers in industrial districts have features rather different from those of wage earners in the standard Fordist model of production. In particular, district workers are usually more skilled and embedded in social relations that considerably diminish their dependence on the employer. As a consequence, this also lowers the economic and social barriers between employer and employee.

The embedding of productive relations in everyday life has other important economic implications. A considerable part of the extra adaptative capacity of district firms is directly or indirectly linked to this feature. This is because the possibility of mobilising temporary and part-time labour – of

family helpers, for example, or of young people, women or elderly people –
damps down the negative effects of economic fluctuations.

However, the most significant consequence of the thickening of multiplex
relations – those, that is, which are economic and social at the same time, like
employment relationships in family businesses – relates to learning. Production knowledge, as well as the rules of behaviour and values that sustain a
district's development – are normally acquired as a by-product of everyday
life. This drives the two distinct but complementary processes of learning
and the local division of labour, both of which give rise to the district's competitive advantage.

As already pointed out, a district labour market comprises not only
dependent employment but also a significant amount of part-time or
occasional work. The latter is carried out by many different people who, for
personal or family reasons, prefer this type of work, rather than permanent
jobs with rigid working hours. On the other hand, however, economic and
cultural reasons (such as the division of labour among the local firms and the
propensity to self-employment) ensure that artisans and small businesses
perform a significant share of the work (blue and white collar) carried out in
the district. Labour mobility, both horizontal and vertical, is high.[17]
Employed and self-employed labour and small entrepreneurial activities do
not constitute separate segments. On the contrary, there is a continual and
sizeable crossover of labour among the various types of work: so much so
that it can be claimed that the passage from dependent to self-employed
work, and sometimes to small business startup, is a normal path of vertical
mobility within industrial districts. As several empirical studies have shown,
the startup of an independent activity is so common and receives such social
approval that family members and even other district entrepreneurs often
help in its attainment (Solinas 1996; Omiccioli and Quintiliani 2000).

The continuum between the various forms of work just discussed is the
basis of the process of new-firm formation. Closely complementary to this
process, however, is another one which consists in the learning, individual
and collective, of the production skills and rules of behaviour which jointly
constitute the 'real' distinctive capital of district firms. It is to this second
process that I now turn.

7. LEARNING OF PRODUCTION KNOWLEDGE AND VERTICAL MOBILITY

Theoretical and empirical research on industrial districts since Alfred
Marshall (1923, pp. 283–8) have highlighted that skills, especially those
learnt by doing and interacting, are relatively more abundant in industrial

districts than elsewhere (Becattini and Rullani 1996). This knowledge differential (mainly related to the localised industry) is the joint result of:

1. the thickening of relations among a great number of subjects (workers and firms) specialised in activities that are partly similar and partly complementary;
2. the fact that these subjects belong to the same community, and therefore share values, rules and institutions that facilitate reciprocal understanding and hence the transfer of tacit knowledge (Maskell and Malmberg 1999, p. 172). As a consequence, the learning process is enhanced to such an extent that Alfred Marshall was led to assert that in industrial districts 'the mysteries of the trade become no mysteries; but are as it were in the air, and the children learn many of them unconsciously' (Marshall 1961, Vol. I, p. 271).

In this connection, it is worth noting that the ease of learning skills, especially those that are not codified and difficult to transfer, is an advantage which is more valuable today than in the past. This is so because the increasing differentiation of consumer demand in developed countries, and exceptional progress in transport and information technologies, have drastically reduced any advantage deriving from the availability of those resources, material or otherwise, that are easily transferable and therefore usable by anybody anywhere.

Here, however, I wish to stress a different point about the value of contextual knowledge: namely that it is an indispensable resource for economic and social mobility through self-employment. As several studies have shown, production skills – acquired mainly by working for some time in a district firm, as well as through social interaction with other members of the same locality – are much more crucial for the startup of an enterprise than money capital (Brusco 1989, pp. 461–88).

The process of learning the mysteries of the localised industry that promotes the rise of new firms is therefore twofold. On the one hand, individuals living and working in the district learn, consciously and unconsciously, production skills that accumulate and eventually enable them to undertake vertical mobility by means of self-employed work or a small business. But on the other hand, the tight interweaving of economic and social relations characteristic of the district milieu, together with the thickening of the inter-firm relations necessary to coordinate the local division of labour, cause a significant part of the production skills to remain 'in mid air', to use Marshall's metaphor. Consequently, these skills become a kind of public good freely available to district members but practically inaccessible to external subjects, except after a long local apprenticeship.

All this highlights how crucial is the learning process to district dynamics. Indeed, the accumulation of skills, partly as individual and partly as collective capital, is at once the cause of new social division of labour and the effect of the specialisation engendered by division of labour itself.

8.   TRUST AND THE BIRTH OF NEW FIRMS

The process of social division of labour, however, could not materialise, let alone sustain itself, if the accumulation of skills were not joined by some kind of insurance, general and specific, against the many risks of the market. The progressive division of labour induces firms to specialise in those activities in which they have acquired distinctive expertise, and therefore a competitive advantage. On the other hand, as we saw in section 5, this process induces each firm to resort to others specialised in areas complementary to its own and easy to coordinate with.

Indeed, it is well known that a social division of labour is advantageous only when it is possible to coordinate effectively, and at low cost, the many specialised activities carried out independently by different firms. In industrial districts, because of close quantitative and qualitative complementarity, and because of the constantly changing variety of the goods produced, the market price mechanism alone is unable to ensure efficient coordination.[18]

Furthermore, the asymmetric information resulting from the different specialisations, together with the uncertainty due to constantly changing demand and to the inevitable incompleteness of contracts, expose the parties to high risks of opportunistic behaviour. Therefore, in the absence of an environment favourable to mutual cooperation, the risks of opportunism may halt the process of social division of labour and lead to vertical integration (Williamson 1985).

Therefore, in order to sustain the formation of new specialised firms, it is necessary not only to diffuse and regenerate the individual and collective capital of production knowledge, but also to guarantee a level of cooperation and reciprocal trust which is sufficient to curb the risks of opportunism.

As in the case of skills, the trust necessary to support district dynamics is of two types that are conceptually distinct yet difficult to separate empirically. On the one hand, there is the kind of trust that springs from belonging to the same community, and therefore from shared values and rules of behaviour: a set of routines arising from the sedimentation of the social and economic practices that have proved effective over time. On the other hand, there is the trust based on repeated interaction between agents in a context where information circulates easily, and in which there are prospects of future gains by the reiteration of trade (Lyons and Mehta 1997).

The first type of trust, unlike the second, cannot be explained by economic calculation alone, since it derives from internalised values and rules from the past which are usually sustained by social rewards and sanctions. This kind of trust, therefore, can be considered as a sort of collective capital, inasmuch as it is available to all district members. The second type of trust is better interpreted as a sort of personal capital. Indeed, not only does its building have costs, but it can also be offered as security against the advance (cash or other) necessary to set up a new business (see Chapter 6 in this volume). The industrial district, with its regular functioning, produces an economic and social environment able to fuel both of the mechanisms at the origin of the two types of trust just considered.

The embeddedness of production in everyday life, the marked division of labour among local firms with the resulting need for integration, the sharing of a common set of values and beliefs: these are all elements that favour the formation of rules of behaviour which encourage cooperation and fairness. On the other hand, the social division of labour and the need to exchange components, services and knowledge with other firms specialised in closely complementary activities multiply the returns deriving from repeated trade. And 'proximity', cultural as well as geographic, helps foster the building of a good reputation as personal capital.

9. LOCAL CONCERTATION AND COMPETITIVENESS

We have just seen that trust as a collective capital is essential for the formation and maintenance of a district as a vital socioeconomic system. Even if this type of trust has its roots in the past, deriving as it does from the sharing of the same social culture, it is not independent of conscious human action, in the way that natural resources can be. On the contrary, it is always also the result of 'political' action in the broad sense. This realisation is of considerable practical importance, since it enables the devising of intervention policies to revitalise industrial districts in difficulties, and to aid the formation of successful industrial districts in those regions that are still economically depressed. An in-depth study of several Italian industrial districts,[19] together with the literature on clusters of small and medium-sized enterprises,[20] shows that the flexible integration of the various specialised activities that takes place within such local systems is normally the result of political-associative regulation. This is regulation in which bargaining takes place not only between individuals (as in the market) but also between associations representing the various economic and political interest groups.

To enable the formation of a dynamic industrial district, and especially its reproduction over time, it is necessary to build, and constantly to renew, the competitiveness of local industry. Such competitiveness cannot be ensured by the automatism of the market alone (competition), not even when it is supplemented by a local culture orienting behaviour towards automatic co-operation. Indeed, the beneficial effects of both automatisms presuppose some conscious forethought, and unified coordination at the local system level. And this, because of the way in which industrial districts are structured, usually requires concerted collective action among the representatives of the different categories in the district and what in section 1 was called the local establishment.

Concerted collective action as a local governance device is necessary for at least three reasons. The first is, in order to allow the fundamental district categories to discuss long-term local development objectives, and the ways to achieve them, with the political and institutional establishment. This is necessary in order to unite interests around a shared, and therefore more credible, vision of development, and in order to promote general commitment to such objectives, so as to strengthen a sense of belonging to the local system.[21]

Secondly, local collective bargaining is necessary in order to institute and maintain over time labour and supplier relations that are essentially cooperative, thereby favouring innovation competition among district firms rather than the exploitation of workers' and suppliers' contractual weaknesses.

Thirdly, local concertation is needed to find institutional solutions for the supply of specific collective goods, such as the organisation of trade fairs to promote local products, or the institution of a technical school for the training of skilled workers: collective goods that, depending on the circumstances, are necessary to create or renew the competitiveness of local industry. This is because such collective goods produce external economies, thus increasing the productivity of existing firms and lowering barriers to entry for new businesses.

Lastly, unlike tripartite national concertation on the so-called neo-corporatist or liberal corporatist model,[22] in the case of local concertation it is not possible to identify precisely which, and how many, collective actors in the various circumstances should sit at the negotiating table. One can only surmise that district concerted action requires the participation of at least the subjects identified in section 1 (the three interests associations and the local establishment). Depending on the specific problem to be tackled, and on the particular history of the district concerned, however, other local and non-local, public and private institutions may join the concertation table.

10. 'NORMAL' CONCERTATION AND SEMIAUTOMATIC ADAPTATION

Considering the multiplicity of reasons in favour of local concertation outlined above, it may evidently take different forms and give rise to an almost infinite variety of institutions, especially as regards the supply of collective goods, which will obviously differ in different places and times. Nevertheless, it is useful to distinguish between two types of concertation according to whether the problem requiring deliberate collective action is permanent or incidental in character. These two types are 'normal' concertation and 'extraordinary' concertation.

'Normal' concertation mainly concerns the local regulation of both labour and supplier relations. Cooperation based on trust as a collective capital is mainly sustained and revitalised over time by 'normal' concertation: that is, by periodic collective bargaining at the district level. In the first case this is between the workers' unions and the employers' association, and in the second between the representatives of the phase firms (usually artisans' associations) and those of the final firms (employers' associations). Should the need arise, the local administration will take part in the bargaining, often in the person of the mayor, who acts as mediator.[23]

As suggested earlier, this type of collective action is fundamental for the maintenance of the district's competitive advantage, since it performs the following important functions.

1. It guarantees a distribution of income that employed and self-employed workers consider, on average, to be satisfactory. This is a necessary (if not sufficient) condition for the renewal over time of both skilled workers and the propensity to self-employment.
2. Satisfactory standards of living promote cooperative labour and supplier relations. Besides lowering coordination costs within and between firms, this favours the sharing of information and the acquisition of contextual knowledge within the district.
3. Local collective bargaining of labour and supplier relations influences not only cooperation but also competition among district firms. Indeed, it considerably reduces the risk of both cut-throat competition during periods of recession and of a costs and prices rise race when, on the contrary, there is high demand for local products.
4. All of this induces firms to compete in ways favourable to development: for example, by introducing new machinery, rationalising production processes, or enhancing the quality or widening the range of their products.

Furthermore, the scope of local collective negotiation is not limited to wages and supplier rates; it also includes regulation of the various aspects of labour and supplier relations. In the case of employed labour, for instance, collective bargaining may concern the regulation of overtime and working conditions in general. On the other hand, the collective bargaining of supplier relations may include rules that set out the procedures for the production of samples, for disputes settlement, for payment, for the identification of production faults, or even for the safeguarding of the local system against 'unfair behaviour'. Therefore, this type of recurrent concertation among the associations representing the principal categories in the district contributes decisively to the periodic definition and evolution of the routines of behaviour on which trust as a collective capital, and the accumulation of contextual knowledge, depend. And it is the key actors in local collective bargaining (unions, employers' and artisans' associations) that control the members of their own category and ensure that not only the letter, but also the spirit of the agreements is respected.

The above considerations show that 'normal' concertation is a sort of political-associative regulatory infrastructure necessary for flexible integration; that is, so that the coordination of the division of labour among district firms may be effectively performed by the market and community automatisms in tandem.

11. 'EXTRAORDINARY' CONCERTATION AND PLANNED ADAPTATION

As already noted, however, negotiations among key local actors cannot concern solely industrial relations in the broad sense. Even when 'normal' concertation functions properly, this may not be sufficient to maintain the local industry's competitive advantage when major changes take place in the outside world. If, for example, the local firms and institutions are unable to respond promptly and adequately to discontinuities in technology, or in demand for district products, this advantage may rapidly decrease and vanish, or even turn into a disadvantage. Indeed, in such cases, a considerable amount of contextual knowledge becomes obsolete. It then becomes necessary to intervene in order to generate new local external economies, so that competitiveness can be regained before the crisis paralyses the district's vital processes, these being the continuous renewal of specialised firms, the generation of trust, and the integration of contextual skills with new codified knowledge. But because of the way industrial districts are structured, and because of the way they work, intervention must take place through deliberate (non-automatic) cooperation among the various social groups, and therefore through local concertation.

Unlike 'normal' concertation, the role of which is to ensure the smooth functioning of the district processes, 'extraordinary' concertation occurs at turning points in the local system's evolution. These are, for example, when an industrial district is formed, or when some external event threatens its survival. The function of 'extraordinary' concertation, therefore, is to define and redefine a shared vision of long-term local development, and to find effective and practicable solutions to the problems that major changes raise for the prosperity of the district as a whole, and not just that of a few firms.

Therefore, because of the great variety of such problems, the issues and the institutions involved in 'extraordinary' concertation cannot be identified *a priori*. On the contrary, depending on the context and on the specific questions to be addressed, concerted action among local groups (often with the participation of external, public and private, actors) must find institutional solutions in order to introduce innovations capable of generating new district external economies. Therefore, in some cases it will be necessary to agree to the creation of a consortium to organise trade exhibitions promoting local products. In other cases, it may be necessary to create an agency for new technology transfer, or to institute a vocational school, or a centre for quality certification. In yet other cases, it will be necessary to find the resources (technical as well as financial) for the construction and management of a centralised purification plant, say, in order to enable local firms to comply with environmental law.

As will be seen from the above examples, 'extraordinary' concertation is often the instrument by which it is possible to mobilise the means and institutional creativity to organise the supply of collective goods and services that will enable the local industry to increase or regain its competitiveness. Considering the quality and quantity of the resources necessary to achieve that goal, one might ask whether local concertation is the appropriate instrument. In this connection, the economic and social advantages of district concerted action and management seem evident, where one considers (a) the extreme variety of the collective goods that need to be produced in the different cases, and (b) the *local* (as opposed to universal) character of such goods. Indeed, the local groups are not only better informed on the specific difficulties that need to be overcome, even if not necessarily on the ways to overcome them, but they are also those most concerned and best able to monitor the effectiveness of the solutions adopted.[24] However, the 'extraordinary' nature of the problems to be dealt with generally requires this type of concertation to avail itself also of institutions and resources (technical as well as financial) external to the district (regional, national or even supranational).[25]

Furthermore, since 'extraordinary' concertation is the device by which major (non-incremental) innovations are introduced into the local system so as to generate, or regenerate, its competitiveness, it is necessarily connected also to 'normal' concertation. Indeed, the representatives of the principal categories in the district and of local government involved in 'normal' concertation cannot be absent from 'extraordinary' concertation either. The link between the two types of concerted action is therefore ensured by the presence in both of them of the same core of key actors. This link is crucial, not only because cooperative industrial relations enable the optimum of semiautomatic adaptation by the district, but also and mainly because such adaptation is not sufficient when it is necessary to cope with discontinuous changes. In the latter case, adaptation requires a new local development project, and usually implies also a new social pact among the different groups involved in its implementation. This is because, in order to maintain competitiveness in radically changed conditions, the local production system must be deeply restructured: many workers and firms specialised in some activities are redundant, while there is a lack of workers and firms specialised in other activities because of changes in products, processes and markets. Consequently, it is likely that district routines will have to be modified as well, with substitution of the previous ones which by now hamper further development. Given that, besides mediating in the disputes between the principal categories, local 'normal' concertation contributes significantly to the definition and redefinition of the explicit rules of behaviour, the two types of concerted action must be interconnected.[26] Even if conceptually distinct, therefore, 'extraordinary' and 'normal' concertation tend to overlap and intertwine during the periods of district formation and at the times of crisis that mark a branching point in the local development path.

12. AN EXAMPLE OF DISTRICT CONCERTATION

A revealing example of local concertation is the collective bargaining of the weaving rates in the Prato district. Here the artisans' associations are the representatives of the phase firms, and, as Prato is a textile district, also of the weaving subcontractors. A great number of such weaving firms started up in Prato in the first decade after the Second World War. During that period Prato's industry went through a cycle of intense growth, followed by a deep crisis which hit especially the larger wool mills. The latter reacted by downsizing and by subcontracting several of the production phases previously carried out in-house, and particularly the weaving.

So, competition among thousands of self-employed weavers lowered dramatically the weaving rates and brought about discontent in local supplier relations. After some attempts to establish fair rates by the artisans' associations, in 1959 the first collective agreement on weaving prices was signed by the Prato employers' and artisans' associations.

Since then, collective negotiation of external weaving prices was repeated yearly or two-yearly until 1997.

Before considering briefly this instance of 'normal' concertation, it is important to stress that the parties involved, right from the start, had a clear awareness of its positive economic effects. Indeed, the preliminaries of the minutes of the first collective agreement stated that 'the contracting parties noticed, in the local weaving market, the existence of an accentuated competition to seize orders, and that such a wild competition is harmful to both the weaving artisans as well as the commissioning firms, with great disturbance of the local market'.[27]

The examination of the minutes of 22 collective agreements in the Prato district enables the reconstruction of this form of local concertation and of its policing role in district market competition. Since the first agreements, besides the prices for the principal weaving operations carried out by the artisans' firms, the minutes contain also some 'general rules'. These concern the production of samples (the price of which is excluded from collective bargaining, since it requires much longer and much greater know-how compared with standard operations) and the settlement of disputes (which was pertinent to the signing organisations). The agreements also contain 'additional clauses' that provide for price corrections for particular work requirements, among which, for example, is an increased remuneration for small batches. This normative structure remained essentially unaltered until the end of the 1970s, when the Prato district had grown enormously (Dei Ottati 1994, pp. 131–8). In contrast, price regulation became much more complex. From the fixing of around ten basic prices in the early agreements, toward the end of the 1970s these had become around 80, not counting the hundreds of extras to be added for the different specifications of each operation.

The changes outside and inside the district that took place in the 1980s (Dei Ottati 1996b), however, required substantial modifications also in supplier relations. The external pressure on the one hand, and the internal differentiation on the other (of the type of fabrics, which were no longer only woollen, but also made of hemp, linen, silk, cotton and so on, and of the type of machinery) had rendered the previous price regulation inadequate. Therefore new clauses were introduced in the collective negotiation of supplier relations, which gradually liberalised the pricing. In 1981 'preferential rates' were introduced for those final firms who ensured continuity of orders and large batches. Later on, there was introduced the possibility for individual firms to negotiate prices lower than the collectively agreed ones for highly productive processes. In 1991, after a considerable restructuring of the local system had occurred, the number of collectively agreed prices dropped considerably (it went back to about ten). Furthermore a new clause was introduced that enabled the individual contracting firms to fix prices different from the collectively agreed ones. Finally, in 1997 the adaptation of the local collective bargaining of supplier relations to the new conditions outside and inside the district came to completion with the signing of the so-called 'gentlemen's agreement', in which the pivot of the negotiation was no longer prices, but rules of behaviour.

The signatories of the 'gentlemen's agreement' were fully aware of the importance of this type of concertation, just as those of the 1959 rates agreement had been. The preliminaries of the 1997 agreement state that 'For the sake of a smooth development of the Prato system, it is necessary to ask the firms that are part of it to act according to criteria of reciprocal correctness and consideration.' And that '*a greater collaboration among firms is an element of rationalisation and growth for the district as a whole*'.[28] To this end, even if the changed conditions made the establishing of homogeneous rates more of a hindrance than a help to the building of correct supplier relations, the praxis of collective bargaining had not become useless. On the contrary, the liberalisation of prices required greater definition and control over the rules of behaviour that the parties must conform to. Indeed, in the 1997 agreement new rules were introduced, and among these, two are worthy of note for their novelty compared with the previous district practice. These are (1) the writing down of orders, and (2) the identification of procedures to reduce faulty production.

The first of these rules particularly, by establishing that the terms of the supplier relation must be written down, introduced a very different contractual practice from the informal one, typical of the local custom. At first sight, this seems to threaten the formation of trust as a collective capital (see section 8). However, in the changed context, this new rule, by lending transparency and certainty to individual contracts, constitutes a safeguard against opportunistic behaviour, which would prove truly destructive of trust as collective capital.

Also, the rule regarding the procedures aimed at reducing production flaws and at solving the resulting controversies is an innovative one. Now that the district products' competitiveness is more and more based on quality rather than on price, it is essential that the different specialised phase firms should each follow precise technical specifications in order to guarantee that the finished good corresponds to the standards required by the client. Indeed, it is exactly for that reason that the prototype supply contract recently agreed by the local artisans' and employers' associations states that the final firm should give to the phase firm 'in writing (even if by fax or e-mail) the technical specifications to be followed for each order'.[29] Therefore district concertation continues, even after the coming into effect of the national law on supplier relations (law number 192/1998) and the liberalisation of weaving prices.

The case just considered shows that the collective bargaining in supplier relations that was started to favour the diffusion of constructive forms of competition and collaboration within the district, was adapted over time to changing conditions, without changing its aim. This example is also relevant as an illustration of how 'normal' concertation, in times of intense transformation, may contribute to the renewal of rules of behaviour, which sustain the maintenance of both local economic competitiveness and social integration.

SOME CONCLUDING REMARKS

On the basis of reflection and evidence accumulated during the study of industrial districts, this chapter has sought to highlight the crucial role played by local concertation, and hence also by the unions in the broad sense (workers' unions, artisans' associations, employers' associations), in economic development. It has noted how the capacity for constant adaptation and innovation, on which the competitiveness of industrial districts depends, is first and foremost the result of ongoing negotiation among the main local categories. Thus conflict of interests, though not eliminated, is mediated in such a way as to develop among those involved (a) greater awareness of their long term interests and (b) closer commitment to the attainment of the goals agreed.

The chapter has pointed out in particular the distinctive features of the district labour market: (a) a wide variety of different types of work; (b) a widespread presence of self-employment and supplier relations; (c) marked mobility among various types and forms of work; (d) the crucial role of skills (contextual and codified, but especially the former) in vertical mobility.

On the other hand, working patterns have generally changed in the developed countries. Recent studies have shown the following tendencies: a shrinking of permanent employment, accompanied by the growth of so-called atypical work (fixed-term, part-time, training contracts); an increase in self-employment and external supplier relations, both in industry and in services; the growing importance of human capital in the form of both skills and trustworthiness.[30]

To the extent that these tendencies are general, the new economic organisation of post-Fordism (Rullani and Romano 1998) seems in significant respects to recall the industrial district model. Therefore, with due caution, starting from the above discussion on local development, I shall try to draw some general conclusions regarding the institutional changes that must accompany the economic and social transformations presently under way.

Firstly, the study of industrial districts shows that when productivity varies across regions, and when differences depend crucially on human capital and on the social context in which production takes place, then it is preferable to have local (rather than national) collective bargaining. This is because the former permits the fixing of prices and rules of behaviour best suited to the specific production context.

In the Italian case, shifting collective bargaining to the local level seems to offer other advantages. It would allow the institutionalisation of a practice that has emerged from past experience of successful local development in the regions of the centre and North East of Italy (Fuà 1983), where the presence of industrial districts is most widespread. Furthermore, local concertation could stimulate greater collaboration between social groups and the establishment, even in those areas of the country that are still depressed, and where a climate of cooperation and trust is necessary in order to promote actions consistent with economic development (Viesti 2000).

Secondly, just as the importance of self-employment in industrial districts forced the artisans' associations to start collective bargaining of local supplier relations, so it is likely that the recent increase in subcontracting and self-employment will favour similar growth in the organisations representing those categories. The enlargement of the concertation table to include the representatives of 'new', legally independent, but often economically dependent workers and subcontractors seems desirable in order to prevent cut-throat competition among them. Moreover, local collective bargaining ensures both higher skills and flexibility, thus promoting continuous innovation. The constant need to protect the weaker parties, and in general the need for social responsibility rules, seem to indicate that the appropriate level for bargaining is not that of the individual enterprise but, once again, that of the local system.[31] This is because the individual firm is too restricted a domain for collective bargaining to continue in its essential role of reconciling particular and contingent interests with general and longer-term ones.

Finally, a third implication of research on local development is that the contents of bargaining should shift from prices to rules.[32] Indeed, the growing variety and variability of working relations and jobs, which is partly due to an increasing variation and differentiation of demand, tends to reduce the effectiveness of detailed collective agreements on prices, even when they relate to a single locality. This does not mean that the interest organisations and collective bargaining have become useless; rather that they need to change considerably. Indeed, in the present situation not only is there a need for new rules able to ensure the correct functioning of the labour market and of supplier relations; there is also a need for rules and institutions able to deliver adequate training at the beginning of a person's working life, as well as periodically, thereby enhancing the knowledge acquired during work experience. Also required in the new context is identification of institutional ways to safeguard the health and life quality of workers in general. The latter are threatened by new diseases and forms of stress connected with the reorganisation of production, which is increasingly intermingled with everyday life (such as telework) without due account being taken of the various needs of human life, including procreation itself.

NOTES

1. There is a vast body of theoretical and empirical literature on industrial districts which, because of its size, cannot be cited here. I shall only mention some collections of essays in English: Goodman and Bamford (1989); Pyke, Becattini and Sengenberger (1990); Pyke and Sengenberger (1992); Cossentino, Pyke and Sengenberger (1996).
   For a wide ranging bibliographical review on industrial districts and local systems of small and medium-sized firms see Nicoletta Tessieri in Becattini, Bellandi, Dei Ottati and Sforzi (2001, pp. 419–77).
2. On the widespread incremental innovation characteristic of industrial districts, see Becattini (1991); Bellandi (Chapter 5 in this volume).
3. On the importance of contextual knowledge for the competitiveness of district products, see Becattini and Rullani (1996).
4. On the distinction between final firms and phase firms see section 3.
5. See, for example, Parri (1997).
6. During the formation of the Prato industrial district, for example, the municipal administration played an important role by promoting local concertation. This was achieved through the institution of a Town Committee (with participation by the representatives of the various local categories) in charge of studying the causes and remedies of the crisis that hit the larger Prato wool mills towards the end of the 1940s. The opportunity that this provided for direct and repeated discussions among the various representatives, with the mediation of the mayor, contributed significantly to general acceptance of local industry restructuring, after the larger wool mills decided to subcontract many of the phases of the production process. This transformed the social conflict triggered by the economic reorganisation into consensus and generalised commitment to the recovery of the local industry. See Dei Ottati (1994, pp. 127–30); Dei Ottati (forthcoming).
7. On the differences between industrial poles and industrial districts, see Russo (1996).
8. For an application of the ecological approach (according to which firms belonging to different phases are different organisational populations), see Lazzeretti and Storai (1999).
9. On the importance of subsidiary activities in the evolution of industrial districts, see Bellandi (1996).
10. For the distinction between 'project-firm' and 'nucleolus-firm', see Becattini (2000c, pp. 17–21).
11. For empirical evidence on Italian industrial districts, see the contributions by the Research Department of the Bank of Italy. In particular see Casavola, Pellegrini and Romagnano (2000, pp. 51–66).
12. The greater importance of family ownership and management in district firms (94 per cent of cases) is also confirmed by recent research by the Bank of Italy. See Omiccioli and Quintiliani (2000).
13. This practice gives rise to interlinking transactions: that is, joint economic exchanges in more than one market among the same agents. On the role of interlinking transactions of subcontracting and credit in industrial districts, see Dei Ottati (Chapter 6 in this volume).

14. On district teams of firms see Becattini (2001); Dei Ottati (forthcoming). On district groups of firms see Dei Ottati (1996a).
15. On Alfred Marshall's thought on the industrial district as a favourable environment for the development of latent capabilities, see Raffaelli (forthcoming).
16. For empirical evidence of the importance of subcontracting and home working in Italian industrial districts, see Omiccioli and Quintiliani (2000).
17. On labour mobility in Italian districts see Birindelli (1999).
18. See Richardson (1972, p. 896). On the coordination of transactions typical of district markets, see Dei Ottati (Chapter 4 in this volume).
19. See, for example, Floridia (1994); Becattini (2001); Dei Ottati (forthcoming).
20. The essential role played by collective action in this development, for example, is stressed by Schmitz (1995 and 1998), and by Scott (1998). Porter himself points out that the development of clusters of firms requires collective action, private and public. See Porter (1998, pp. 88–9).
21. For an example of this function, see Dei Ottati (1994, pp. 127–30).
22. See Lehmbruch (1977), and Alacevich (1996). Neocorporatism is a model of the manner in which the different interests of the main social groups (typically workers and employers) in a nation-state are regulated with the mediation of the central government. Often, the objective of the agreement is income distribution, in order to control inflation. For a brief account of national-level concertation in Italy from the 1960s to the 1990s, see Salvati (2000).
23. On the role of industrial relations in the development of the Prato industrial district, see Trigilia (1989); and in that of the Biella district, see Locke (1995). For the case of the Emilian districts, see Russo et al. (2000). On industrial relations in local systems of small firms, see Perulli and Trigilia (1990).
24. On the relevance of local concerted action and planning, and of the intermediate institutions, for economic development, see Arrighetti and Seravalli (1999); Seravalli (1999, pp. 79–92).
25. Solution of the problems raised by environmental law in the tanning district of Santa Croce sull'Arno (Tuscany), for example, required the local groups – gathered in an 'Emergency Political Committee' formed for the purpose – to involve both the national government and the regional government. It was necessary to resort to the national government to obtain first the deferment, and then the modification of the so-called Merli law (number 319/1976) which restricted the discharge of pollutants into public waters, thereby obliging tanning firms to make heavy investments to reduce pollution. The regional government's participation was also important for the realisation of the depolluting investments, since the modification of the law (also thanks to pressure by local groups) endowed the region with the powers to regulate, and to allocate funds for investments in purification plants. For a highly revealing account of this case of local concertation, see Floridia (1994).
The participation of external actors in local concertation may be crucial for other reasons as well. Indeed, it may be necessary to introduce a truly innovative, and hence effective, solution to local problems. Moreover, it may avert the risk of political lock-in effects of the kind exemplified by Grabher (1993, pp. 263–4) with reference to the Ruhr area.
26. Obviously, local concertation must somehow be coordinated with national concertation, as well as with national and European Union legislation, at least as regards labour, industry and environment. These issues, however, are not considered in this chapter.
27. Collective agreement on weaving rates in Prato, 12 June 1959.
28. Agreement on procedures and initiatives to improve relations between final firms and phase firms in the Prato textile district, signed by the representative organisations on 29 September 1997 (italics added).
29. Text of the prototype supplier contract agreed between the artisans' and employers' associations of Prato, 27 June 2000.
30. See Rullani (2001). For a wide-ranging report on recent changes in working patterns in Europe, see Supiot (1999). On changes in work and its conceptualisation, see Strath (2000).
31. See also Supiot (1999, p. 188).

32. On the importance of collectively negotiated rules and also of written contracts in generating an environment favourable for the development of trust relations in business, see Burchell and Wilkinson (1997).

REFERENCES

Accornero, A. (1999), '"Poter" crescere e "voler" crescere: piccoli imprenditori ex-dipendenti', in F. Traù (ed.), *La questione dimensionale nell'industria italiana*, Bologna: Il Mulino, pp. 149–212.
Alacevich, F. (1996), *Le relazioni industriali in Italia: cultura e strategie*, Rome: La Nuova Italia scientifica.
Arrighetti, A. and G. Seravalli (1999), 'Sviluppo economico e istituzioni', in A. Arrighetti and G. Seravalli (eds), *Istituzioni intermedie e sviluppo locale*, Rome: Donzelli Editore, pp. IX–XXVII.
Becattini, G. (1984), 'Ispessimenti localizzati di esternalità', *Studi e informazioni*, 1: 180–6.
Becattini, G. (1991), 'The industrial district as a creative milieu', in G. Benko and M. Dunford (eds), *Industrial Change and Regional Development*, London: Belhaven Press, pp. 102–16.
Becattini, G. (2000a), *Il distretto industriale: un nuovo modo di interpretare il cambiamento economico*, Turin: Rosenberg & Sellier.
Becattini, G. (2000b), 'I distretti industriali: un arcipelago di economie sociali di mercato', in A. Quadrio Curzio and M. Fortis (eds), *Il made in Italy oltre il 2000: innovazione e comunità locali*, Bologna: Il Mulino, pp. 221–4.
Becattini, G. (2000c), *Dal distretto industriale allo sviluppo locale: svolgimento e difesa di un'idea*, Turin: Bollati Boringhieri.
Becattini, G. (2001), *The Caterpillar and the Butterfly: an Exemplary Case of Development in the Italy of the Industrial Districts*, Florence: Le Monnier.
Becattini, G., M. Bellandi, G. Dei Ottati and F. Sforzi (eds) (2001), *Il caleidoscopio dello sviluppo locale. Trasformazioni economiche nell'Italia contemporanea*, Turin: Rosenberg & Sellier.
Becattini, G. and E. Rullani (1996), 'Local systems and global connections: the role of knowledge', in Cossentino, Pyke and Sengenberger (1996), pp. 159–74.
Bellandi, M. (1989), 'The industrial district in Marshall', in Goodman and Bamford (1989), pp. 136–52.
Bellandi, M. (1996), 'Innovation and change in the Marshallian industrial district', *European Planning Studies*, 4(3): 357–68.
Birindelli, L. (ed.) (1999), 'Mobilità del lavoro nei distretti: elementi teorici, metodologie ed evidenze fattuali', Mediocredito centrale, Osservatorio sulle piccole e medie imprese, *Quaderno di politica industriale*, 29.
Brusco, S. (1989), *Piccole imprese e distretti industriali*, Turin: Rosenberg & Sellier.
Burchell, B. and F. Wilkinson (1997), 'Trust, business relationships and the contractual environment', *Cambridge Journal of Economics*, 21(2): 217–37.
Casavola, P., G. Pellegrini and E. Romagnano (2000), 'Imprese e mercato del lavoro nei distretti industriali', in Signorini (2000), pp. 51–66.
Cossentino, F., F. Pyke and W. Sengenberger (eds) (1996), *Local and Regional Response to Global Pressure: The Case of Italy and its Industrial Districts*, Geneva: International Institute for Labour Studies.

Dei Ottati, G. (1994), 'Prato and its evolution in a European context', in R. Leonardi and R.Y. Nanetti (eds), *Regional Development in a Modern European Economy: the Case of Tuscany*, London: Pinter, pp. 116–44.

Dei Ottati, G. (1996a), 'The remarkable resilience of the industrial districts of Tuscany', in Cossentino, Pyke and Sengenberger (1996), pp. 37–66.

Dei Ottati, (1996b), 'Economic changes in the district of Prato in the 1980s: towards a more conscious and organized industrial district', *European Planning Studies*, 4(1): 35–52.

Dei Ottati, G. (forthcoming), 'Exit, voice, and the evolution of industrial districts: the case of the post-war development of Prato', *Cambridge Journal of Economics*.

Floridia, A. (1994), 'Continuità e mutamento nel distretto conciario di Santa Croce sull'Arno', in A. Floridia, L. Parri and F. Quaglia, *Regolazione sociale ed economie locali: attori, strategie, risorse: il caso dei distretti conciari*, Milan: Franco Angeli, pp. 106–208.

Fuà, G. (1983), 'L'industrializzazione del Nord Est e del Centro', in G. Fuà and C. Zacchia (eds), *L'industrializzazione senza fratture*, Bologna: Il Mulino, pp. 7–46.

Goodman, E. and J. Bamford (eds) (1989), *Small Firms and Industrial Districts in Italy*, London: Routledge.

Grabher, G. (1993), 'The weakness of strong ties: the lock-in of regional development in the Ruhr area', in G. Grabher (ed.), *The Embedded Firm: On the Socioeconomics of Industrial Networks*, London: Routledge, pp. 255–77.

Lazzeretti, L. and D. Storai (1999), 'Il distretto come comunità di popolazioni organizzative: il caso Prato', *Quaderni IRIS*, 16, Prato.

Lehmbruch, G. (1977), 'Liberal corporatism and party government', *Comparative Political Studies*, 10: 91–126.

Leibenstein, H. (1966), 'Allocative efficiency vs "X-efficiency"', *American Economic Review*, 3: 392–415.

Locke, R.M. (1995), *Remaking the Italian Economy*, Ithaca, NY: Cornell University Press.

Lyons, B. and J. Mehta (1997), 'Contracts, opportunism ad trust: self-interest and social orientation', *Cambridge Journal of Economics*, 21(2): 217–37.

Marshall, A. (1923), *Industry and Trade*, fourth edition, London: Macmillan.

Marshall, A. (1961), *Principles of Economics*, ninth (variorum) edition, Vol. I, London: Macmillan.

Marshall, A. (1975), *Early Economic Writings, 1867–1890*, edited by J.K. Whitaker, 2 vols., London: Macmillan.

Maskell, P. and A. Malmberg (1999), 'Localised learning and industrial competitiveness', *Cambridge Journal of Economics*, 23(2): 167–85.

Montfort, J. (1983), 'A la recherche des filières de production', *Economie et statistique*, 151: 3–12.

Omiccioli, M. and F. Quintiliani (2000), 'Assetti imprenditoriali, organizzazione del lavoro e mobilità nei distretti industriali', in Signorini (2000), pp. 339–58.

Parri, L. (1997), 'Risultati di azione umana ma non di progetto umano. I distretti industriali per Hayek e la Scuola austriaca', in C.M Belfanti and T. Maccabelli (eds), *Un paradigma per i distretti industriali: radici storiche, attualità e sfide future*, Brescia: Grafo edizioni, pp. 175–89.

Perulli, P. and C. Trigilia (1990), 'Organizzazione degli interessi e relazioni industriali nelle aree di piccola impresa', in P. Perulli (ed.), *Le relazioni industriali nella piccola impresa*, Milan: Aisri-Franco Angeli, pp. 73–88.

Porter, M.E. (1998), 'Clusters and the new economics of competition', *Harvard Business Review*, November–December: 77–90.
Pyke, F., G. Becattini and W. Sengenberger (eds) (1990), *Industrial Districts and Inter-Firm Cooperation in Italy*, Geneva: International Institute for Labour Studies.
Pyke, F. and W. Sengenberger (eds) (1992), *Industrial Districts and Local Economic Regeneration*, Geneva: International Institute for Labour Studies.
Raffaelli, T. (forthcoming), *Marshall's Evolutionary Economics*, London: Routledge.
Richardson, G. (1972), 'The organisation of industry', *Economic Journal*, 82: 883–96.
Rullani, E. (2001), 'Lavoro e sindacato nella società postfordista', in A. Ninni, F. Silva and S. Vaccà (eds), *Evoluzione del lavoro, crisi del sindacato e sviluppo del paese*, Milan: Franco Angeli, pp. 115–48.
Rullani, E. and L. Romano (eds) (1998), *Il postfordismo: idee per il capitalismo prossimo venturo*, Milan: Etaslibri.
Russo, M. (1996), 'Units of investigation for local economic development policies', *Economie appliquée*, 1: 85–118.
Russo, M., G. Allari, S. Bertini, P. Bonaretti, E. De Leo, G. Fiorani and G. Rinaldini (2000), 'The challenges for the next decade: notes on the debate on the development of the Emilia-Romagna region', University of Cambridge, ESRC Centre for Business Research, *Working Paper* 176.
Salvati, M. (2000), 'Breve storia della concertazione all'italiana', *Stato e mercato*, 60: 447–76.
Schmitz, H. (1995), 'Collective efficiency: growth path for small-scale industry', *The Journal of Development Studies*, 31(4): 529–66.
Schmitz, H. (1998), 'Collective efficiency and increasing returns', *Cambridge Journal of Economics*, 4: 465–83.
Scott, A.J. (1998), 'The geographic foundations of industrial performance', in Proceedings of *Las regiones ante la globalización: Competitividad territorial y recomposición sociopolítica*, El Colegio de Mexico, Mexico City, 25–27 April 1995, pp. 71–99.
Seravalli, G. (1999), *Teatro regio, teatro comunale: società, istituzioni e politica a Modena e a Parma*, Rome: Donzelli editore.
Signorini, L.F. (ed.) (2000), *Lo sviluppo locale: un'indagine della Banca d'Italia sui distretti industriali*, Rome: Donzelli editore.
Solinas, G. (1996), *I processi di formazione, la crescita e la sopravvivenza delle piccole imprese*, Milan: Franco Angeli.
Strath, B. (ed.) (2000), *After Full Employment: European Discourses on Work and Flexibility*, Brussels: Presses interuniversitaires européennes.
Supiot, A. (1999), *Au-delà de l'emploi: transformations du travail et devenir du droit du travail en Europe*, Paris: Flammarion.
Trigilia, C. (1989), 'Il distretto industriale di Prato', in M. Regini and C.F. Sabel (eds), *Strategie di riaggiustamento industriale*, Bologna: Il Mulino, pp. 283–333.
Viesti, G. (2000), *Come nascono i distretti industriali*, Rome-Bari: Laterza.
Williamson, O.E. (1985), *The Economic Institutions of Capitalism: Firms, Markets, Relational Contracting*, New York: The Free Press.

10. The multiple paths of local development

Marco Bellandi and Fabio Sforzi

INTRODUCTION

A territorial re-reading of the Italian economy, with its variety of places that changes over time in sometimes surprising ways, suggests the idea of a kaleidoscope. The first surprise is the appearance of signs of coherence in change which is particularly apparent in some places. The latter are not fortuitous clusters of activities and needs governed by external principles and factors. Rather they are 'local reproductive systems' in which local exchange between production and consumption, private and public, follows its own logic, albeit in tandem with different external conditions (technological, market). Some images of the kaleidoscope visibly follow a specific path of change: metaphor aside, a path of local development. The images that have attracted the most attention in Italy in recent decades correspond to well-established industrial districts.

The second surprise is in a certain way an effect of the first. The study of district 'images' tends to 'educate the eyesight' into perceiving – amid the change and the diversity that characterise those many other local realities in which national production activities are concentrated – certain features of local development proper. The intuition that some of these features are extremely general has led to the formulation of an appropriate territorial scale to be used as a benchmark when studying the potential and limits of local development.

In their daily lives, most people commute from their home to work and vice versa on a regular basis and within a relatively small geographical area. The use of their leisure time outside the home, too, usually involves travel across only short distances. The interweaving of these recurrent movements marks out territorial units which constitute stable ambits of shared everyday experience among resident human groups. A first approximation of these units are 'local labour market areas' identified by looking for highly self-contained patterns of daily commuter movements (ISTAT 1997). From now on we shall use the general term 'local systems' to refer both to places customarily regarded as displaying the logic of local development, and to those other local areas in which the daily life and work experiences of the resident population display nonetheless a significant density.

In what follows, after brief discussion of the processes of district development, we shall examine processes of a different kind, which more typically characterise local systems that do not fit the image of a district (they may be pre- or post-district forms). The conclusions will set out some considerations on policies for local development.

1. DISTRICT PROCESSES

The rise of individual industrial districts – at least in the Italian experience of the last few decades – is often accompanied by a fortunate merger between customs rooted in the experience of local communities and contingent political circumstances: for instance, the emergence of local leaders intent on creating economic opportunities to tap local resources (Trigilia 1990). Local customs must allow a generally-endorsed distinction to be drawn between spheres of collective interest, where a spirit of cooperation is required, and spheres of individual interests, where a spirit of economic independence and a sense of self-responsibility are necessary. Moreover, the development of an industrial district necessarily entails a distancing from its initial social conditions, if nothing else because of generational turnover and an influx of 'fresh energies'. A satisfactory capacity for collective action is maintained – according to a logic not deterministic but 'endogenous' in type – by processes that produce external economies which graft themselves onto initial social propensities.

Principal among these processes is the progressive and relatively localised division of the district's central production processes and of those complementary and instrumental to them. This articulation is shaped in technical and commodity terms by the dynamic nexus between the district's specialities and a core of needs formed over time and expressed by groups and strata of world populations which the district has learnt to stimulate and to satisfy (Becattini, Chapter 1 in this volume). In organisational terms, the division of labour among specialised enterprises, and therefore the extension or adaptation of the relative market institutions, is driven by the experiences of producers with marked entrepreneurial abilities operating in the more structured enterprises; in teams of enterprises connected by ties of reciprocal knowledge and trust; and in relationships with a set of technical consultants, commercial and financial intermediaries, public agencies, and so forth. The set of complementary and reciprocally adapted activities helps focus local society's attention on the existence of a communitarian dimension to the local 'industry' (Dei Ottati, Chapter 4 in this volume).

A second important process is the locally diffused learning – in the home and at school, and in the many local enterprises, also of small size – of specific knowledge (technical, commercial, organisational) which helps the reproduction of suitably-skilled labour but also fosters social mobility, the emergence of economic responsibility, and the growth of entrepreneurial projects. All of which also means the reproduction of a spirit of cooperation and a sense of independence (Becattini, Chapter 3 in this volume).

A third process concerns the generation of opportunities for innovation through interaction among complementary skills utilised when undertaking product projects. This comparison draws on the conditions inherent in the first two processes that facilitate the exchange of tacit knowledge – or at any rate knowledge difficult to transfer at a distance. However, systematic engagement with global markets and external organisations also induces the exchange of more codified and transferable knowledge. This fosters both the local growth of new productive knowledge and the standardisation of some local production processes. Cognitive openness hampers the onset of collusive arrangements and induces the institutions to support new opportunities to enhance local resources, rather than protect rent positions (Becattini and Rullani 1996).

The circle is closed when one considers that the three classes of external economies produced by the above three processes – economies of specialisation, education and creativity – and their concrete manifestations[1] are not immediately transferable to competing organisations external to the district. This gives rise to a localised competitive advantage which justifies the greater remuneration of local resources and fuels the enlargement of the local division of labour (Sforzi, Chapter 8 in this volume).

Is should be emphasised that the virtuous circle is not deterministic. Internal and external challenges constantly arise; and a positive response to them is not guaranteed, although private and collective actors may be aided by the local factors (Bellandi, Chapter 7 in this volume).

2. LARGE AND SMALL ENTERPRISES, URBAN AND RURAL ENVIRONMENT

'Structural' definitions of the industrial district provide, in greater or lesser detail, a list of features arranged along two axes. The first consists of the ways in which production is organised (the system of specialised enterprises and the localised division of labour);[2] the second spans the local socio-institutional environment (marked by the density of the reciprocal relations with the system of enterprises). This structure is coherent with the district-formation processes described in the previous section, and in the case of a virtuous circle, its more virtuous features are reproduced (systematically but not invariably) by the processes themselves, together with a series of minor adjustments and innovations. This, therefore, is a *self-reproducing* model of development. And it concerns *local* development because the strategic factors consist of progressive relations between enterprises and local society.

Besides the experiences of dynamic industrial districts, are there other tools with which to interpret local development? Candidates are the industrial pole and the Fordist city, the large dynamic city, the rural local system. They suggest particular manifestations of the same features that are also combined within the general definition of the district. Figure 10.1 gives an illustration of these combinations. The features exemplify the classical extremes of the modes of production (large enterprise versus small enterprise) and the local environments in which that production takes place (urban versus rural). These extremes should not be taken as antithetical, but rather as ideal-typical forms, combinations of which yield relatively distinct types of local systems: the city and the rural system, in which large and small enterprises coexist; the large-scale, industry pole and clusters of small marginal or dependent enterprises, in which urban and rural features coexist.[3]

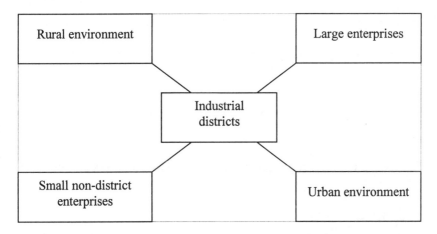

Figure 10.1 Pairings of environments and firms interpreted according to the industrial district approach

It is then possible to imagine hybrids, so that if the diagram is read starting from the extremes of the axes, the industrial district appears as a hybrid of hybrids.[4] This explains the scepticism about the industrial district shown by those (among industrial economists, economic sociologists and economic geographers) who assume that one of the foundations of the specialist study of society is the classical duality of their respective disciplines. The interpretation outlined in the previous section instead claims that it is in the industrial district that one finds a self-reproducing model of local development.

It is also useful to compare the extreme forms, and then perhaps the various empirically significant hybrids, against this model. The first step is to define the change processes that operate in places different (at least partly) from districts. The second step is to cross-reference these processes with typical forms of local systems, in order to determine the nature of other self-reproducing models of local development. Although this second step is still largely unexplored, one may nevertheless attempt to plot a multiplicity of 'paths of local development' which combine, with some degree of coherence, aspects of production processes at least partly rooted in places and forms of local systems.

A self-reproducing model of local development cannot be invented on paper. Rather, it is the result of a constant shuttling between theoretical reflection and empirical research. What we propose here is only a framework within which to explore paths of local development in not typically district settings. Our analysis – which will necessarily not take full account of all the interpretative dimensions – will be organised around one of the two axes mentioned earlier: that of the organisation of production. We shall consider some types of non-district enterprises, taking care to make their territorial dimension explicit. Then these types will be combined with sociocultural features of specific local settings.

3. THE PLACES OF THE LARGE ENTERPRISE

The distinction between 'district enterprise' and 'large enterprise' tends to be blurred by the fact that (virtually) all sectors have seen a shift from mass production to differentiated and customised processes. As a consequence of this change in contemporary capitalism, the relative importance of productivity has given way to that of innovativeness.

The variability and personalisation of demand by broad categories of consumers in the industrialised countries has set value on the ability to explore, propose and react to shifts in preferences, while curbing final prices. This capacity constantly to offer variety and variations is matched by the diffusion of tacit productive knowledge. However, price containment requires the relatively efficient organisation of a sufficiently extensive division of labour. This mode of production – which, as said, is typical of industrial districts – is becoming increasingly common in other local manufacturing systems, like large-firm ones.

If a large external enterprise acquires and maintains economic and social dominance over an economically weak local society, new firms will arise as its 'dependants' (Brusco 1990). The enfranchisement of the latter – should it be possible and convenient to the neo-entrepreneur – will be a slow and difficult process. It will ultimately depend more on conditions external to the local environment – for example the localisation of new firms in the locality in search of specialised sub-suppliers – than on internal dynamics.

Alternatively, alliances may be created by 'same-rank' enterprises but also by independent specialists. If innovativeness and personalisation are the key factors in profitability, 'capital' goes in search of arenas comprising enterprises able to develop transferable tacit and codified knowledge. The rise in average income levels over the last few decades has enabled large numbers of people to acquire substantial levels of productively valid technical-scientific knowledge, especially in urban settings. However, when an advanced ability to deploy sophisticated tacit knowledge for industrial purposes is required, it is industrial districts, or district-like local systems, that are the 'ideal' places for cross-fertilisation (Vaccà 1996).

Although large enterprises increasingly structure themselves as multi-local network-enterprises – in the sense that they belong to many different places simultaneously – they tend to give priority to their relationship with the place (the industrial pole) where they began their development. The vertically integrated process by which they initially created their productive formulas has gradually shaped local society, which displays cultural features and institutions wholly functional to company needs.

4. THE PLACES OF SMALL AND MEDIUM-SIZED NON-DISTRICT ENTERPRISES

Compared to large enterprises, small and medium-sized ones tend to have a different relationship with the place in which they undertake their production, a relationship which derives in large part from the organisational model of low vertical integration that typifies them.[5] This makes them 'naturally' more open, making the local society, with its values-systems and customs, and their relative institutions, more influential over enterprises.

The district enterprise is the archetype of the small and medium-sized enterprise that co-penetrates with local society and depends on reciprocal relations with the places in which it arose and developed. This is made possible by permeability between the population of enterprises and local society, which share knowledge, values, typical behaviours and institutions. Socioeconomic interpenetration may make change slower, but it prevents the onset of irremediable cleavages between the population of enterprises and local society.

However, not all small and medium-sized enterprises are district enterprises; nor are all local systems of small and medium-sized enterprises industrial districts. There are small enterprises, individual or part of geographical concentrations, with a low level of vertical integration, which localise in metropolitan or rural local systems.

4.1 The Small High-Tech Metropolitan Enterprise Supplying Advanced Services

We pointed out in the previous section that a first category of non-district small and medium-sized enterprise is comprised of the increasing number of specialists in advanced knowledge (technology, business organisation, design, and so on) providing services to production – whether they are key nodes in the network of some larger enterprise or whether they 'navigate' with relative independence among diverse corporate or virtual networks. What are the places of these specialists?

The image of the professional comfortably ensconced in a country cottage, using the Internet to work with the whole world, is certainly effective but tells only part of the story. To recall district-forming processes, active and continuous exchange among the numerous technical-scientific skills required by the development of new technologies and new products is easier in an environment which fosters innovative entrepreneurship and trust relationships within temporary research groups, and which is made up of a variety of complementary skills in design, management and finance. Interactions among agents with backgrounds like this often provide the basis for virtual networks, sometimes operating on a world scale.

The places congenial to this activity are numerous and diverse; but they are mainly particular zones of large cities in which innovative companies, polytechnics and universities are located.

4.2 Neighbourhoods of Artistic Crafts Enterprises

A second type of small enterprise brings us to a feature of Italian development. Connected in numerous concrete situations and in a thousand different ways with the development of industrial districts, the wide variety of small artistic crafts enterprises in Italy is a feature of extraordinary importance. These enterprises have contributed greatly to reinforcing the image of Italy deeply impressed by its history on the collective imaginations of numerous other countries.

As Giacomo Becattini points out, Italian silversmiths, furniture and art restorers, producers of articles in wrought iron or alabaster, intaglio carvers, decorators, and thousands of other craftsmen besides, constitute a veritable galaxy of specialised producers operating on the blurred boundaries that separate art from craftsmanship and industry.

Better than others, this sector highlights the continuity that ties contemporary production to the mainstream of the Italian cultural tradition. Compared to the enterprises embedded in district processes, more than the complementarity of skills – although this is important – it is the individual capacity to draw on a shared historical-artistic-architectural heritage, by definition difficult to transfer, that is paramount. More than innovative entrepreneurship, it is the pleasure of inventing new variations on the tradition that counts; more than trust in relationships among enterprises, what matters is the prestige of fine workmanship and the satisfaction of exhibiting and comparing one's achievements.

As in the previous case, these are generally not enterprises that permeate the entire local system, guiding its evolution. They are instead confined to one part of the local system: a neighbourhood, for example. However, these are not areas that can be likened to technological parks or to university campuses, because the crafts (or high-tech) neighbourhood is comprised not only of enterprises but also of an (almost) complete system made up of small local sub-communities.

4.3 Enterprises Embedded in Rural Settings

A third type of small and medium-sized enterprise has been examined by the recent literature of rural local development (Basile and Cecchi 2000). These are enterprises which share a stock of work-related and social experiences in local settings, engaged in the utilisation of natural resources (as well as traditional activities in forestry, fishing, and so on). Ramifying out from this experience are locally interweaving patterns of the production and marketing of local wines and foods, environmental and cultural goods; patterns which may be agricultural but also concern agro-industry and wine tourism, or a mix of the two. The countrysides, coasts and mountains of the Italian regions are 'naturally' dotted with these bases of experience.

4.4 Non-Embedded Enterprises

The sub-supplier dependent on vertical control by a large firm belongs to a broader class which is made up of enterprises tied to local demand for goods or services, or to the local supply of labour and infrastructures. These enterprises are not embedded in the socioeconomic and institutional relations that define a place. This class naturally consists of numerous large agricultural, manufacturing, commercial and general service enterprises, which may be either part of the large firm's network or depend on various sectoral conditions.

By extension, units and subsidiaries controlled by a multi-local firm can be distinguished between those that belong to the network of social, cultural and institutional relations of a place and those that remain substantially extraneous to it. The latter are often controlled units which enter a large firm's strategies with very narrow margins of organisational and entrepreneurial autonomy. The former can be further differentiated into those that dominate (such as the driving firms) local relations and those that establish symmetric relations – sometimes 'camouflaged' – within a system of locally-rooted small firms (Vaccà 1996; Tessieri 2000).

5.   PATHS OF LOCAL DEVELOPMENT

We have seen that enterprises can be considered from various points of view; and that the places to which they belong help define the production methods that they adopt and which guide its change. We have seen in particular that the notion of 'small enterprise' is so ambiguous that it is an unreliable basis for any analysis of contemporary industry. Classifications based upon it are simplifications that fail to take adequate account of the 'real continuity' between one form and another. With the inevitable risk of schematism, we may draw up the following classification:

Multi-local enterprises:
(a) network-enterprises

Embedded local enterprises:
(b) district enterprises
(c) high-tech enterprises supplying advanced services
(d) crafts enterprises with high historical-cultural content
(e) enterprises utilising natural resources

Non-embedded local enterprises:
(f) dependent sub-suppliers and units controlled by network-enterprises
(g) enterprises tied to local demand for goods and services or to the local
     supply of labour and infrastructures.

These various types of enterprise are to be found in various combinations in local systems, with the prevalence of one or other signalling the particular economic and social mechanisms at work. It is fairly straightforward to cross-match them with the quadrilateral of non-district local systems (Table 10.1). Type (a) characterises and dominates industrial poles; types (f) and (g) typify dependent local systems; type (e) rural local systems. Large dynamic cities may be settings characterised by relatively complex combinations of (c), (d) and (a). Industrial districts, of course, correspond to (b).

Table 10.1 Forms of local system and related types of enterprise

Forms of local system	Distinctive types of enterprise	Secondary types of enterprise
Industrial pole	a	f, c
Dependent local system	f, g	e, b
Rural local system	e	d, b, f, g
Dynamic large city	c, d, a	f, b, g
Industrial district	b	c, f, a

However, a cross-matching of this kind between the predominant types of firm and local systems is not enough to define the distinctive features of specific patterns of local development. The literature suggests that the paths of development followed by local areas also depend on the presence and role of secondary types of productive organisation.[6]

In the following sections we shall discuss certain aspects of possible paths of local development on the basis of the combinations suggested by the above scheme.

5.1 Large Dynamic City and Discontinuous Change

The large dynamic city is made up of a wide variety of productive, social and cultural patterns. However, this plurality may give rise to the disorganisation and fragmentation of local reality if the patterns are juxtaposed or contraposed rather than standing in positive interaction (Bagnasco 1999). Hence, if plurality is to be an advantageous redundancy, it must transform itself into an 'interacting plurality'. And because urban congestion inevitably pushes the production of excessively bulky goods to the margins of the city, this interaction may be only non-material in type, and so too its results. Consequently, cognitive interaction is of crucial importance in fostering the adequate involvement of local society in the change process, and in ensuring a certain degree of social cohesion. This accounts for the importance of the geographical concentration of high-tech enterprises, and of the headquarters of network-enterprises, as the entry and exit portals for large masses of transferable knowledge.

How does a local system of this kind work? Of help here is reference to the industrial district as a model of localised learning and the cognitive spiral that drives it. We may, that is, think of the large dynamic city as a particular kind of industrial district. If we do so, it is possible to discern within its plurality of models, industries and services, a core of activities which closely complement each other in the production of knowledge useful for product or process innovations in sub-populations of the overall population of enterprises tied to local demand.[7] The material output from these activities leads to the creation of new industries which may be 'exported' throughout the world. From this point of view, the diversification of the manufacturing sectors in large cities is more the outcome of cognitive interaction than a decisive factor in their dynamism.

High-tech industry may be the most striking result of metropolitan cognitive interaction, but it is certainly not the only one, nor necessarily the economically most important. Many of the large Italian (and European) cities have long histories, which if not interrupted by catastrophes have bequeathed a considerable historical, artistic and architectural heritage. This heritage may be the basis for a network of relations with tourist activities[8] – and, directly or indirectly via these, with traditional crafts – with cultural organisations, including university faculties, a variegated set of business services, and industrial activities. As regards the latter, consider the image that this heritage imparts to certain industrial brand names, or the attractiveness to business persons, international managers and scientists of an art city equipped with up-to-date communications technologies. Crafts enterprises with high non-material content are enabled to reproduce themselves in new forms by the connection between knowledge of a historical-artistic heritage and the use of new technologies and formal knowledge: today, for example, through relations with specialised services (CAD-CAM software for the restoration of antique furniture, the conservation of frescoes, and so on).

On the interpretation proposed here, the large dynamic city is a model of local development which displays a pattern resembling that of the district but which extends to include diverse kinds of enterprise and for this reason is less coherent. Enlargement fosters innovative processes which are generally beyond the range of districts. However, greater fragmentation may easily give rise to discontinuity in the path of local development; and it cannot be taken for granted that cognitive interaction and satisfactory levels of social cohesion will persist over time.

The emergence, within contemporary industrial districts, of a variety of high-tech enterprise clusters, the strengthening of medium-sized enterprises, and the localisation of the headquarters of large firms in search of specific innovativeness, have manifold outcomes, the interpretation of which may be facilitated by the model of the large dynamic city.

From another point of view, the large dynamic city *qua* a federation of local subsystems furnishes a useful basis for the study of supra-local, but regionally circumscribed, change processes. Relevant here is the literature on the 'regional innovation systems' and 'innovative milieux'.

5.2 The Reorganisation of Industrial Poles

In large enterprises, although their individual production units may have some degree of autonomy (more so in network-enterprises), strategic decisions flow mainly from company top management to the controlled units, from the centre to the places in which these units are located. The home base of headquarters and other strategic units displays a stable path of development as long as the large enterprise is able to rely on local society for the production of important amounts of technical, human and social capital, and as long as it is not hit by some crisis (Porter 1998). However, this is development that depends in large part on the corporate organisation. What has just been said also applies to peripheral places characterised by the presence of units controlled by a large firm. But in this case the path of development is less stable than that of the centre. In fact, as a result of changing geographical and productive convenience, the latter may decide to close one of its large plants, with repercussions on the local system that 'depends' on it. These repercussions are the more damaging, the more the plant has impoverished local professional and entrepreneurial skills or inhibited their development.

When a large firm reorganises itself even rapidly through processes of deindustrialisation (outsourcing in the same place, or delocalising else-where), the inevitable inertia of a local society shaped by the institutions of corporate dependence impedes any positive response to change. However, if the local system has accumulated a stock of organisational and scientific culture, and a propensity to technological innovation, these factors may mean that it is still convenient for the large firm to keep managerial functions *in loco*. The opportunity of doing so may be increased if the local system already consists of secondary clusters of small, dependent, but above all innovative enterprises.

On the other hand, if the large firm's local dominance substantially diminishes, the secondary clusters may provide the platform for entrepreneurial ventures which shift local society onto development paths different from those of the past. Maintaining social cohesion will not be easy, however, because there are likely be large sections of the local population who regard the change as socially deleterious.

Favourably disposed public agencies, and strategies by the large firm to support small-scale entrepreneurship – also under the impetus of national-level schemes – may facilitate the transition to district-like forms.

5.3 The Possibilities of Local Development in Rural Areas

In predominantly rural areas, trust relations, entrepreneurial patterns and stocks of hard-to-transfer skills all relate – directly or indirectly – to the presence of natural resources suited to the production of raw food materials, and of services to production and consumption. In Italy, this presence is often enriched by the long-standing traditions of craftsmanship of the country's numerous medieval towns (type (d) enterprises). This feature highlights a major difference with respect to the industrial district.

The core of complementarity relationships does not directly link a set of nuclei of industrial and commercial skills (production, the exporting of products and consumer services). The decisive links are those between each nucleus of skills (agricultural, industrial, commercial, tourist) and a tradition of life and work in contact with a set of local natural resources. Of course, these linkages may produce supply chains and productive interweavings where the local culture – if it creatively taps into its tradition by considering it not as a stereotype but as something alive and evolving – may play a crucial role in gaining competitive advantages. Some industrial districts have originated from this process, but a local system can be called rural as long as its development path is distinguished by linkages with agricultural tradition. This influence is subtle but significant.

On the positive side, a local endowment of natural resources, if suitably exploited, allows the solid reproduction of the linkage between local specialities (from wine and food products, including quality raw materials, to agrotourism services) and particular needs to be satisfied or stimulated. On the negative side, local markets for intermediate goods and services are less dense, institutions less focused, and cognitive interactions less easy. And the reproduction of entrepreneurial attitudes is constantly threatened by the possibility that the relationship with natural resources may shift towards the passive protection of rent (spread of type (g) enterprises).

In these circumstances, investments by external enterprises in innovative economic initiatives or in sub-supply relationships foster the openness of the local system, with outcomes which, though ambiguous, can be understood in the light of the above discussion of industrial poles (accumulation of entrepreneurial skills versus a culture of dependence).

At the same time, of increasing importance is light-handed but specific intervention by the State to shift local political action towards supply of the public and collective goods that accompany the embedding of nuclei of local organisational and entrepreneurial skills.

6.   ON POLICIES FOR LOCAL DEVELOPMENT

The experience of contemporary industrial districts suggests that the set of specialised public goods that support local enterprises[9] is not the inevitable outcome of deliberate action undertaken by enlightened organisations. Thus, for example, the success of policies promoted by local authorities to give impetus to the social reality to which they belong also depends, and in large measure, on the way in which they target support on the production activities with effective potential for development; on the extent to which they are able to pursue objectives of a general nature; and on the determination that they display in enforcing decisions, overcoming inertia and misgivings.

Policies for local development targeted on the formation of specialised public goods are facilitated by the force of the district-forming processes that they themselves help foster and steer. This is one of the main virtuous circles that operate within industrial districts in good marching order. It is therefore no coincidence that little attention has been paid to the 'autonomous dimension' of policies in the district literature, which initially focused on the factors accounting for the success of Italian industrial districts in the 1960s and 1970s. However, the idea sometimes re-proposed of an initial 'spontaneous' phase – all path dependency, animal spirits and pure market – that purportedly characterised Italian districts seems to have been gainsaid by every really thorough case study. Policies and local institutions have always been essential, but during the stages of take-off, success and ongoing development they are, so to speak, 'immersed' in the flow of economic-social relations of the local area.

It is instead the case that policies for local development are more difficult, and therefore become more obviously essential, when a 'strong' local system is passing through a restructuring phase, or when a local system is 'weak' because it is socially depressed or in decline. If local society is not entirely fragmented, there will be clusters of activity in which district-forming processes – or those others compatible with local paths of development discussed in previous sections – are in operation. However, these activities may be weakly connected, and not evidently dominant in the social and economic system of the place concerned. The difficulties will be accentuated by the fragility of territorial identification, and therefore by resistance to concerted action by organisations connected in various ways to the local system. These factors will heighten the ambiguity of interpreting local potential, and the action to take, and they will also increase the obstacles raised by opportunist exploitation of collective resources; while the jealousies provoked by interests unconstrained by a shared endeavour will obstruct every reasonable solution, or they will give rise to a costly – and clientelistic – jumble of partial and contradictory projects.

The presence of a political, cultural and economic leadership, rooted in the place and able to cope with these difficulties, makes a major difference. It may produce a project which offers prospects for development based on the place's potential and shared by the majority of local society. Connected with this project must be the creation of sets of local public goods linked by various relationships of time and level. Understanding of these relationships is vital if the efficiency and efficacy of collective action is to be assured in these circumstances. As a consequence, the growth of appropriate organisational skills – to be applied not in the individual enterprise but in the local system as a whole – is important for broadening the margins of success for collective action.[10] Even when awareness of the potential and limits of local development gives rise to the creation of suitable administrative capabilities, there still remains an element of political subjectivity that evades 'local planning'.

Even more so does this element evade policies for local development formulated at the centre, by the State or national agencies, although these can heighten the impact of local policies if they are combined with the latter by 'light' regulation and negotiation (Becattini, Chapter 11 in this volume). Such 'lightness' entails that interventions by the centre must be declaredly partial and subsidiary. They must not be implemented through the *ex ante* selection of firms or local actors deemed deserving of support, nor through the attraction of those merely seeking to acquire financial subsidies. Centrally-promoted policies acquire leverage in three ways: by defining the rules of the game among private, collective and public local actors; by influencing the definition of the windows of opportunity offered by development paths rooted in local potential (including redistribution policies); and by monitoring and assessing the efficacy of local initiatives financed by public money.

These policies should also be 'complex' in that they orient and sustain the vitality of entire local societies. Consequently, besides areas of direct intervention, consideration should be given to numerous others that require indirect support. And, of course, in this case too intervention may have negative outcomes.

We began our discussion of locally-defined policies for local development by emphasising that public and collective measures are conditioned by the strength of the socioeconomic relations on which they are targeted. The same consideration applies to policies formulated at the centre. In this case, however, the argument merges with analysis of more general problems relating to the socioeconomic changes now taking place in contemporary societies. This therefore brings us to the 'final frontier', which we can only briefly touch upon in this concluding discussion.

Because its driving force resides in the entrepreneurial division of labour, the industrial district is not a dirigiste alternative to the market. But insofar as its proper development requires deliberate intervention by human agents – policies and politics, that is – it is not the triumph of pure market either. The a-critical extolling of market mechanisms, or alternatively of dirigiste methods, tends to deplete – in one respect (as an invitation to 'hit and run' investments by multinationals, for example) or the other (in the past, incentives for the 'rationalisation' of small firm systems) – the resources of local diversities. The experience and analysis of district processes offer solid grounds for multiculturalism and they therefore gainsay the standardising thesis. The extension of debate to a multiplicity of local paths of development may be a further step in this direction.

NOTES

1. For example, external economies of variety in the production of a range of products which varies in relation to changeable and fragmented demand.
2. The enterprises in a district do not constitute a uniform population in which each of them competes and exchanges equally with the others according to 'community market' mechanisms valid for all of them. The population comprises groupings of varying type, extension and stability which take the names of federations, progressive alliances, groups or teams. Each team forms around a leader or a 'product project' in the broad sense, and includes a set of suppliers, some tied by 'cascade' shareholdings, cross-shareholdings, or similar, and others, for varying periods of time, by other types of agreement.
3. In the industrial pole, the organisational sphere of the large leading enterprise extends into spaces which are not necessarily contiguous and often non-urban.
4. As pointed out in Note 2, as regards well-established industrial districts, and therefore as regards the model of the industrial district, it is a mistake to identify the basic organisational unit with the individual small enterprise. It should also be stressed that industrial districts comprise an often inextricable blend of urban features (intensification of communication channels and a variety of what may even be sophisticated knowledge) and rural ones (the strength of the institutions that prompt local actors to valorise – in different yet socially recognised ways – contextual knowledge and traditional productive activities).
5. Low vertical integration applies to numerous craft enterprises – if not to their main production process – because of the large number of external services required by a micro-enterprise if it is to remain competitive.
6. Note that the types of enterprise not included in the scheme (either as distinctive or secondary) in correspondence to some form of local system are to be taken not as absent from the corresponding concrete case (type (g), for instance, is ever-present), but as marginal to definition of the form of development. The significance of including the secondary types will be briefly discussed in the points that follow. The list is merely intended to provide an example of a general framework for analysis.
7. A preponderance of type (g) enterprises, together with clusters of large firm subsidiaries and dependent enterprises, characterises instead the case of large dependent cities.
8. The tourist business involves a variety of enterprises, often of type (g) or (f).

9. For example: the local network of markets and enterprise teams; technical standards and reputation; the local educational and training system; and in general the institutions that regulate openness to extra-local knowledge, dedicated industrial infrastructures, and so on.
10. Advanced training programmes to develop these skills are already being run or devised in various parts of Italy.

REFERENCES

Bagnasco, A. (1999), *Tracce di comunità: temi derivanti da un tema ingombrante*, Bologna: Il Mulino.
Basile, E. and C. Cecchi (2000), *La trasformazione post-industriale della campagna: dall'agricoltura ai sistemi locali rurali*, Turin: Rosenberg & Sellier.
Becattini, G. and E. Rullani (1996), 'Local systems and global connections: the role of knowledge', in F. Cossentino, F. Pyke and W. Sengenberger (eds), *Local and Regional Response to Global Pressure: The Case of Italy and its Industrial Districts*, Geneva: International Institute of Labour Studies, pp. 159–74.
Brusco, S. (1990), 'The idea of the industrial district: its genesis', in F. Pike, G. Becattini and W. Sengerberger (eds), *Industrial Districts and Inter-Firm Co-operation in Italy*, Geneva: International Institute for Labour Studies, pp. 10–19.
ISTAT (1997), *I sistemi locali del lavoro 1991*, edited by F. Sforzi, Rome: Istituto Poligrafico e Zecca dello Stato.
Porter, M.E. (1998), *On Competition,* Boston, MA: Harvard Business School Press.
Tessieri, N. (2000), 'Multinazionali e distretti industriali in Italia', *Sviluppo locale*, 7(13): 77–99.
Trigilia, C. (1990), 'Work and politics in the Third Italy's industrial districts', in F. Pike, G. Becattini and W. Sengerberger (eds), *Industrial Districts and Inter-Firm Cooperation in Italy*, Geneva: International Institute for Labour Studies, pp. 160–84.
Vaccà, S. (1996), 'Imprese transnazionali e contesto socio-culturale ed istituzionale', *Economia e politica industriale*, 23(90): 37–82.

11. Towards a geographical redefinition of the form of the State

Giacomo Becattini

PREMISE

I shall address the problem of development policies from one particular viewpoint: the geography of public intervention. The problem has been addressed more than once since the Second World War, but mainly in relation to institutional aspects or legal technicalities. I intend to address it from a different standpoint, one that takes account mainly of the socio-economic analyses which have so deeply and unusually affected the Italian experience. I am referring of course to the debate over the last two decades on industrial districts and on local development, but I shall also draw upon the debate in the 1960s about national and regional planning.

The problem is made more complicated and less easy to fit into any framework by the fact that it spans several disciplinary fields which happen to be fairly distant from one another (such as economics and law). Being well aware of this I shall put forward some provisional observations which I derive both from the study of socioeconomic phenomena in Italy (and especially in Tuscany) which I have carried out mainly on a geographical basis, and from my reflections as a citizen of Italy about what has been happening to our Republic. I must stress again that these are no more than reflections, indeed no more than starting points for reflection, which I shall briefly marshal around three topics.

One of the key concepts underpinning the observations which follow is the widely held idea of the existence of a multiplicity of legislative and administrative levels, ranging from European to national, regional and generically local. At each of these levels there normally arises a problem of rational delimitation of its boundaries, which is often resolved in practice by what appear to be long-established political and administrative frontiers. I shall concentrate especially on the last of these levels, although I do not regard the subject as closed, even at local level, without a full specification of the architecture of the State.

1. THE ENVIRONMENTAL BALANCE

The pressures of population growth and of economic activities on the natural environment, whether in the sense of the consumption of non-renewable resources (for instance, saturation of all building land in the few existing plains) or in that of the reduction in the natural container's capacity to absorb and repair the effects, have in the last two decades led to an explosion of the environmental problems that had been building up for a long time.

Some environmental problems are on a global scale and suggest the need, if they are to be dealt with effectively, for a world government of some kind, able to impose a long-term or very long-term plan for the use of the whole of planet Earth (and even of the space around it). There is no need to point out that this set of problems is inescapable and of critical importance, but since I do not possess the necessary knowledge I shall not attempt to deal with them. In any case this aspect of the problem does not appear to be on the agenda of this volume.

Other environmental problems, however, concern our immediate environment, what might be termed our kitchen garden. Here it would seem to be logical to establish procedures for the management and regeneration of the environment such as to ensure that each of the components (the house and garden of my metaphor) maintains a certain balance between the activities of human consumption and pollution of the environment on the one hand, and the mechanisms of purification and regeneration provided by nature, along with human repair activities, on the other.

The point on which I shall concentrate my attention is how to establish the boundaries of the 'house+garden' unit, always bearing in mind, let me repeat to avoid any misunderstanding, the importance of the interdependence of neighbouring houses and gardens.

The problem of the most appropriate natural unit to adopt when we are seeking a balance between human activity and the environment has long been with us. It was posed for Tuscany, for example, as early as Targioni Tozzetti's famous *Introductory Treatise on the Physical Features and Topography of Tuscany* (*Prodromo della corografia e della topografia della Toscana*, Florence, 1754). In this work the division of Tuscany is linked to its natural division into the many valleys which compose it.

> The most natural and convenient division of Tuscany, it seems to me [writes Targioni Tozzetti] is to be made according to the different valleys of its principal rivers, that is those both large and small which flow directly into the sea. There is not a yard of land that may not be included within the category of some valley; since there is almost not a yard of land from which the rain falling upon it does not drain into some river.

The years and centuries that followed have refined and complicated this definition of Targioni Tozzetti, but the concept of valley, or in more recent parlance of rain basin, has retained, and indeed consolidated in the course of the latest accounts of environmental problems, its centrality. It is not my task here to report upon the strictly scientific developments of this aspect of the subject, nor would I be equipped to do so. What I want to pick out here is simply that in the new division of the territory of Italy that we are looking for, the natural dimension of the rain basin remains a benchmark which, albeit open to corrections and additions, is inescapable.

2. THE LOCAL VARIETIES OF A REGIONAL SUBCULTURE

If we move on to a consideration of the social and economic aspects of the problem, two approaches are needed: (a) the identification of culturally homogenous areas (a homogeneity which must obviously be taken with a pinch of salt), and (b) the identification of self-contained areas of exchanges and commuting for personal and employment reasons (a self-containment also to be taken with a pinch of salt).

Cultural homogeneity (often called a shared subculture) imparts a significance, albeit always a relative one, to the scale of values and major objectives of a given population. Conversely, lack of cultural homogeneity, ' that is the random coexistence of different and incompatible scales of value and functional preferences prevents us, strictly speaking, from deciding whether a given change occurring in a given area is to be regarded for those who live there as an improvement or a worsening of their conditions of life. Hence the desirability of at least an indicative delimitation of areas in our country which are roughly homogenous in cultural terms. There are plenty of statistical indicators available for this task that could be supplemented by surveys and enquiries as needed.

Naturally this does not mean that in any area that is culturally homogenous (always in a very relative sense as we have seen earlier), there are no disparities and conflicts of interest and aspirations; but rather that such disparities are to be found for the most part within a network of basic common values that are shared by the vast majority of the permanent residents of the area, and which differ, in their systemic patterns, from those which are found in other culturally homogenous areas of the country.

Within areas of cultural homogeneity, mainly fairly large, one can identify areas of intense and continuous interaction between the conditions of daily life (the places and conditions of work, the places and conditions of living, studying, worshipping and so forth) and the specific 'philosophy of life' (in other words, the system of behaviours, values and conscious aspirations) prevailing among the inhabitants. Geographers have sought to define the concept alluded to here, if I am not mistaken, in terms of daily urban systems. Another conceptual benchmark may be represented by the 'local labour markets'. If within a large area of approximate cultural homogeneity sub-areas can be found where the great majority of the population both lives and works, each of the latter will display, in general terms, a differing intensity of some characteristics rather than others of the subculture concerned, leading to the development of what may be termed 'local variants' of that subculture.

The actual measurement of the basic social and economic units that roughly correspond to these local variants is a very complex operation that may not, and normally will not, give unambiguous results. It would involve the use of a large set of statistical indicators, the carrying out of a wide range of targeted surveys, and recourse, if need be, to referenda, in order to clarify points which there was no other way to ascertain. It would involve in fact working to identify local systems with sensitivity, discernment and a clear sense of the interdependence of cultural, social and economic phenomena.

3.   CENTRES OF PRODUCTION OF TACIT KNOWLEDGE

A third order of considerations may be derived from a global reconsideration of the process of production of knowledge and goods. Modern industrial civilisation is built upon an endless process of conversion of contextual or tacit knowledge into codified or explicit knowledge, and vice versa. The overall process referred to may be broken down schematically into the following phases: (a) *socialisation* of tacit knowledge, typified by apprenticeship within a craftsman-learner relationship, which takes place through observation, imitation and practice (contextuality) and only applies in specific situations and within precise limits; (b) *externalisation* of tacit knowledge, when the latter is given expression and can be made usable for others via the use of metaphor, analogies and mental models, tacit knowledge ripened through action; (c) *combination* of explicit knowledge, involving the manipulation (such as by incorporation in textbooks and transmission through teaching) of information codified in a language that makes them easily transferable, although such transferability, however accessible, is nevertheless not completely free from distortion due to the cultural filters which almost always occur between different individuals; (d) *internalisation* of explicit knowledge in the course of real action, thereby producing new tacit and explicit knowledge, that is using science and technology at the same time as tacit knowledge in the creation of specific products.

The formation of world markets which carry potential competition to every corner of the Earth has created close links between the processes of production of goods and services and the process of production of knowledge, in the sense that it is no longer possible to produce and sell goods and services without becoming involved in the overall process of production of new knowledge. Mere repetition, which is in any case strictly speaking impossible, no longer pays. Innovation in process and/or product, which was the exception until a few decades ago, has become the unavoidable norm in industrial production. Correspondingly, productive activity may be seen as one phase in a process of cognitive experimentation whose products are jointly knowledge, goods and services. Alongside this cognitive experimentation linked to the production of goods and services, and therefore self-financing, there is 'pure' cognitive activity, not directly and consciously related to the production of goods and services.

As a result of historical development, tacit knowledge is always found in specific locations (this remains true for knowledge located in firms); and since production is always the result of a combination of tacit knowledge (socialised and externalised) and explicit knowledge (combined and internalised), the marketability of the product will crucially depend upon the quantity and quality (the appropriateness for the product concerned) of the tacit knowledge stored in any given location. The explicit knowledge incorporated in machinery, in textbooks, in organisational patterns, may be acquired by anyone and easily passed on; what cannot be acquired and passed on so readily is the accumulated tacit knowledge incorporated in any given local system of production. And it is the latter which, when it successfully interacts with the relevant explicit knowledge (that is, with the scientific and technological knowledge which, jointly with the tacit knowledge to be found on the spot, produces goods and services for the world market), confers a specific competitive advantage upon a given local system.

Now to assume that local systems of production (including production of services as in tourist districts) are actually the real basis of the economic potential of a country gives rise to two kinds of consequences. In the first place there is the need to be equipped to draw upon the historical cultural specificity of any local system of production. A local system has to become capable of identifying precisely what it is and then to organise itself to make the most of it, at least as far as that it possible for a local system. The perspective in which the problems of local systems can best be considered envisages a concentration of study and research on the processes of the formation (but also of the dissipation) of local tacit knowledge (which is an indirect way of studying the local processes of production) and on the specific ways in which the latter combines with general explicit knowledge. Production, research, training, marketing and selling of the products (goods and services), and around them all the aspects of social life, have to converge in a single project for the continuity and renewal of the local system.

In parallel with this, from the regional, national or supranational viewpoint, account has to be taken of where the processes of production of knowledge and goods in a particular country (or region or supranational entity) are located; and consideration must be given to their geographical distribution and mutual influence as crucial factors in efficiency, and hence as a primary objective for economic policy at supra-local levels. In other words the interdependence between specific forms of production and social and cultural conditions (proximity and distance, communications and transport, and so on) has to be used to stimulate multiplying and synergetic effects. The country is not seen here either as a mosaic of statically coexisting areas, nor as a single undifferentiated block of territory, but essentially as a dynamic and interactive system of local systems. The national spiral of production of knowledge and goods, being part of the world spiral, is here broken down into a large number of local systems producing either or both, each aspect containing its own evolutionary impulse and participating in a network (which is also continuously variable) of relations between those systems.

This type of analysis requires the basic unit, from the standpoint of the cognitive-productive mechanism, to contain: (a) at least one area of accumulation of tacit knowledge; (b) at least one area where living conditions are such as to discourage the emigration of the bearers of tacit knowledge ripened in production.

The problem becomes more complex in fact in relation to very large areas where there is no social process going on of production of knowledge and goods. Such areas may participate, perhaps via a university, in the process of production of codified knowledge (especially knowledge furthest away from productive processes), but there is no accumulation of tacit knowledge of a kind and to an extent likely to produce economically efficient combinations. In such areas the identification of geographical units of the kind discussed above may become difficult or impossible, and it may be necessary to adopt other criteria.

A further complicating element arises in the case where large 'outsize' urban conglomerations exist which exhibit characteristics unrecognised in modern economic development and which require, since they are where the upper levels of administration reside, special treatment. Similarly, special treatment, albeit with different aims, is needed for areas which house the country's historical heritage.

CONCLUSIONS

All in all, a new division of Italy leading to a more rational and more democratic (in the sense of more accountable to and more closely monitored by the electorate) management of the power and the resources of its citizens should result from a series of factors which derive, respectively, from the logics of environmental conservation, from a community of shared and conscious values and aspirations, and from the production and circulation of knowledge and goods.

A problem which can be posed in more general terms is that of the average size of these sociocultural units. Whole blocks of administrative regions? Whole regions such as Tuscany? Or smaller entities, the size of a province, or, to be clearer, of a consortium of local authorities? In my opinion the basic unit has to be relatively small if it is to mobilise a sufficiently strong sense of belonging and identification. And a sense of belonging and of identification are certainly needed if we wish to create a clear linkage between the powers and duties of local communities and obtain the genuine support (not rhetorical, formal and superficial) of the citizens of Italy today. So I am thinking of middling-sized areas ranging, roughly, from the present province to consortia of local authorities. This implies, I repeat, a hierarchy of levels (local, regional, national and European) among which are divided the various functions, responsibilities and powers. But the basic building brick, in this conception, remains for me that of the local level outlined above.

This is where the analysis I have barely sketched out meets up with current discussions about federalism, or administrative and/or legislative devolution. I would not dream, in my ignorance of these matters, of proposing legal frameworks for solutions to our problems. But I believe that I can express my basic conviction in simple terms. To make local government truly accountable to the electorate they must be given the executive and legislative powers, and the resources (such as tax revenues of their own or from elsewhere); and their voters must be given powers of democratic control capable of making the concept of local autonomy a reality. In my view there is nothing to prevent a substantial amount of the legislative powers devolved by the central State being conferred upon an intermediate level such as the region.

In conclusion, the new division of the country, aimed at bringing power and responsibility closer to the citizen, has to divide the country into areas and blocks of population such as to: (a) allow each unit an overall balance between its economic life and its ecology (apart from factors intrinsically national or supranational); (b) bring together individuals who, because of the place where they live, the work that they mainly do and the life that they lead, perpetuate and develop, by responding actively to the total evolution of the world, the distinctive characteristics of a common sociocultural heritage; (c) do not dissipate but on the contrary jealously guard the conditions of production and reproduction of tacit knowledge linked to productive processes located in their areas but also well positioned in the world division of labour.

Index

and internal economies 23, 54, 149,
    166
local 1, 31, 157, 159, 166, 175, 178,
    180, 184, 198
of scale 77, 138, 140, 144, 148, 149,
    150, 151, 152
of scope 138, 140, 144, 148, 149, 150,
    151
of specialisation, education, creativity
    211, 212

Fabiani, S. 180
Falorni, A. 29
Fama, E. 124
Fantappié, R. 66
Fasano Guarini, E. 65, 66
financial intermediaries 3, 122–4, 212
firms
    final 102–105, 185–9, 197, 201–202,
        205, 206
    nucleolus 188–9, 205
    project 188, 205
    service 55, 187–8
    teams of 63, 86, 92, 190, 206, 211,
        225, 226
flexible specialisation 29, 36–8, 54–
    7, 135–8, 145–8, 152, 182
Floridia, A. 206
Fontana, G.L. 163
Fordism 163, 166, 186
four Tuscanies 32–6, 39, 40, 49, 51,
    59–60
Frey, L. 90
Fuà, G. 37, 90, 125, 127, 204

Galimberti, F. 162, 164
Galluzzi, P. 27
Gangopadhyay, S. 126
Georgescu-Roegen, N. 25
Goglio, S. 90
Good, D. 119
Goodman, E. 125, 205
goods
    collective 137–8, 144–5, 150, 196–7,
        199, 223
    household 164, 173, 175, 177
    personal 173
    personalised 165
    public 4, 224
    specialised public 223

standarised 55, 99, 165
Grabher, G. 206

Harris, J.E. 79
Harrison, B. 132
Hippel, E. von 106
Hirschman, A.O. 91, 111, 115, 117

implicit partnership 116–17
implicit rules 75, 77–8, 92, 111
industrial district
    district processes 199, 211–12, 217,
        225
    features of 109–11, 158–62, 185–6,
        191, 212–14
    Italian 2, 3, 5, 90, 105, 132, 139, 143,
        150, 157–82, 195, 205, 206, 211,
        223
    Marshallian 3, 95, 98–101, 104
industrial pole 58, 158, 159, 179,
    180, 187, 205, 213, 215, 219,
    221–2, 225
industrial relations 41, 99, 159, 198,
    200, 206
industries
    auxiliary 31, 32, 40, 55, 99, 105, 159
    districted 175
industry
    light 20, 30–40, 49, 59–60
    localised 36–8, 54, 133, 159, 185,
        188, 193
Inman, R.P. 138
innovation 2, 3, 24, 31, 57–8, 76, 82,
    84–5, 89, 92, 95, 98, 100, 101,
    125, 135–6, 141, 144, 152, 161,
    184, 187, 203–205
integration 186–7
    entrepreneurial vertical 131–2, 140–
        42
    flexible 195, 198
interdependencies
    traded 161
    untraded 161
interlinking transactions 108–27, 205
    of subcontracting and credit 109, 114–
        22, 126, 127, 205
internal economies of scale 136, 159,
    180

Jacquemin, A. 151